Praise for *Beyond Mars and Venus*

"No one delivers greater wisdom about relationships than John Gray. In *Beyond Mars and Venus*, he provides much-needed guidance as to how to navigate the path of love in complicated times like these."

—**Marianne Williamson, #1** *New York Times*
bestselling author

"A true expert understands that as times change, tried-and-true methods must be reexamined and updated. John Gray not only embraces the unique challenges in modern relationships, but his tools and wisdom are every bit as helpful today as ever."

—**Jack Canfield,** *New York Times* **bestselling author**
of the Chicken Soup for the Soul series

"Twenty years after his earth-shaking *Men Are from Mars, Women Are from Venus*, John Gray has opened up a whole new universe of helpful relationship advice in *Beyond Mars and Venus*. His explanation of love and intimacy in the 21st century will rock your world."

—**Harvey Mackay, #1** *New York Times* **bestselling author of**
Swim with the Sharks Without Being Eaten Alive

"Leave it to John Gray, whose creativity framed gender differences in planetary terms as Mars and Venus, starting a never-ending conversation about the differences between men and women, to go *Beyond Mars and Venus* and make the discussion relevant for contemporary couples. All couples, traditional or modern, will be informed by this perceptive thinker about relationships."

—**Harville Hendrix, PhD and Helen LaKelly Hunt, PhD,**
authors of *Getting the Love You Want* **and**
Making Marriage Simple

"How do we achieve true love in today's stressful, chaotic world? How many times have we attempted to explain the inexplicable by saying, *Well, you know, 'men are from Mars'*, a term so frequently used it's part of pop vernacular? Here's the deal, men are from Mars and women are from Venus; understanding that traditional roles have changed and evolved, and being able to adapt to the shift is key to a successful relationship. John Gray's *Beyond Mars and Venus* captures this evolution from both perspectives. Becoming comfortable in our new roles allows for each of us to be seen, heard, and affectionate with one another. Being able to express these inherent sides of ourselves clearly determines our strengths and need for stress management and choosing balance. Greater intimacy and deep love are the gifts. I love this book."

—Suzanne Somers

"John Gray's famous book *Men Are from Mars, Women Are from Venus* has changed countless lives for the better (including mine) and has helped so many people live in greater happiness. This new guide offers tools and wisdom that are as helpful today as ever."

—Marci Shimoff, professional speaker, #1 *New York Times* bestselling author of *Happy for No Reason* and *Love for No Reason*, and coauthor of *Chicken Soup for the Woman's Soul*

"John Gray is always ahead of the curve. He teaches from what he lives, what he has learned from his own marriage and family, and from his countless clients and seminar participants. I know the man quite well. Sometimes in a book you get a bunch of untested words and concepts. Here you get the real deal: from a man who walks his talk and uses every day to live as love. If you want to understand yourself better and sweeten your relationship, this book will take you to the next level."

—Arjuna Ardagh, founder of Awakening Coaching and author of *The Translucent Revolution*

"John Gray provides brilliant guidance for the rapidly changing state of gender roles in our relationships. *Beyond Mars and Venus* is required reading for all couples who are serious about growing and thriving in love together."

—Arielle Ford, author of *Turn Your Mate into Your Soulmate*

"John Gray's new book applies his work and wisdom to the lives of modern couples, picking up where the classic guide left off. His new book has the power to change lives. It changed mine."

—Barnet Bain, author of *The Book of Doing and Being: Rediscovering Creativity in Life, Love, and Work* and director of *Milton's Secret*

"*Men Are from Mars, Women Are from Venus* changed the way we looked at relationships and this completely new version cracks the code for today's ever more complex relationships. Read it—you and your partner(s) will be glad you did!"

—Dave Asprey, founder and CEO of Bulletproof and author of the *New York Times* bestseller *The Bulletproof Diet*

"More than any author, thought leader, or master facilitator/teacher, John Gray has been on the front lines and in the trenches—doing the work with real people—since he wrote *Men Are from Mars, Women Are from Venus* twenty-five years ago. The deep wisdom, spiritual richness, authenticity, and practical guidance of *Beyond Mars and Venus* cannot be overstated. Another must-read for the ages!"

—Dr. Ken Druck, author of *The Secrets Men Keep*, *The Real Rules of Life, Courageous Aging*, and *Healing Your Life After the Loss of a Loved One*, and the original Executive Coach

"My wife and I read *Men Are from Mars, Women Are from Venus* many years ago. The book positively changed the way we communicate with one another and we've now been married for more than twenty-seven years. We have always recommended that book to couples we know. Having read *Beyond Mars and Venus*, we will now be adding this outstanding book to our recommendation."

—Dr. Ivan Misner, *New York Times* **bestselling author and Founder of BNI**

"John Gray's wisdom, insight, and lifelong experience have drastically impacted my health, mind-set, and success. In this fabulous new book, he provides groundbreaking tools for deepening intimacy and our capacity to love. Clearly, there's nothing more important."

—Marcia Wieder, CEO of Dream University

"By guiding each of us to support our partner to be his or her authentic self, *Beyond Mars and Venus* deepens our love and helps us become the best partners we can be."

—Warren Farrell

Beyond

MARS

and

VENUS

Beyond
MARS
and
VENUS

RELATIONSHIP SKILLS FOR
TODAY'S COMPLEX WORLD

JOHN GRAY

BenBella Books, Inc.
Dallas, TX

Beyond Mars and Venus copyright © 2017 by John Gray
First trade paperback edition 2020

BENBELLA
BenBella Books, Inc.
8080 N. Central Expressway
Suite 1700
Dallas, TX 75206
www.benbellabooks.com
Send feedback to feedback@benbellabooks.com

BenBella is a federally registered trademark.

Printed in the United States of America
10 9 8 7 6 5 4

ISBN 978-1-953295-13-2 (trade paper)

The Library of Congress has cataloged the hardcover edition as follows:
Names: Gray, John, 1951- author.
Title: Beyond Mars and Venus : relationship skills for today's complex world / John Gray.
Description: Dallas, TX : BenBella Books, Inc., [2017] | Includes bibliographical references and index.
Identifiers: LCCN 2016049061 (print) | LCCN 2017002319 (ebook) | ISBN 9781942952299 (trade cloth : alk. paper) | ISBN 9781942952305 (electronic)
Subjects: LCSH: Man-woman relationships. | Sex differences (Psychology) | Sex differences. | Interpersonal relations. | Interpersonal communication.
Classification: LCC HQ801 .G6679 2017 (print) | LCC HQ801 (ebook) | DDC 306.7--dc23
LC record available at https://lccn.loc.gov/2016049061

Editing by Leah Wilson and Glenn Yeffeth
Copyediting by James Fraleigh
Proofreading by Michael Fedison and Cape Cod Compositors, Inc.
Author photo by Glade Truitt

Cover design by Bradford Foltz
Text design by Aaron Edmiston
Text composition by PerfecType, Nashville, TN
Printed by Lake Book Manufacturing

Special discounts for bulk sales are available.
Please contact bulkorders@benbellabooks.com.

*This book is dedicated with greatest love and admiration
to my daughter Lauren Gray.
Her insights for women in relationships
inspired me to develop many of the new ideas in this book.*

CONTENTS

CONTENTS

INTRODUCTION

I wrote *Men Are from Mars, Women Are from Venus* twenty-five years ago, and it has remained a bestseller ever since, with millions of readers around the world. It continues to touch people's lives in fifty languages and over 150 countries. During my interviews around the world, the most frequent questions I get are: How have relationships changed in the last twenty-five years? Do the insights in your book still apply?

**How have relationships changed
in the last twenty-five years?
Do the insights in your book still apply?**

The short answer: The world has changed dramatically, with significant implications for our relationships. The increasing pace of work and life has increased stress for both men and women. And with millions more women in the workplace and men taking on more responsibilities at home, relationship dynamics have shifted.

What we need in our relationships to experience lasting fulfillment has dramatically changed. Both men and women require a new kind of emotional support that embraces greater authenticity, intimacy, and personal expression. Gone are the days when a woman was required to be submissive and dependent on men, and a man had to carry the burden of providing for his family alone.

This change has created incredible new opportunities, both for relationships and individuals. People have the opportunity to be themselves in ways they never could before, and to embrace characteristics beyond those of their traditional gender roles, allowing for relationships of more profound intimacy than ever before.

But these changes also bring significant new challenges. We must learn to successfully express our masculine and feminine qualities in ways that reduce, rather than increase, our stress. And we must learn how to support our partners' new needs as they do the same for us.

In some ways, men are still from Mars and women are still from Venus, and many of the insights of my first book are still quite valid. But with greater freedom to express ourselves, we need a new set of skills for successful relationships. *Beyond Mars and Venus* will teach you these skills.

Just because women today work side by side with men in the workplace and men participate more in raising their children, it does not mean men and women are the same. Our roles are certainly changing but our biology is still very different. And because men and women are different, we react to the changes in our roles in different ways, ways that are often misunderstood and misinterpreted by our partners. In *Beyond Mars and Venus* we will explore in great detail our new needs for emotional support as well as the added challenges that inevitably arise in modern relationships as a result.

**Our reactions to change are
often misunderstood because we
are different from each other.**

These challenges relate to single people as much as to couples, because the changes in our modern relationships are a reflection of the changes that are currently happening within us as individuals. The new insights we receive by going beyond Mars and Venus are necessary not just for romantic relationships but also for our own happiness as well as that of our children. They help us to be better coworkers and, by understanding others better, be more successful. Whether you are single or in intimate relationships, you are always relating to people of the opposite sex.

If you are single and searching for someone to spend your life with, this book will help you be a better partner to that person when you find them. If you are single and not looking for a partner, this book will help you to understand your own emotional needs so that you can lower your stress and experience increasing happiness.

**These new insights are necessary
for romantic relationships
as well as our own happiness.**

Many single people long to be married, while just as many married couples long for the freedom they had and the excitement they felt when they were single. But whether we are single or in a relationship, our lives can be harder today than ever before. Harder not just on a material level but because we are seeking a higher level of emotional fulfillment, and when that level is not attained we feel a higher level of disappointment.

What we are witnessing is a dramatic shift in the context of our relationships. Trying to have successful relationships today while using the skills and insights developed for traditional relationships over thousands of years is simply not enough and does not work.

For both men and women, providing each other the new support necessary to create a fulfilling relationship is a tall order. Most men have no role models for providing this kind of support. I know I certainly didn't. Our relationship training came from watching our fathers, who may have been skilled in the old model but not in this new one. By going to work every day to provide for their families, our fathers could fulfill most of our mothers' relationship expectations.

By going to work every day to provide for their families, our fathers could fulfill most of our mothers' expectations.

Likewise, women do not have role models for getting the support they require today or giving men the support they need. Effective communication skills to ask for more were not part of a woman's training. If a woman's husband fulfilled his role by providing for their family, there was nothing more for her to ask for. If he didn't fulfill his role, her only recourse was to complain and nag, which certainly didn't bring them closer.

Our modern role models come from TV sitcoms and movies, which provide great entertainment, but do not show the sometimes challenging and difficult road to actually creating fulfilling relationships. In the popular sitcom *Modern Family*, we laugh as characters behave and communicate in ways that exaggerate our own modern challenges and experiences—but in the last five minutes, everyone miraculously reconnects and feels happy and loving. They show the outcomes we long for but not the practical process of transformation.

In classic romantic movies like *When Harry Met Sally*, *Titanic*, *The Notebook*, and my favorite, *Somewhere in Time*, by identifying with the characters, we get to glimpse the deep love that is possible when the tension of unrequited love is released. We get a peek into the possibilities of happiness and fulfillment that love can bring when the characters are able to overcome some obstacle to finally find the one they are looking for. What we see on the big screen, we feel within ourselves and long to experience in our lives. But what the movies don't show is what happens next when the realities of daily life set in.

Our role models for new relationships come from TV and the movies; they don't give a realistic picture of real romance.

We imagine that the characters live happily ever after, but we are not shown how. We are temporarily uplifted by a vision of possibilities, only to be disappointed by the clash of our dreams and the reality of our lives. To create a lifetime of love, to actually grow in love together, we need to learn new skills not demonstrated in the movies.

Men are not shown the importance of affection and positive feedback in bringing out the best in their partners, how to make decisions together when their partner has a different point of view, how to schedule time together when one partner has more work responsibilities, how to plan dates and not wait to the last minute to keep the romance alive, or how to resolve arguments or listen to his partner's feelings without getting defensive.

Women are not shown the practicalities of how to bring out the best in their partners, how to fulfill their partners' different needs, how to communicate their own needs without complaining, or simply how to play their role in creating lasting romance. In the movies, the romantic hero always says the right things and the heroine only needs to respond. In real life, romance is not all up to just one partner—it's a two-way street.

**In real life, romance is not all up to just
one partner—it's a two-way street.**

This journey of transformation into someone who knows their own needs and is able to support their partner's is not immediate. But you can begin this journey now; you don't have to wait for your current partner, or a future partner, to join you. All it takes is for one partner to change and the relationship will change. Eventually, as one person becomes a better partner, the other comes along.

When I wrote *Men Are from Mars, Women Are from Venus*, a question I heard for years was: How do I get my partner to read this book?

My answer: Don't. Trying to get your partner to read the book can imply that your partner is not good enough and he or she may become defensive. Instead, read it for yourself, and practice the tools that will help you to be happier without needing to change your partner at all. Chances are, your partner will eventually become curious and want to know what you are reading.

The same is true for this book. Your focus should be on changing yourself, not your partner. As long as your happiness depends on changing your partner, you make it more difficult for them to change and grow. Just as you want the freedom to be yourself, they, too, need that freedom.

Sometimes if we give more, we will get more, but other times we get more by doing less. When we give more because we aren't getting enough, we run the risk of giving more solely to change our partners, and that just doesn't work. It feels to your partner like manipulation rather than support!

Giving more to change your partner feels like manipulation rather than support.

There is nothing wrong with wanting more in a relationship, but trying to change your partner is not the way to get it. When you are not getting enough in your relationship, the first step is to give less to your partner and instead give more to yourself. Instead of trying to change your partner, change yourself. Making a change will always bring forth another part of your partner. When you change what you do, you will always get a different result, but when you change how you feel, the result is even more dramatic. Throughout *Beyond Mars and Venus* you will learn new strategies for changing your feelings so that you can bring forth the best in your partner. By developing your ability to find happiness in your life without demanding a change from your partner, you are then free to give more and eventually get more.

By finding happiness without demanding that your partner change, you are then free to give more and still be happier.

Quite often, couples in troubled relationships have a long list of legitimate complaints. When this is the case, there can be no solution unless both parties can back off from blaming each other and take responsibility for their part in the problems. Blaming is our only recourse when our happiness is dependent on our partners. Couples often get caught in a blame game that looks a little like a tennis match: she gets upset about something, he defends himself and gets upset with her. And then the blame goes back and forth. The only way out is to stop blaming your partner by learning a new way to come back to love. And this is exactly what the insights in *Beyond Mars and Venus* will show you how to do, by providing the necessary new knowledge to create a mutually supportive, complaint-free relationship.

When you are coming from a place of fulfillment, you have more to give. When your heart is fully open, and you have new gender-specific insights regarding your partner's new needs, not only will you experience a higher level of fulfillment but also, with your help, your partner will be able to respond better to your own new needs. It rarely works to ask for more when you are dissatisfied with what you are getting. But even more important, it never works to ask for more when your partner is not getting what they need.

It doesn't work to ask for more when your partner is not getting what they need.

To improve your relationship, your first step is to find your way back to opening your heart without depending on your partner to change. Your second step is to feel, say, or do what you can to help them. By giving them what they need, they will be way more inclined to give you what you need in return. Your third step is to ask for more in small increments while giving your partner big rewards for giving more. This is your formula for success; expecting more without giving more first is a formula for failure. In addition, expecting too much too soon will also sabotage all your efforts.

Many women feel they are already giving more and they are not getting any results. That is often because what they are giving is not what their partner needs most. Without new insight, a woman instinctively gives the kind of support she is wanting but not what her partner really needs. Without a deeper under-standing of how men think and feel differently from women, her efforts go unappreciated, as she is unable to provide the new support a modern man needs.

Likewise, most men think they are giving plenty because they are often giving more than their fathers gave. But because today a woman's needs are different, duplicating his father's behaviors and attitudes for providing loving support is not enough to fulfill her.

In previous generations, husbands provided a kind of lov-ing support that fulfilled a woman's needs for survival and secu-rity. But today, a modern woman requires a new expression of love that supports her emotional needs for affection, sharing, romance, intimate communication, and equal respect as well as an increased need for independence and self-expression. For clarity, I call this new kind of support "personal love."

**Women today require a new kind of support
to fulfill their needs for *personal love*.**

In a similar but different manner, men also have new emo-tional needs to feel successful and appreciated for their attempts to fulfill their partner's emotional needs while also fulfilling their own needs for increased independence and self-expression. In the past, a man could feel successful in life by providing for the material fulfillment of the family, but today a man has new needs: to feel trusted, admired, and appreciated for his efforts to provide the new emotional support a woman and his children need. I call this new requirement a man's need for "personal suc-cess." He needs positive feedback that lets him know he is suc-cessful in his efforts to support his family not only on a material level but emotionally as well.

**Men today require a new kind of support
that fulfills their need for *personal success*.**

In *Beyond Mars and Venus*, we will explore in great detail modern men's and women's new but different emotional needs for a more personal love and personal success. This insight is essential to creating a complaint-free relationship, because by understanding what is most important to your partner's fulfillment, you can target your energies to provide the love and support that they will value and appreciate most.

**By understanding what is most important
to your partner's fulfillment, you can
more successfully target your energies and love.**

In practical terms, take a couple of months after reading this book to first apply your new insights to experience greater happiness and better stress management without depending on your partner to change. The next step is to begin giving a little more love and support in small doses according to the specific *personal love* or *personal success* your partner needs. Last, as you are giving your partner what they need, you can begin to apply your new skills for asking for more in small increments while giving them big rewards.

Both men and women in relationships need to find their own happiness first without depending on their partner changing. Likewise, a single person must find their happiness without depending on finding the perfect partner for them. If you are single, during this first step of increasing your self-reliance, let go of trying to find the perfect person and instead practice your new relationship skills by creating a series of positive dating experiences. It is much easier to develop new skills when there is not a lot at stake. By changing your intention from finding the perfect person to instead focusing on having a positive experience, you will be free from being too picky or judgmental about who you choose to practice your new skills with.

Changing your intention to just having positive dating experiences will free you to enjoy practicing your new skills.

To be happy and fulfilled in our relationships, we first need to be happy and fulfilled in our lives. It is unrealistic to depend on our intimate relationships as the sole source of fulfillment. When we create a life rich in friendships, family, exercise, good food, meaningful work, or service to the world, and have plenty of opportunities for fun, entertainment, education, personal growth, and spiritual devotion, then having a loving relationship can make us even happier. To experience lasting love in relationships today, you must find a baseline of happiness by fulfilling your other needs separate from your needs for an intimate relationship.

To be fulfilled in an intimate relationship, you must first find a baseline of happiness by fulfilling your other needs separate from your partner.

Many people mistakenly assume that success alone in the outer world brings happiness in our personal world. But this is not true. It takes love and new relationship skills. If success were enough, why then are the tabloids so full of stories of famous, successful people going in and out of rehab centers? Why are so many successful people divorced, single, or estranged from their children? Why are the rich not exempt from the symptoms of unhappiness: depression, anxiety, and sleepless nights?

By taking greater responsibility for your happiness, you become free to provide the personal love and messages of personal success that are required for your relationship to thrive. Until you have experienced the greater fulfillment that comes with the deeper intimacy achieved through expressions of personal love and success, it can be impossible to imagine. You can't know how good ice cream tastes until you taste it. Many men and woman today are lost in the trance of the modern world that says more money or things will make them happier, and they are unable to recognize the power of love.

It is hard to imagine the power of personal love until you experience it.

I remember when I first recognized the power and value of personal love. Certainly I have always loved my wife and that love was very fulfilling, but I didn't realize how important giving personal love was. I was still overly focused on making money to be a good provider and be loved for that.

One day, in the sixth year of our marriage, after making love, I said to Bonnie, "Wow, that was great sex. That was as good as it was in the beginning."

After a longer pause than I expected, Bonnie said, "I thought it was better than in the beginning."

Then I said, "Really, why do you think that?"

She said, "Making love in the beginning was great, but we really didn't know each other. Now after six years you have seen the best of me and the worst of me. And you still adore me. That makes sex much better."

In that moment I realized that the deeper intimacy we had experienced over the first six years had made sex even more fulfilling. For me this was an important revelation. Particularly for men, sex is a doorway to feel their deep love for their partner. But with greater intimacy from years of expressing a more personal love, sex becomes only one of the many expressions of love. With the new insights in *Beyond Mars and Venus* for fulfilling our modern needs for personal love and success, you will learn there are many ways to experience intimacy—and sex is only one of those ways.

After thirty-one years of marriage, I continue to experience a deeper and more intimate love for my wife, not only in the bedroom but also through regular hugs, affection, mutual support, and kind and supportive communication, along with fun dates and spending time with our children and grandchildren. I am no longer dependent on sex as the only doorway to connect with my love for Bonnie. Sex has become one of the many ways we experience and share our love for each other.

There are many ways to experience intimacy and sex is only one of those ways.

My wife's comment that sex was better after six years helped me realize that it was love that made sex so fulfilling. That day I realized the power of personal love and the greater fulfillment that it provides. When I saw that my character was appreciated more than my physical or material support, I learned to appreciate my own personal power to give love as much as my power to make money.

With this insight, a man's heart opens more. No longer does he have to give up all his own wishes and wants to provide monetary support for his wife and family. As they share this financial responsibility together, he is free to discover the power of his heart and not only his wallet. He is no longer just a "human doing" but a "human being" as well.

**When a man's personal love is appreciated
by a woman, he discovers the power of his heart
and not only the power of his wallet.**

Many men stay single primarily because they are not confident that a woman will stay happy in their relationship. They don't know their inner potential to provide exactly what a modern woman today needs. In marriage, without these new skills the passion disappears; men give up trying to make their partners happy and women stop depending on their partners for love and support.

With this new understanding of the modern woman, a man knows what he can provide and what he can't. He doesn't take responsibility for her happiness so he doesn't feel a sense of failure when she is upset or unhappy. With this insight, at times when there is little he can do, he is then free to "not make it worse" as he patiently allows her to find her way back to love. At other times, when she is open to his love, he knows just what to do to make her happier.

So many women today don't want to get married because they have given up on men. They are hungry for a man who can provide the kind of personal love that a girlfriend cannot give them or that they cannot give to themselves. With no clear pathway to success, they have given up. But with the new insights in this book, a woman can access her female power to get what she needs, and her man can discover his inner power to give her what she needs while getting what he needs in return.

Jimi Hendrix is often quoted as saying, "When the power of love overcomes the love of power, the world will know peace." I personally believe that people who strive to find and develop the power of love at home are the new heroes of our time.

When the power of love overcomes the love of power, the world will know peace.

It is much easier to drop a bomb than to drop our egos and find love. It is much easier to escape the pain of our broken hearts by running away from love. But those who continue to try are the most noble and deserve more love and encouragement, even—especially—when they make mistakes.

Today we all want more—from our lives, and from our relationships.

The good news is that we *can* have more. But first, we must learn how to get it.

Beyond
MARS
and
VENUS

1

BEYOND MARS
AND VENUS

Men Are from Mars, Women Are from Venus explored the most common challenges and misunderstandings between men and women and offered solutions for the world as it was twenty years ago. Since then, our relationships have changed dramatically—we are more free than ever before to go beyond limiting male and female stereotypes, and as a result, the common Mars and Venus qualities and characteristics assigned to men and women are no longer so clear-cut.

Our needs have changed, both as individuals and relative to each other, and because we are not aware of these changed needs or how to meet them, we're experiencing rising stress and dissatisfaction in our relationships and lives. We need new insights, tailored to how we have moved beyond the old concepts of Mars and Venus, that still honor the differences between men and women and the challenges that arise from not understanding our differences in a positive way.

The many ideas of *Men Are from Mars, Women Are from Venus* are still relevant in a variety of ways, but they need to be updated and applied to our new challenges. The Mars/Venus ideas have become part of popular culture, and they've helped millions of men and women communicate better, but with popularity and time their meanings have been watered down, oversimplified, and even distorted and narrowed.

Many people who haven't read *Men Are from Mars, Women Are from Venus* mistakenly assume the title means that we are so different we will never understand each other. Nothing could be further from the truth. When we encounter shared differences, if we have a way to understand those differences in a positive way, one that can makes sense to us, then communication improves. Understanding differences alone is not a magic solution to every problem, but good communication can make any situation better.

Understanding our differences in a way that makes sense is the foundation of good communication.

Before diving into what's new about Mars/Venus, it's important to recap the essential principles explored in *Men Are from Mars, Women Are from Venus*. Listed below are twelve key factors that commonly lead to misunderstandings between men and women in more traditional relationships. However, in our complex modern world, as women take on the traditional roles of men, quite automatically they relate more to many of the Mars tendencies. In a similar way, men may also take on the Venus tendencies as they begin to share traditionally female roles at home. As you read this list, reflect on which ones you relate more to. In what ways are you or your partner from Mars or Venus?

Factor	Mars Tendency	Venus Tendency
1. Values	Self-reliance	Sharing
On Mars, they value independence, accomplishment, and success. Making a difference is a high priority. On Venus, they value sharing, nurturing, and interdependence in relationships. Giving and receiving love is a high priority.		
2. Handling Stress	Withdraw	Connect
On Mars, they retreat into their "caves" to recharge when stressed. They use this time to get away from their problems or to subconsciously work out solutions. On Venus, they handle stress by discussing their problems with people close to them, seeking empathy and support.		
3. Giving Support	Keeps it fair	Gives as much as they can
On Mars, they give the support they see as fair and then relax to receive an equal amount of support in return. On Venus, they give as much as they can, but often give more than they get and as a result feel overwhelmed and ultimately resentful.		
4. Showing Love	Cyclical	Continuous
On Mars, they get close, pull away to take space, and then spring back full of love. On Venus, they feel a greater need for ongoing feelings of closeness, attachment, and intimacy.		
5. Scoring Points	Thinks big	Appreciates many small gestures of love
On Mars, they give points based on the size of the expression of love. When they give thirty-two roses, they expect thirty-two points.		

On Venus, little expressions of love are just as important as big expressions. They give one point for each expression of love. If they receives thirty-two roses, they give one point. If they receive one rose, they give one point. To get thirty-two points, Mars needs to give one rose thirty-two times.

6. Moods	Steady	Waves

On Mars, their mood is usually even. They require less reassurance, but their need for intimacy regularly decreases and then increases. Like a rubber band they pull away but eventually spring back.

On Venus, their moods rise and fall like waves. They have a greater need for reassurance that they are loved. With understanding and acceptance, negative feelings and insecurities automatically shift into positive feelings.

7. Reason for Communicating	Practical	For connection

On Mars, they talk to solve problems or gather information to achieve certain goals.

On Venus, they talk to solve problems but also to feel connection and empathy.

8. Needs	Direct	Indirect

On Mars, they are direct; they speak up and ask for what they want.

On Venus, they follow the golden rule and give to others what they want to receive; they expect their needs will be met without having to ask.

9. Intimacy	Sex	Romance

On Mars, they want a partner who wants and enjoys sex as much as they do. (This is a change from previous generations.) Sex helps them to feel their love.

On Venus, loving gestures outside the bedroom are just as important as what happens inside the bedroom. Love helps them to feel their desire for sex.

10. Problem Solving	Takes actions	Appreciates support

On Mars, when faced with a big problem, they either take immediate action or, if there is nothing they can do, simply let it go until they can do something.

On Venus, they talk about the problem to attract support to face the challenge together.

11. Mistakes	Corrects actions	Gives more

On Mars, when mistakes are made, they reflect on what they did or did not do. They decide what they can then do to solve the problem.

On Venus, when mistakes are made, they feel a greater sense of empathy and regret and then reflect on how they can give more to make up for their mistake or make the current situation better.

12. Happiness	Goal-oriented	Relationship-oriented

On Mars, they are happiest when they're successful in achieving meaningful goals. They feel great satisfaction and pride through overcoming challenges.

On Venus, they are happiest when their personal needs for love are fulfilled. They can then freely enjoy giving their love and support, trusting they will receive what they need in return.

Men and women have always related in different ways to these Mars/Venus tendencies, but as you have probably noticed, with every passing year more women can relate to the male tendencies and more men can relate to the female tendencies. That's because this chart only describes Mars and Venus *tendencies*. As individuals, we are each a unique blend of these tendencies. There is no right or wrong blend.

In the case of your relationship, it may appear that now the tables are turned and *women* are from Mars and *men* are from Venus. Or it may be in your relationship that men are still from Mars and women are still from Venus.

In either case, a greater awareness of our different tendencies, when and if they show up, makes us better prepared to deal with them. The following chapters will explore how these tendencies may have changed or be different for you and provide new insights that will support you and your relationships regardless of how much you identify with one set of tendencies or the other.

Changing Roles

The growing number of men and women who reflect their opposite gender tendency is a good thing, because it means we are experiencing increased freedom to be who we truly are, independent of social expectations. But in shedding the shackles of our traditional Mars/Venus roles, in some cases we have let go of one role to simply take on another that is just as limiting.

In shedding the shackles of our traditional Mars/Venus roles, in some cases we have let go of one role to take on another that is just as limiting.

Many women today have moved too far to their male side and then complain that they are stressed, exhausted, depressed, or simply can't relax and enjoy their lives.

Joan is a lawyer in a big law firm. Joan is often overwhelmed with too much to do and can't relax when she gets home. She makes more money than her husband Jack, so they decided he would work part time and stay home to raise the children. They love each other and are mutually supportive, but, like many couples, the passion is gone in their relationship.

Joan felt gender differences were not significant at all. At a small party, I mentioned to her that I was writing a new book.

Joan said, "I don't relate to Men Are from Mars, Women Are from Venus *at all. I don't think men and women are so different."*

Jack responded by saying, "I think there is a lot of truth to it. If you just reverse the title to Women Are from Mars, Men Are from Venus, *I think it describes our relationship perfectly. We are very different!"*

Later on, I spoke privately to Jack and asked, "How are you and your partner different?"

Jack laughed and then said, "In a hundred different ways. I read Men Are from Mars *and my wife is definitely from Mars. You say women want to talk more, but when Joan comes home she is too busy to talk, and when she does talk she wants solutions. She doesn't just want to share about her day.*

"I am the one who wants to connect; I want to talk about my day but when I try she becomes impatient or she interrupts me with solutions and suggestions and can't just listen. She tells me I shouldn't feel what I feel.

"When it comes to romance, affection, or hugs, she could care less. Most of the time when she is home she is in her cave either watching the news or working online. We really don't have much of a personal life and she doesn't seem to mind.

"We would not even have a social life if I didn't insist on it. Trying to create time for just us is like pulling teeth."

The kind of role reversal we see in Joan and Jack's relationship is an extreme example but similar shifts in roles and needs have become more common today. Free from outdated social expectations, people today are more capable of embracing both male and female qualities within themselves and in a potential partner. Men are commonly more supportive of a woman with a career, and women are more supportive of a man whose ambitions are less about making money and more about following his heart, which often includes spending more time parenting as well as creating quality relationships.

Free from outdated social expectations, people today are more capable of embracing both their male and female qualities.

With this openness to change, men and women have more flexibility to take on different roles according to their financial needs, age, relationship status, or personal preference. As women take on more traditional male roles that support the expression of their masculine qualities, it actually changes parts of their brains, as well as what hormones their bodies produce. Research into brain plasticity over the last decade reveals that what we do during the day changes our brains, which in turn stimulates different hormones in the body.

Most traditional male occupations will stimulate more male hormones. Working on a construction site or defending a client in the courtroom will stimulate high levels of testosterone for both men and women, while teaching a kindergarten class or nursing a patient will stimulate more estrogen. When women take on traditional male roles, at home they will often exhibit more of the Mars tendencies described in *Men Are from Mars, Women Are from Venus*, because these roles stimulate more male hormones and fewer female hormones. The same is true of men who take on more traditionally female roles; they may relate more to the Venus tendencies.

But when women take on traditional male jobs, it becomes even more important for them to express their female side at home to find a healthy balance of their male and female hormones. Without the right balance of hormones, a woman's feelings of boredom, dissatisfaction, emptiness, and restlessness increase. However, when a woman takes some time to feel, embrace, and express her female qualities after a long day of expressing her masculine side, it will actually lower her stress levels.

Likewise, when men spend more time in nurturing activities during their workday, it becomes even more important for them to access and express their Mars qualities in their personal romantic relationships.

One of the big reasons couples lose the passion in their romantic relationships is that they are missing the insights and new skills to find this balance of male and female qualities within themselves. If a man is suppressing his masculine side or a woman is suppressing her female side, it will create boredom or restlessness and kill the passion. He becomes too soft or emotional and she becomes too hard and detached. His energy levels may drop at home and she may become more and more overwhelmed, feeling she has too much to do. In later chapters we will explore the many different symptoms of suppression along with new insights and strategies for finding a healthy balance.

Finding Balance to Sustain Passion

One of the biggest challenges to finding balance is that for most people, balancing our male and female sides is not automatic and does not always immediately feel good. This shift to balance one's male and female sides is not automatic but often takes a clear act of will.

At the end of the day, when Joan returns home, she is more interested in going to her cave, a Mars tendency, while Jack is more interested in talking to connect, a Venus tendency. These automatic tendencies may feel like they are required to feel good, but they are more often counterproductive and kill the passion.

**Balancing our male and female sides
is not automatic and
does not always immediately feel good.**

At the end of their workdays, both Jack and Joan are automatically doing what feels good. But doing what feels good or is automatic is not always good for us. It may feel good to go shopping, but it will certainly create additional problems if you can't afford what you buy. During an argument, it may feel good to yell at your partner, but it certainly doesn't create a better outcome. It may feel good to counter your partner's complaints with your own complaints, but it usually just pushes them away.

We automatically do many things in our relationships that just make things worse. Without a clear alternative that could work better, we tend to mindlessly repeat our mistakes, not because they work but because they are automatic or just feel good.

**It may feel good to counter
your partner's complaints with your own,
but it usually just pushes them away.**

Everyone knows some foods are good for us while others taste good but are not good for us. If you eat a few cookies, it raises your blood sugar. Each cookie feels good, so it takes willpower to resist eating another and another. But with each cookie you eat, your blood sugar level goes further out of balance. Doing what feels good is not always the right path to take.

If a woman is too far on her male side, she needs to first recognize that she is out of balance, and then she needs a clear awareness of what complementary female quality she needs to express to find balance. Without clear insight regarding the different complementary qualities of her male and female sides, finding this balance is nearly impossible. (We'll explore the twelve most common different male and female qualities in detail in a later chapter, to help both men and women find their inner balance.)

When Joan returns home, she either keeps working or goes to her cave to relax and forget the problems of her day. What she doesn't know is that she can actually relax better and leave her work problems behind by learning new skills for sharing her feelings and connecting with her partner.

Jack faces a similar challenge. If a man suppresses parts of his male side during the day, then he, too, needs to find balance in his personal life. At the end of the day he needs to reconnect more with his male side. After nurturing his children during the day, Jack wants to connect more with his partner by sharing his feelings, but he can actually connect better by first taking some cave time or by listening to Joan talk about her day, rather than talking more about his own. And, although it can sound shocking at first, men who talk too much about their feelings can actually kill the romance in their relationships. (In later chapters we will explore why in much greater detail.)

**Although it can sound shocking at first,
men who talk too much about their feelings
can actually kill the romance in their relationships.**

Without new insight into our need for balance, Joan automatically moves more to her male side at home and Jack automatically moves more to his female side. Unless these automatic tendencies are reversed, Joan and Jack will unknowingly create more distance and stress in their relationship. And with new insight on how to find that balance, Jack is still free to express his female side and share about his day, just not when his partner needs to share more. Joan is also free to express her male side and take her cave time, just in a new way that allows her to really relax and fully enjoy it.

Joan and Jack are only one example of the different ways modern men and women may go out of balance and lose the passion in their relationship. Without new relationship skills that specifically support our changing roles, this new dynamic, even as it increases our personal freedom, can also increase our stress. This added stress takes a toll on our relationships, happiness, and health.

Of course I'm not suggesting that to overcome our new challenges we switch back to our traditional roles. Regardless of what roles we choose, our intimate relationships can be greatly enriched by understanding our specific emotional needs according to the hormonal needs of our biological sex. By accepting and appreciating our differences, we can support each other and ourselves in a new way that lets us better meet our new challenges and find balance.

Again, there is no one right way to relate to these Mars and Venus tendencies. Each man and woman does so in their own unique way. One woman will have a greater need to connect with her partner by sharing feelings, while another will have a greater need to be more independent and take more time for herself. Some men will have a greater sense of independence, while others will want to share more time with their spouse. But with a greater understanding of our differences, and of our gender-specific hormonal needs, regardless of our changing roles during the workday, we are better equipped to get the support we need in our personal lives and give the best support to our partner.

Regardless of what roles we choose, with the right insight we can still find balance in our lives.

The Problem with Changing Roles

While our increased ability to choose our roles means we are more able to express parts of ourselves that our traditional roles did not allow, taking on different roles can also suppress other parts of who we are. When we are too masculine, we are suppressing parts of our female side. When we are too feminine, we are suppressing parts of our male side. This inner suppression causes additional stress. Finding balance is the answer, although everyone's balance is different. If you are suppressing one part during your workday, then to lower your stress levels, you need to find your balance at home in your personal life.

The problem with our changing roles is they can suppress other parts of who we are.

Without understanding practical ways to find this balance, we tend to get further out of balance. This prolonged suppression eventually leads to chronic stress and burnout. Situations that are already challenging become even more stressful. Without these insights for finding balance, it is harder to give and receive the love and support that can lower our stress and enrich our lives.

Consider, again, Joan and Jack's story. During the day at work, while solving urgent problems and being tough and competitive, Joan suppresses her more feminine, vulnerable, and cooperative side. While taking care of the kids at home, her husband Jack is able to express his more sensitive and nurturing side, but is also suppressing many of his masculine qualities.

Even though Joan loves her job, because she suppresses many of her feminine qualities at work, she feels extra-stressed and overwhelmed when she returns home. Coming home ideally should help her to find balance and reduce her stress, not be another source of it.

Joan loves her job, but when she comes home she is exhausted, overwhelmed, and more stressed.

Jack has a different challenge. Without the pressure to fully provide financially for his family, and with the freedom to spend more time with his children, his nurturing side can unfold. While this can feel really good and in some ways is very fulfilling for him, by suppressing his masculine, competitive qualities his nurturing responsibilities can eventually make him extra tired or needy.

The new insights in *Beyond Mars and Venus* not only help couples like Joan and Jack to balance the expression of their male and female sides, but also support couples in more traditional relationships where the man is the primary financial provider and the woman is the primary caretaker of the children.

In a more traditional relationship, a man's daily work responsibilities can easily suppress his feminine side. Likewise, a woman staying home with the children can easily suppress her masculine side. For both men and women, the suppression of our authentic self inhibits our ability to experience lasting passion.

Fortunately, the changes in our expectations for men and women have made it much easier for us to find the balance we need. For example, many women today who could depend on their husband's salary and be stay-at-home mothers choose to take on part-time jobs to support the expression of their male side; in this way they are much happier. Likewise, many men who are the main financial providers in the relationship are choosing to work less, spend more time on recreation, and participate more in raising their children

These changes can liberate us and lead us to greater balance. Barbara Marx Hubbard, an author and inspirational teacher and my friend, dealt with her changing role as she grew older and wiser in a very positive way. As she told me, "When my children had all grown up, I suddenly felt like a teenage boy, energetic and wanting to make a difference in the world. I was vocationally aroused."

Having supported her female side as a mother, she was now able to express more of her male side by starting a successful career as a public speaker and author while staying grounded in her feminine ability to nurture. This allowed her to remain happy and emotionally fulfilled.

But these changes can also suppress parts of who we are. At "retirement age" too many men give up having meaningful work each day and instead focus primarily on enjoyment and relaxation. This suppresses their male side, increasing their stress, which is exactly what they thought retirement would let them avoid! This increased stress can have serious consequences: men's risk of heart disease in the first three years of retirement skyrockets.

Besides understanding our own changing needs as we take on new roles, we also need to understand how our partner's needs differ from our own. The right kind of love and support can be instrumental in helping our partners find their own balance, and *Beyond Mars and Venus* will show you how to support your partner while finding your own balance.

Our New Possibilities

In the following chapters, we will explore the many new challenges and possibilities that arise as both men and women are released from the limitations of a traditional relationship. With greater access to our inner feminine and masculine characteristics, we now are living in a time when the possibilities of increasing love, success, and happiness are within our reach.

So often people feel they can't make a relationship work because they and their partner are too different. By understanding our different tendencies in a positive way, we can begin to make sense of our partners and discover new strategies for giving and receiving love and support.

The truth is, we are all different, and that is why we are attracted to each other. Complementary opposites attract. It is the foundation of chemistry. It is why we need each other; we all have something special to contribute to each other and the world. What we take for granted in ourselves provides a special kind of support for others.

What we take for granted in ourselves provides a special kind of support for others.

By clearly understanding your unique balance of masculine and feminine characteristics, you will have greater validation, permission, and clarity to express who you are and a new perspective from which to get the specific support you need. Not only will you be happier, you'll become a better partner, too.

2

FROM ROLE MATE TO
SOUL MATE

I n my seminars I ask audiences, "Who had parents who stayed together and didn't get divorced?"

Usually about half the people raise their hands.

I then ask that group, "Who thinks you have better communication and relationship skills than your parents?"

In response, almost everyone raises his or her hands.

This common response begs the question, "If we have better skills, why are we more challenged in our relationships? Why are more people single? Why is there so much divorce?"

The answer is twofold. The world has changed in the last fifty years in ways that have radically increased our stress. What we want in our relationships has changed as well. While our communication and relationship skills are often better than our parents', our relationships are under stress in new ways, and so our challenges are even greater. Couples today long to have a new kind of relationship. They have higher expectations, and unless they understand how to fulfill those expectations, they have greater disappointment.

**Couples today have higher expectations
and greater disappointment
when their new needs are not fulfilled.**

Our parents or grandparents were often content as long as their partners fulfilled a specific role. This is a Role Mate relationship. But today we want to experience a higher level of emotional fulfillment that comes from a relationship in which we are able to freely express our authentic and unique selves. This is a Soul Mate relationship.

In a Soul Mate relationship we are able to freely express our authentic and unique selves.

In a beautiful twist of fate, it turns out that the most effective way for couples to reduce the rising stress caused by modern changes in the outside world is by coming together as Soul Mates. And by joining together as Soul Mates to overcome these increased levels of stress, we can actually rise to greater heights of love and fulfillment than were possible in the Role Mate relationship. As with any challenge, if we are prepared to meet the one presented by today's new reality, we become stronger and wiser.

The Role Mate Relationship

A traditional Role Mate relationship is based on stereotypical male and female roles in which the man is the provider and the women is the nurturing homemaker. The primary purpose of a Role Mate relationship was to divide responsibilities between men and women to ensure the survival and security of their tribe or society as well as their individual families. Simply put, partners were picked primarily on their ability to fulfill these roles and not on romantic chemistry.

Shakespeare's Romeo and Juliet are the classic examples of romantic love because they died right after getting married. If they had lived, they would have ended up in a passionless marriage like everyone else at that time in history. They would have been pushed into a traditional Role Mate relationship and the passion they felt in the beginning would have dissipated.

In our modern relationships, without new skills for creating a Soul Mate relationship, our passion will be as temporary as it was in the days of Romeo and Juliet. But with the freedom and emotional support to fully and authentically express ourselves, the passion we feel in the beginning of a relationship can be sustained for a lifetime.

Romeo and Juliet are only examples of romantic love because they died right after getting married.

In the sixteenth century, during the time of Romeo and Juliet's short-lived affair, romantic chemistry or the euphoric feelings of new love were commonly known to be fleeting and therefore insignificant. Parents picked their children's marriage partners. These arranged marriages were very common throughout the world until the eighteenth century, and are still common in parts of China, India, and other developing countries. In an arranged marriage, the determining factors for picking a Role Mate are less about romantic love and more about practical qualifications. At different times in history and in different cultures around the world, the requirements for a Role Mate were often the same. Here is a list of the most common, which were considered more important than romantic feelings:

1. A woman's youth, virginity, and ability to have children
2. A man's strength and height
3. Mental, emotional, and physical health
4. Wealth
5. Family's social status
6. Same race
7. Same religion
8. Parental approval

While Role Mate relationships benefited society, many men and women were left unfulfilled because it meant suppressing parts of themselves that didn't fit their roles. Men who wanted to care for their children or who might have preferred a lower-paid but more fulfilling job kept this to themselves because they were needed to support their family. Women who wanted more intellectual challenge or who had ambitions beyond home life had to stifle this part of themselves to focus on caring for their family.

Today we no longer find this self-repression acceptable. In the last 200 years, and particularly in the last fifty years, we have come a long way. With women becoming more financially independent, educated, and self-reliant, both men's and women's emotional requirements for selecting a suitable partner have changed.

Because a woman is no longer fully dependent on her husband to fulfill her needs for survival and security, she has greater freedom to pursue her own dreams and act on her feelings. If a marriage is not working, it is now much easier to get a divorce. In 1969 the rate of divorce in America went from 10 percent to 50 percent in one year. The rates skyrocketed partly because this was the year no-fault divorce policies were instituted, but also because women were already more financially independent and so had the means to survive on their own.

For women, a man's strength, size, social status, or wealth are no longer dominant factors in her selection process. They are still factors, but she is also looking for romantic chemistry. A dominant requirement for getting married is "falling in love." Women are especially looking for a partner who can provide a new level of emotional support. Men's requirements have changed as well. A woman's domestic skills are no longer a major requirement for men in picking a marriage partner. He is more interested in how a woman makes him feel than in her abilities to cook and clean or her race, religion, or social status.

A man is more interested in how a woman makes him feel than her abilities to cook and clean or her race, religion, or social status.

Without the many pressures of being a sole financial provider, a man feels a greater freedom to follow his dreams, or at least strike a balance in his life between working hard to make money and taking time for his own personal fulfillment. He is released from the self-imposed burden of sacrificing his own emotional needs to financially support his wife and family, as well as from the social pressure to do so. Unlike his predecessors, he has the luxury of feeling his emotional needs for love, recreation, and greater participation in raising his children.

A man today feels a greater freedom
to pursue his dreams and enjoy his life more.

With wider and cheaper access to birth control and the sexual revolution in the sixties, millions of men and women were freed to fulfill their sexual needs and postpone having children and getting married. Prior to this time, without birth control, if a woman got pregnant, a man was obligated to marry her, and she became dependent on him for his support. Shotgun weddings were the norm; social norms dictated that to have sex, a man and woman first had to get married.

The radical shift in social permission to have sex before marriage gave men and women extra time to pursue their education and potential careers. It also gave them more time to select a suitable partner who would provide them with the maximum emotional fulfillment.

Because men and women today are less dependent on each other to ensure the survival and security of the family, they are free to feel higher needs: for emotional support and for the opportunity to freely and authentically express themselves. Ironically, as men and women have become less dependent on each other in the material sense, they have become more dependent on each other for emotional support and personal fulfillment.

Both men and women feel higher needs:
for emotional support and for the opportunity
to freely and authentically express themselves.

Psychologist Abraham Maslow popularized the concept of needs as existing in a hierarchy in 1943. He introduced the idea that at any particular time, a certain need dominates. Our lower, more basic needs for heat, shelter, food, and safety must be satisfied before our higher needs for love and emotional fulfillment can be fully felt or dominate our awareness. Because men and women no longer need each other to meet their basic needs, higher needs have become more dominant in their awareness. The fulfillment of these higher needs is the primary requirement for relationships to thrive today.

Because a woman no longer needs a man for her food and safety, her higher needs for emotional fulfillment, love, and personal expression dominate her awareness and give rise to new wishes, wants, and motivations. Likewise, because a man is no longer required to be the sole provider for his family's food and safety, he begins to feel his higher needs for emotional fulfillment, love, and personal expression. For modern men and women, these higher needs now prevail and guide their choices, not only for picking a partner but for keeping them. Couples today are not satisfied with the status quo of a safe and secure relationship. They want more but have not yet discovered how to get more.

With modern conveniences and new opportunities to be self-sufficient, our dependence on a Role Mate decreases and the requirements of a Soul Mate relationship take center stage. Deep and lasting love, romance, emotional support, and good communication have become paramount.

With new opportunities to be self-sufficient, the requirements of a Soul Mate relationship take center stage.

The Soul Mate Relationship

Both men and women are looking for a new level of emotional fulfillment in their intimate relationships—a Soul Mate relationship. Couples today fall in love and want to stay in love. A partnership designed only to ensure their material needs is not enough. Couples hunger for a relationship that goes beyond the limitations of a Role Mate relationship to fulfill a deeper need for emotional intimacy and authentic self-expression.

Couples today fall in love and want to stay in love.

Love and its many expressions have become the deciding factor in picking a partner and staying in a relationship. Likewise, the common reasons for ending a relationship today have much more to do with a lack of emotional fulfillment than in our parents' and grandparents' time.

Let's explore a few examples:

Carol wants to divorce her partner. She says, "I give and give and I don't get back."

As her therapist I ask, "What is it that you don't get back? Help me understand that better."

Carol says, "He is no longer affectionate. I feel disappointed that he is not even interested in my life or my feelings. Everything has changed. All the romance is gone. I still love him but I am not in love.

"He wasn't this way in the beginning. We are now like two disconnected roommates leading separate lives but living in the same house. I want more in my life. I want to feel loved and appreciated."

Carol is not complaining that her partner has failed as a Role Mate. He has a good job. She is unhappy because her emotional needs are not being met. She wants him to be more affectionate and interested in her life. She wants to feel connected; she wants to feel special and in love.

Tom also wants to divorce his partner. He says, "No matter what I do, it is never enough to make her happy. When she is so stressed it is hard to feel good when I come home."

As his therapist I ask, "Why can't you feel good? Help me understand why her happiness is so important to you."

Tom says, "When she is happy, everyone is happy. But when she's unhappy she looks at me like I am the problem. I want to feel good and not feel like I am not good enough.

"She used to be really happy to see me when we returned home from work. I felt happy that I made a difference in her life. I felt appreciated and loved.

"Now it seems she is always overwhelmed. We used to really enjoy being together but that has changed, both outside and inside the bedroom."

I then ask, "How has it changed in the bedroom?"

Tom says, "When I am interested in having sex, she will almost always say yes, but her response is more from obligation rather than her delight."

I then ask, "How has that changed your sex life?"

Tom says, "Sex has become routine and boring. I don't want to give up having a great sex life. I don't want to live in a passionless marriage. I want to feel a mutual love and connection, like in the beginning."

Tom is not expecting his partner to be a better homemaker, cook, or mother to their children. They both participate in cooking, cleaning, and parenting. His disappointment has to do with his lack of emotional fulfillment, which is directly linked to her emotional fulfillment.

Unlike his father, who was content if his wife merely satisfied his sexual needs, Tom wants his partner to be lit up by his presence and enjoy sex as much as she did in the beginning of their relationship.

Tom and Carol are common examples of the challenges that arise for couples that have gone beyond the traditional roles of Mars and Venus. They want lasting passion but they haven't learned how to sustain the romantic love they felt in the beginning.

Our Modern Challenges

Besides learning to fulfill our new needs and expectations to create lasting love and passion, we must also learn to minimize the negative effects of modern stress on our relationships.

In the last fifty years, life has become more complicated and stressful. Longer working hours, intensified by grueling commutes and more traffic; the increased cost of health care, housing, food, and rising credit card debt; and the combined responsibilities of work and childcare in two-career families are only a few of the sources of stress in our fast-paced modern lives. More than ever we need to learn new ways of supporting each other and ourselves.

In spite of new technologies designed to connect us like the internet and cell phones, information overload and round-the-clock accessibility have reduced much of our communication to the equivalent of sending postcards. Both men and women are stretched to the limit with little energy for our personal lives. With increased independence and opportunities for success at work, we are often left with a sense of isolation and exhaustion at home.

**With increased opportunities for success at work,
we are often left with a sense
of isolation and exhaustion at home.**

The unprecedented levels of stress men and women are experiencing is taking a toll on our romantic relationships and limiting our ability to be successful at work. Whether single or in committed relationships, we are often too busy or too tired to sustain feelings of attraction, motivation, and affection. Everyday stress drains our energy and patience and leaves us feeling too exhausted or overwhelmed to enjoy and support each other at home, or to provide the best support for coworkers and clients.

Stress magnifies our problems at home.

We are often too busy to see how we are making choices every day that sabotage our ability to find fulfillment in our relationships. A man will give his heart and soul to make enough money to provide for his family and return home too tired even to talk with them, much less offer support. A woman will work all day and then return home to give the support she thinks her husband requires, but when he doesn't give the kind of support she needs, she feels resentful and her heart closes.

Under the influence of stress, men and women forget why we do what we do. We forget that the reason we work so hard is to provide for and care for the people we love the most. We love our partners, but we are no longer in love with them.

Too Busy and Too Tired

As I travel the world, teaching the Mars and Venus insights, I have witnessed a new trend in relationships linked to increasing stress. Both couples and singles believe they are too busy or too exhausted to resolve their relationship issues, and often think their partners are either too demanding or just too different to understand.

Attempting to cope with the increasing stress of our fast-paced lives, men and women feel neglected at home. While some couples experience increasing tension, others have just given up, sweeping their emotional needs under the carpet. They may get along, but the passion is gone.

The more traditional causes of divorce like economic problems, adultery, drug addiction, or physical abuse still exist, but they are now fueled by a growing emotional dissatisfaction, which is amplified by our increasing stress.

Global studies reveal that as women become more educated and financially independent, their risk of staying single or getting a divorce increases, their happiness decreases, and their stress levels rise. This does not have to be the case. While increasing divorce, unhappiness, and stress are the statistical norm today, many educated and financially successful women are happily married and experience less stress. The problem is not education or financial independence, but that we have not learned how to support the new needs that arise from these changes.

Certainly better conditions in the workplace can help lower our stress, but outer stress is inevitable. Our work life will always present new challenges and problems. For men and women, it is the quality of our personal relationships and home life that most determines our ability to cope effectively with that stress. My day can be filled with frustrations, disappointments, and concerns, but that can all melt away when I anticipate returning home to a loving wife and a happy family life.

**It is the quality of our home life
that most determines
our ability to cope effectively with stress.**

Certainly, too, there are many personal growth strategies that can help us to lower our stress and build our self-esteem, but the most important is giving and receiving love in our relationships. Different techniques can help us to open our minds and hearts, but without new relationship insights it is hard to sustain our positive feelings.

Learning to improve communication in our personal relationships to manage our stress effectively frees us to experience what we are all seeking in life . . . a feeling of aliveness, happiness, love, and fulfillment, along with a sense of mission, meaning, and purpose.

Instead of being another problem we have to solve, relationships can actually be the solution. Instead of coming home to a new set of problems and stress, coming home can mean entering a safe haven of loving support and comfort.

**Instead of being another problem to solve,
relationships can actually be the solution.**

We can easily feel victimized and blame the outer world for our new relationship challenges. Or we can recognize that by learning new relationship skills, we will not only cope better with increasing stress but also thrive. By facing our new sources of stress as a partnership, we can not only lower our stress but also grow closer with greater love and passion.

By learning to lower stress with
better communication skills, we can grow
closer with greater love and passion.

Growing Together in Love

When we give a part of our heart to someone, how he or she holds us in their awareness has a big effect on how we feel about ourselves, as well as our willingness to give love. If a stranger rejects you, it has little effect, but when someone you care about rejects you, it can be so painful that, to protect ourselves, we withdraw and close our hearts as we automatically put up walls and defenses.

Then, as we hold on to our various reasons for closing our heart, the result is we continue to feel a deep pain in our hearts. But this time it is no longer the pain caused by another; it is the pain caused by withholding our love. The greatest emotional pain we can experience in life occurs when we stop sharing our love with the people we love the most.

The greatest pain we can experience
occurs when we stop sharing our love
with the people we love the most.

With the new insights this book provides, you can learn to reopen your heart through compassion and appreciation rather than defend yourself with blame and resentment. You'll learn to better understand and love yourself, so that you will not be so emotionally bruised or defensive when your partner is stressed and therefore unable to support you in the ways you need. At times your Soul Mate will still frustrate and disappoint you, but with new insight regarding their unique gender-specific challenges, empathy and compassion will soften your heart and give you a greater power to look inside yourself and let go of your sometimes petty demands, unrealistic expectations, one-sided accusations, and unloving judgments.

With new insight for understanding your partner's new challenges for lowering their stress, you can be more patient and forgiving.

Then, on days when your partner is able to provide their loving support, it will shine a light on the real you and reaffirm that you are worthy of love—both theirs and your own. But at other times, when your partner is stressed and unable to provide the love you need, you will be able to shift gears and take time to do something that makes you feel good. With this approach your partner can no longer bring you down, so when you do feel their love he or she can take you higher.

Even with self-love, receiving love still makes a big difference. It is like knowing you are beautiful or handsome and then looking in the mirror to be extra delighted by seeing the true radiance of who you are. Seeing yourself in the reflection of your Soul Mate's eyes creates a greater fulfillment than you can experience alone.

Your partner's love can give you the love you need to awaken within you a greater and higher love.

When you can access your own inner happiness that is not dependent on your partner's love and support, you are free to feel compassion for their struggles, accept their imperfections, and appreciate their efforts to do their best. You discover your power to bring out the best of them over time.

With this foundation of self-love and inner happiness, you do not need your partner's love to feel happy, but you do need their love to feel *happier*; on a good day your partner's love can make you feel even happier and more willing to give your love. In this way relationships enrich our lives in ways that would be impossible for us alone.

When you can embrace and appreciate your own virtues and have compassion for your own limitations and inner challenges, you are ready to grow in love and intimacy. With this increased self-awareness and self-love you can sustain an open heart and grow together with your partner in deeper love, acceptance, and trust. With this new power you can create a true Soul Mate relationship.

This kind of growth is not possible in casual relationships. It was a surprise to me, after several years of marriage, how much better my marriage with Bonnie could be. As we continued to overcome our challenges in learning to recognize and appreciate each other's strengths while accepting, understanding, and having compassion for our limitations, our journey together has had many twists and turns. By staying together and growing in our ability to love, we have thrived.

For us, the journey of love has been like driving up and around a mountain. With every turn there is a new vista that we could never have imagined. Since beginning our journey with each other forty years ago, we have gotten lost many times, run out of gas, experienced an overheated radiator, and gotten a few speeding tickets and several flat tires. Somehow, in making it through these challenges, it has made the different views even more rewarding and beautiful.

**Overcoming our relationship challenges
has made our life together
even more rewarding and beautiful.**

Creating a Soul Mate relationship is not something that happens automatically; it is earned through our inner commitment to be true to ourselves and find a higher love, a willful intention to let go of past mistakes with forgiveness, the wisdom to correct what doesn't work in our own actions, the understanding and compassion to unconditionally accept our partner's limitations, and finally the courage to open our hearts again and again.

3

YOUR UNIQUE SELF

One of the main benefits of the Soul Mate relationship is its potential to awaken and support the natural unfolding and expression of our unique selves.

A Soul Mate relationship supports the natural unfolding and expression of our unique selves.

As we let go of traditional male and female roles, we suddenly have access to parts of ourselves we had previously suppressed or hidden. Instead of being limited to expressing characteristics related to their traditional roles, men now have greater access to their female side and women now have greater access to their male side.

A modern man is no longer required to suppress his female side to be considered a "real" man, and a modern woman is no longer required to hide her male side to be considered a "real" woman. As a result, we gain access to our authentic, unique selves: our own unique blends of masculine and feminine characteristics.

A man is no longer required to suppress his female side to be considered a "real" man. A woman is no longer required to suppress her male side to be considered a "real" woman.

The expression of our suppressed male or female side releases a tremendous energy. Expressing even a taste of our authentic self dramatically increases our sense of aliveness, energy, and passion for love and life.

For a woman, this access awakens her masculine sense of mission in harmony with her feminine sense of purpose. A woman's masculine mission is to make a difference by expressing her unique talents, while her feminine sense of purpose is ultimately to love and be loved. While love is always a priority in her life, she wants to express that love in a way that makes a difference. Just as she strives to be more loving at home, she brings that love to her work by wanting to be her best self and bring out the best of others.

For a woman, access to her unique self awakens her masculine sense of mission.

For a man, access to his unique self more fully awakens his feminine sense of love and devotion. It is now quite common for men to freely admit they are "falling in love." The growing love in his heart gives more meaning to his mission as his purpose extends beyond his own needs to serve the needs of others.

For a man, access to his unique self awakens his feminine sense of love and devotion.

Even as recent as when I was growing up, a "Real Man" didn't freely admit his need for love, nor did he admit to vulnerable emotions. He was a man of action, tough and capable of enduring hardships and danger without complaint. This suppression of vulnerability was clearly expressed in the heroes of 1950s Westerns, who, after saving the woman, would ride off into the sunset . . . alone.

But in the sixties, a major shift in gender roles began to unfold. As women were creating support groups to develop and express their independence and power, men were starting to grow out their hair, wear pink shirts, and demonstrate for peace. "Make Love Not War" was their motto.

The power of this mass awakening was most clearly demonstrated by the orgasmic response of young women screaming to the new sound of the Beatles and other rock bands of the sixties.

On Sunday night, February 9, 1964, teenage girls in America were first introduced to the Beatles on the historic *Ed Sullivan Show*, and their dramatic response startled everyone. Onstage were four young male musicians, with long hair, singing in harmony and freely expressing their innocent and unabashed love and devotion for women. The lyrics of their most memorable breakthrough song, "I Want to Hold Your Hand," say it all.

This mass awakening was clearly demonstrated in the orgasmic response of young women screaming to the new sound of the Beatles.

The Beatles were able to declare a man's love in a way that was rarely heard before. My wife Bonnie remembers that she, too, was spontaneously crying while watching the Beatles.

She said, "Finally, someone was speaking to me."

The Beatles were singing from their hearts in a way that connected with millions of young women. As these four talented young men were connecting to their own romantic female sides, it released in women a new freedom to come out and express their authentic selves, which meant the freedom to express more of their masculine side. This growing wave of independent women in the sixties and seventies freed men from the age-old traditional pressure to be sole financial providers. Likewise, the rising wave of loving and romantic men, as expressed in the music of the Beatles and other rock bands during the sixties, set a generation of young women free to break from traditional stereotypes.

In this way, the music of the Beatles released—particularly in women—a tidal wave of energy that had never been witnessed before. Beatlemania was the dramatic release of this energy. During that time, I also felt the surge of new energies. I can remember this awakening when I attended a Beatles concert at fourteen years old.

Before the concert, I vowed not to stand up and scream, but as soon as the Beatles walked onstage, I stood up and screamed like everyone else. Clearly something new had been unleashed in me and in my generation.

The changes that began in the 1960s have continued to expand through the present day. Thanks to increasing equality between the sexes and a growing societal acceptance of a broader range of norms and behaviors, people today have a greater degree of freedom to be themselves than ever before.

Freely Expressing Our Unique Selves

In prehistoric times, women and men had mutual and equal respect for each other's mutually supportive but different roles. A woman depended on and appreciated a man's willingness to die in battle to protect his family or to endure discomfort and hardship while hunting for the family. Likewise, a man depended on and appreciated a woman's willingness to lovingly care for his children's physical needs as well as his own.

Throughout most of history, our separate roles felt less restrictive because they served our most important needs: to survive and be secure. But as time marched on, and as the need for separate roles has lessened, the Role Mate relationship has become too restrictive. Both men and women have felt an increasing desire to express all parts of their being without suppression, individually and in our relationships. This new requirement has shaped and defined our new needs for a Soul Mate relationship.

**In the distant past, our separate roles
felt less restrictive because they served our
most important needs: to survive and be secure.**

This (still ongoing) transformation, from Role Mates to Soul Mates, is unprecedented in our history, and it is as significant as our shift from being hunter-gatherers to farmers and merchants, or from the agrarian age to the modern industrial and computer ages. It creates a new foundation for true equality between the sexes, and has the potential to usher in a time of peace, love, and understanding throughout the world.

The shift from Role Mate to Soul Mate creates a new foundation of equality between the sexes.

But the emergence of our unique selves comes with more than just increased potential for happiness. The potential for pain also increases. After we get a taste of free and authentic expression, suppressing aspects of our male and female sides can become our greatest source of emotional pain and suffering.

For example, because women now have the opportunity to express their *independence* (a characteristic of her male side), it can cause great suffering for a woman to restrict herself to the role of being fully *interdependent* (a characteristic of her female side) in her relationship.

Likewise, because men now have the opportunity to express their interdependence and follow their hearts (a characteristic of his female side), it can a cause great suffering for a man to restrict himself to sacrificing his own wishes, wants, and dreams to fulfill his traditional role of sole financial provider.

When we suppress any of the characteristics of our male and female sides that are seeking expression, we lose touch with our feelings of happiness and aliveness. From this perspective, a major source of our inner pain, biological stress, and suffering is our own conscious or unconscious resistance to expressing different aspects of our unique selves.

Our suffering comes from our own inner resistance to expressing aspects of our unique selves.

Our New Challenges

Women have expressed masculine characteristics like independence and detachment throughout history, but it certainly was not common, particularly if they were planning to have a family. Without access to birth control, women were commonly pregnant or breastfeeding most of their lives. To care for her children, a mother was dependent on her husband to provide both financial support and security. It would be nearly impossible for her to raise her family without the help of a provider.

But today, women are freely expressing their male independent side. This has enormous benefits. By taking time to educate themselves before getting married or having children, women are freer to choose a career that follows their inner passions and to discover and express their talents in the world, as well as become financially independent. They have the luxury of taking more time to find the right relationship for themselves rather than marry the first man they have sex with. They experience the joy of greater self-reliance and the ability to explore their different interests without depending on others' approval.

**With increased independence,
women have the luxury of taking more time
to find the right relationship.**

Because women are no longer repressing important parts of themselves, they can enjoy a greater sense of pleasure and fulfillment both at work and at home. But with this newfound freedom, men and women are also in danger of suppressing other aspects of their unique selves.

As important as it is for a woman to be able to express her male side, it is equally important for her to express her female side. To be fully happy, she must, after expressing her male side, return to her female side to achieve her proper balance; every women or man has their own unique balance of masculine and feminine qualities. If a woman's need for balance isn't being met, she will experience increasing stress, dissatisfaction, and a variety of expressions of emotional pain, from depression and anxiety to sleeplessness and food addictions. Without new insight to restore balance, she will attempt to cope with this pain in a way that increases her imbalance and her pain.

For example, to avoid the pain of loneliness she feels when her feminine need to be loved and in love isn't met, a woman may cope by relying on her independent male side, which looks to success rather than love for fulfillment. Rather than devoting more time to creating a loving relationship, she focuses on creating more success in her career.

By focusing more on her male side, which seeks to be independent and successful, she disconnects further from her female side, which needs to be loved and loving. She becomes further disconnected from her feminine side and so cannot resolve the source of her pain.

To avoid feeling the pain of loneliness, women disconnect from their vulnerable needs to feel loved and in love.

Men can also experience a greater fulfillment as they move beyond their independent and detached masculine side to more fully acknowledge and feel their needs to love and be loved. By accessing their female side they are able to more fully feel their love for their romantic partner, their family, and their work.

Rather than mindlessly following the rules and expectations of society and doing what has always been expected, men are free to follow their hearts to discover what makes them happy. Without the traditional pressure of getting married before fulfilling their sexual needs, men also have greater choice in picking a mate.

But as men open their hearts to access their feelings, it brings new risks and challenges. With an open heart, his needs are suddenly greater. It is no longer enough for a man to earn a living and provide for his wife and children. He wants to follow his heart rather than sacrifice his own needs and wishes for his family; he wants to enjoy his life as well.

With this greater access to his female side, he runs the risk of going out of balance and focusing too much on his own needs and not his partner's. And if he expresses more of his female side while disconnecting from his male side, it will create increasing stress and dissatisfaction.

When men follow their hearts, they risk going out of balance.

In moving too far to their female side and following their feelings, men easily run the risk of becoming too needy or too confronting and demanding. Too many times, I have witnessed men unknowingly sabotage their relationships by demanding more from their partners and then blaming them, rather than accessing their own masculine independent side, which is not overly dependent on their partner to be happy. In other cases, men are unable to make a commitment in relationships because they focus too much on their own needs, emotions, and feelings rather than learning new ways to succeed in meeting their partners' needs.

Because we are presently in transition from letting go of traditional ways of relating to fully expressing our unique selves, we should not expect this process to always be easy or automatic. As we raise our expectations, our relationship challenges become greater, but so do the benefits of meeting those challenges. With this new insight, we can use our loving relationships to guide us back into balance.

Our new quest for a Soul Mate relationship to support our authentic self-expression presents many new challenges, but it also promises a much higher level of fulfillment. A successful traditional Role Mate relationship could certainly bring happiness and contentment, but it could not provide the increased level of passion and aliveness that occurs when a man or woman freely express both sides of their unique self.

A Role Mate relationship can bring happiness and contentment, but only a Soul Mate relationship creates lasting passion.

Falling in love feels so good because it is a moment when we feel safe enough to fully express ourselves. The new blending of our male and female sides lets us glimpse a higher and unconditional love that includes passion, compassion, and wisdom. But to sustain this wonderful love, it takes new skills and insights that let us bring our male and female sides into balance.

To sustain lasting passion, a relationship must support the ongoing expression of both our male and female sides.

Our Male and Female Sides

In later chapters we will explore in greater detail different attributes of our male and female sides and the consequences of their suppression, but for now a simple description of our male and female characteristics follows. Keep in mind that every man and woman has both a male and female side.

Our authentic and unique self is our own internal balance or blend of these complementary characteristics. There is no perfect balance that is the same for everyone. Every man has his own unique balance of male and female characteristics and every woman has her own blend as well. And by recognizing, accepting, and expressing your unique blend, you can find a higher love and happiness.

Every man and woman has their own unique balance of male and female characteristics.

Below are twelve characteristics or qualities of our male and female sides. I use the terms "sides," "qualities," and "characteristics" for variety but they are all intended to have the same meaning and their use is interchangeable. There are certainly many more qualities, but for the purpose of easy identification and discussion I have just listed twelve.

A person's authentic unique self may be any degree or combination of these different characteristics, regardless of their biological sex. In addition, our unique male and female balance may be expressed differently in various situations. For example, I may express my male side more at work and my female side more with my children. And as we pass through different stages of life, our needs change, and the side we tend to express more often may change with them. When we are single we naturally develop our independent side, and when we are married we tend to express more of our interdependent side.

Twelve Male and Female Characteristics

The Male Side	The Female Side
1. Independent	1. Interdependent
2. Detached	2. Emotional
3. Problem solver	3. Nurturer
4. Tough	4. Vulnerable
5. Competitive	5. Cooperative
6. Analytical	6. Intuitive
7. Powerful	7. Loving
8. Assertive	8. Receptive
9. Competent	9. Virtuous
10. Confident	10. Trusting
11. Accountable	11. Responsive
12. Goal-oriented	12. Relationship-oriented

The potential for discovering and then expressing our own unique blend of these different characteristics is what attracts us to certain people and situations.

A person (man or woman) who is more confident (a masculine quality) will be attracted to a person (man or woman) who is more trusting (a feminine quality) and vice versa. Through growing together in love, the more trusting person will grow in their ability to be more confident and the confident person will grow in their ability to be more trusting.

A person who is more independent (a masculine quality) will be attracted to someone more relationship-oriented who greatly values interdependence (a feminine quality) and vice versa. Through growing in love together, the more independent partner will grow in their ability to appreciate the value of relationships and intimacy, while the more interdependent partner will grow in their ability to value and express their qualities of independence.

In this way, we often feel chemistry with a person who more fully expresses qualities that complement the qualities we ourselves more often express. Through embracing the complementary qualities in our partner, we awaken those qualities within ourselves. This helps us grow in wholeness and passion as we continue to find ways to sustain our love and to understand, accept, and appreciate our partners.

Masculine and Feminine Are Not Just Social Constructs

While some may consider naming our different characteristics masculine and feminine to be arbitrary or artificial, these distinctions are actually grounded in biological male and female differences.

The naming of our male and female qualities is grounded in biological male and female differences.

Expressing any of the twelve male qualities in the list opposite increases the male hormone testosterone in both men and women. Testosterone levels are much higher in men and therefore it is appropriately regarded as the male hormone. Expressing any of the twelve female qualities in the list above increases the female hormone estrogen in women and men. Estrogen levels are much higher in women and therefore it is appropriately regarded as the female hormone.

The concept of gender is not merely a "social construct," as some would have us believe. Certainly our traditional male and female roles have been strongly determined by culture, but breaking free from our traditional roles to discover and express our unique selves does not mean that men and women are suddenly the same. When a woman accesses and expresses her masculine qualities, she is still a woman and is very different from a man. A man with full access to his feminine qualities is still a man and is different from a woman.

Because our biology is different, men and women have different hormonal needs. And because different behaviors stimulate different hormones, men and women have different priorities regarding certain kinds of emotional support. Men and women require distinctly different brews of hormones to be stress-free, happy, and fulfilled.

Men and women require distinctly different brews of hormones to be stress-free.

Understanding these differences in our biological hormonal needs can dramatically increase our ability to give and receive the love and support essential for successfully managing the increased stress in our lives.

There are two kinds of stress: internal and external. As discussed, we are all facing new and greater external stressors. External stress, like traffic jams and deadlines or disappointments and arguments in your marriage, then creates the hormone cortisol, which produces internal stress and inhibits our ability to feel peaceful, loving, happy, or fulfilled. Throughout *Beyond Mars and Venus*, the word "stress" refers to our internal stress response to external stressors.

By lowering our internal stress (as measured by cortisol) through stimulating gender-specific hormones, we are then better able to keep our minds and hearts open to express our unique blend of masculine and feminine characteristics and support our partners in doing the same.

By creating hormonal balance, we experience a greater freedom to express our unique selves.

Testosterone is often called the male hormone because every man, regardless of his childhood conditioning, cultural training, or sexual preference, has at least ten times more than a healthy woman. Some men will be born with a greater degree of masculine qualities, which is determined by his DNA as well as his mother's hormone levels while his body was developing in the womb. With more masculine qualities and fewer female qualities, he will need to sustain higher testosterone levels to feel his best. Other men with a greater degree of feminine qualities will have less of a need to sustain higher testosterone levels. While some healthy men have ten times more testosterone than women, other healthy men with more masculine qualities will have thirty times more testosterone.

In a similar manner, some women are born with a greater degree of feminine qualities and a greater need for activities that produce estrogen and other female hormones in order to feel their best, whereas other women with a greater degree of masculine qualities have less of a need to sustain higher estrogen levels. Estrogen is often called the female hormone because every healthy woman, regardless of her childhood conditioning, cultural training, or sexual preference, has at least ten times more than a healthy man. Too much testosterone can lower women's estrogen levels. To balance the increased testosterone produced during their workday, they will need more estrogen in their personal life.

Nurture or Nature?

Some would say it is our social conditioning or early life experiences that determine how we express our masculine or feminine qualities. This perspective is true because how well we can express our unique balance has everything to do with how we are nurtured. Our unique balance of male and female qualities is natural but how we express ourselves is determined by the nurturing we receive or don't receive. Our male and female differences are both natural and nurtured.

We are each born with our own unique and authentic balance of male and female qualities depending on DNA and exposure to hormones in the womb. This unique balance of male and female qualities is our natural and authentic state. Some men will have more feminine qualities and some women will have more masculine qualities.

With lots of love and support in childhood we are then able to express our authentic balance. However, experiencing a lack of love and support to express our authentic balance of male and female qualities can cause us to suppress particular qualities.

For instance, a woman who felt abandoned or neglected as a child may have been forced to care for herself, and so her male confident and independent side is overexpressed while her female trusting and interdependent qualities are suppressed. Unable to trust a potential partner, she is unable to open her heart and feel "in love." If she does get involved in a love relationship, she may then move too far in the opposite direction, overexpressing her female side and becoming overly needy, demanding, bossy, or critical.

Likewise, a man who as a child was missing a supportive father as a role model and never experienced a happy mother may suppress his independent male side and become overly interdependent and needy in relationships, or he may rebel in the other direction by becoming "macho," suppressing his feminine side in an attempt to find his masculinity.

These are just two examples of the many ways we can suppress our authentic selves due to social pressures or a lack of loving support in childhood. While denying or disowning parts of our authentic self in the short term may help us to survive, in the long run this psychological suppression affects our hormonal balance by suppressing our stress-reducing hormones. Without the correct balance of hormones, we cannot effectively cope with stress and keep our hearts open. By learning to embrace our different male and female qualities, we hold the key to experiencing a lifetime of lasting love and passion.

The Power of Hormones

Testosterone and its balance with estrogen (and other female hormones) dramatically and directly affects a man's moods, feelings, emotions, energy levels, reaction times, muscle growth and physical strength, motivations, health, libido, endurance, happiness, and feelings of love, well-being, and attachment.

Testosterone dramatically and directly affects a man's moods, feelings, energy levels, strength, libido, and happiness.

Estrogen and its balance with testosterone and other female hormones dramatically and directly affects a woman's mood, feelings, emotions, energy levels, reaction times, fat storage, endurance, motivations, health, libido, happiness, and feelings of love, well-being, and attachment.

Estrogen dramatically and directly affects a woman's moods, libido, energy levels, and feelings of love, well-being, and happiness.

For a man or woman, the expression of male qualities in the earlier list stimulates the production of testosterone: independence, emotional detachment, problem solving, and so forth all stimulate testosterone. Expressing these male qualities, which produce testosterone, may feel equally good to men and women, but when we are stressed they will lower a man's internal stress reactions, but not a woman's. It takes the expression of female qualities, which produce female hormones, to lower her stress.

For a man or woman, the expression of female qualities stimulates the production of estrogen. Trusting a partner to support you, depending on others, emotional expression, nurturing activities, and so forth all stimulate estrogen. Certainly these things may feel equally good to men and women, but when we are stressed they will lower a woman's internal stress reactions but not a man's, because it takes testosterone to lower a man's stress.

In Role Mate times, internal stress often came from overexpressing characteristics associated with one's gender role. For men, the cultural pressure to suppress their female side was a source of great stress. In a variety of ways a man had to be "macho": he had to support his family without complaint or expressing worry or fear. For women, pressure to be heavily feminine and to repress their desire for independence and intellectual achievement created great internal stress.

**In Role Mate times, internal stress
often came from overexpressing characteristics
associated with one's gender role.**

But things have changed. Today, women tend to move too far to their male side, suppressing their female side, and men tend to move too far to their female side, suppressing to various degrees their detached and independent male side.

**In our modern complex world, women move too far
to their male side and men move too far
to their female side, both of which increase stress.**

With a greater freedom to express their female emotional and interdependent side, the major cause of internal stress for men is suppressing their masculine side and overexpressing their female side, while the major cause of internal stress for women is suppressing their feminine side and overexpressing their male side.

From my own clinical observations in over forty years of counseling men and women, I have repeatedly observed the inevitable consequences of this hormonal imbalance in men and women. When a man experiences any of the symptoms of internal stress like anger, loss of libido for his partner, dissatisfaction, boredom, or loss of passion in his life, it is usually because he is temporarily too far on his female side: he is feeling too much, and so his testosterone has dropped and his estrogen is too high.

Learning to focus on activities that increase his testosterone and decrease his estrogen will lower his internal stress.

When a man is stressed, increasing testosterone and decreasing estrogen will always lower his stress.

Contrary to this, if a woman is stressed, increasing the expression of her male side and raising her testosterone will not lower her stress but actually increase it.

When a modern woman is stressed, increasing activities that raise estrogen and decrease testosterone will always lower her internal stress hormones.

When a woman is stressed, increasing estrogen and decreasing testosterone will always lower her stress.

Contrary to this, if a man is stressed, increasing the expression of his female side and raising his estrogen will not lower his stress but actually increase it.

Developing Authenticity

As discussed, every man and woman is born with his or her own unique balance of male and female qualities. At each stage of life, from childhood to adolescence to adulthood, if we are allowed and supported to freely express our authentic selves, then we are able to gradually discover, express, develop, and even simultaneously blend these different qualities. Through simultaneously blending our authentic male and female qualities we are able to grow into the experience of a higher love, which we will explore in greater depth in the last chapter.

Through simultaneously blending our authentic male and female qualities, we are able to experience a higher love.

In a general sense, the purpose of the first half of our lives is to discover, develop, and express the many male and female qualities of our authentic selves with an emphasis on our biological differences and related needs. At puberty a boy's testosterone levels increase up to twenty times as high as previous levels, while a girl's estrogen levels increase to six times previous levels. When these levels are not sustained, they will experience unnecessary internal stress.

An adolescent girl with more male qualities will need less stimulation of her female side to sustain her healthy level of estrogen, while a girl with more female qualities will need more support. But regardless of the degree of masculine qualities, if either girl is stressed, her solution to lower her internal stress is to temporarily give more support to her female side to restore healthy estrogen levels. Likewise, if an adolescent boy is stressed, he needs to temporarily focus on expressing his male side to restore his testosterone levels, regardless of what his healthy balance is in relation to other boys.

Beyond adolescence, a woman's estrogen levels will gradually begin to decline as her testosterone levels increase and peak around age thirty-five. (Many women report reaching their sexual prime around age thirty-five.) An opposite change occurs in men. At thirty-five, a man's testosterone levels may begin to drop. Prior to this drop, his estrogen levels have been gradually increasing and will continue to increase. (This gradual drop in testosterone is quite common in men in our society but uncommon in indigenous men.)

It is at this point in life, when a man naturally makes more estrogen and a woman makes more testosterone, where we begin our new journey to blend our male and female qualities to create a higher love.

If a woman has not learned to sustain and support the production of her female hormones, then as her testosterone naturally increases in relation to her declining estrogen levels, she will suffer a variety of menopausal symptoms. Hot flashes, sleepless nights, anxiety, or depression are common menopausal symptoms in today's society, but in indigenous societies where women are supported in expressing their female sides, they do not experience these symptoms. Before, during, and after menopause, if a woman is not grounded in her female side, she becomes testosterone dominant and her stress levels increase, causing dissatisfaction, unhappiness, anger, and a lack of fulfillment.

**Before, during, and after menopause
a woman can become testosterone dominant
and her stress levels increase.**

At midlife and beyond, if a woman is grounded in her female side, fully expressing her female qualities, then the increased expression of her male hormones will not overshadow and suppress her female qualities. She is then able to begin learning how to simultaneously blend her male and female sides in every feeling, thought, decision, and action. This balance opens a new door to experiencing a higher love along with sustained energy and passion.

A similar but opposite scenario is true for men. After puberty, a man's testosterone levels remain ten or more times higher than a woman's his whole life. Then, as he goes beyond midlife, his estrogen levels naturally increase. If he has not fully developed his masculine qualities to the degree that is unique to him, the rise in estrogen will begin to suppress his testosterone.

A man's testosterone levels are designed to stay ten or more times higher than a woman's his whole life.

If a man learns to sustain his testosterone levels in the first half of his life, then when his estrogen levels start to rise at midlife, he can sustain his testosterone levels as well. This simultaneous balancing of hormones allows him to experience a higher love, wisdom, compassion, and unconditional love along with lasting vitality, virility, and health.

Cultural Norms and Self-Expression

The free expression of a man's female side at midlife while keeping his testosterone levels high, and the free expression of a woman's male side at midlife while keeping her estrogen levels high, was not possible in previous generations because both men and women were restricted by cultural norms to suppress themselves throughout their entire lives. To various degrees, men were required to suppress their female side and women were required to suppress their male side. As a result, lasting passion was not possible after many years of marriage.

If a woman's unique blend of masculine and feminine qualities included more masculine qualities, she felt more restricted and suppressed throughout her lifetime, and as a result experienced less peace of mind, love, happiness, and fulfillment in life. She also would be highly stressed—unless she was able to break free of social norms and express her masculine side. But this was not always a sure road to happiness, because to express her masculine side, she often had to suppress her interdependent female qualities. Thus she often stayed single because it was hard to find a man who would lovingly support her independence and self-reliance.

A more masculine woman could decrease her inner stress by defying cultural norms.

Today women are free to express their masculine qualities, but women who have more feminine qualities are more stressed because, by trying to fit into or compete in the workplace, they end up suppressing their female side. Their need to nurture and be nurtured is greater than that of women with more masculine qualities.

This does not mean that women with more masculine qualities are stress-free today. They often handle stress in the workplace better, but in their relationships they can be much more challenged. Because their female side is not as strong, they have not developed ways to support it. They are not good at receiving support or asking for help.

A woman with a high degree of male qualities is usually not good at receiving support or asking for help.

Again, men have a similar but opposite story. More men are following their hearts and doing what they love. This activates their female side but can also suppress their male qualities of independence and detachment. Instead of being cool, calm, and collected, they are insecure and easily become angry, demanding, or needy in their relationships.

When men move too far to their female side and suppress parts of their male side, they are often too emotional and easily dissatisfied in relationships. These men stay single because they feel no woman is good enough. They are very romantic and excited when they first meet a woman but then quickly lose interest. In many cases, they just can't make up their minds: one minute they can't live without her (interdependence), and in the next moment they swing back to their independent, detached side and lose interest.

One minute he can't live without her and in the next moment he swings back to his independent, detached side and loses interest.

Other men get married, but, in their quest to please their partners, suppress their male qualities. While doing so may feel good in the moment, over time they lose their sense of aliveness and passion for their partner.

On the other hand, some men refuse to expand themselves within their relationships to include their female side, and the outcome is the same: they lose the passion they felt in the beginning.

To sustain passion, all of us, men and women both, must continue to grow in greater awareness and expression of our unique balance of male and female qualities.

**To sustain passion we must continue to grow
in greater awareness and expression
of our unique balance of male and female qualities.**

The reason for this is that, without a clear understanding of our male and female sides, when we go out of balance it is more difficult to come back to our unique balance of male and female qualities. The common outcome for men and women is, rather than growing together in love, they are becoming more stressed.

The good news is that with new insight, we can take specific actions to regulate our hormones that are not dependent on our partners. In later chapters we'll explore these, as well as what you can do to support your partner's need to find hormonal balance. You will learn how to help them lower their stress, as well as get the support you need to find your own balance.

First, though, let's take some time to understand more deeply why recognizing these differences between men and women is so important.

4

DIFFERENCES ATTRACT AND CREATE LASTING PASSION

Couples start out in their relationships with complete confidence that they have a special love and they will never lose their passion. But in most cases, that passion is lost, even when the love persists.

The number one question couples have about today's complex relationships is how they can create lasting passion. The answer is simple to say but not so easy to achieve: differences attract. By learning to express our unique self, which is different from our partner's unique self, passion can not only be sustained, but grow.

Falling in love with your partner is similar to passionately loving a new song. At first you just can't get enough of it and it feels like you will always love it, but if you hear that same song over and over, even though it excites every cell in your body at first, after a while it loses its impact. The passion you felt in the beginning is lost. When a song is new and different, it automatically stimulates specific brain chemicals and hormones that make you feel more alive. When a song is no longer new and different, those brain chemicals and hormones are no longer stimulated.

If you hear the same song over and over, even though it excites every cell in your body at first, after a while it loses its impact.

The good news when it comes to relationships is that people are not recorded songs. Unlike a static recording, people can and do change and grow. When a relationship supports the authentic expression of our unique selves, then we continue to change and grow every day. This continual newness can support our attraction and passion.

But when we suppress aspects of our male and female sides in order to earn a living, fulfill social pressures and expectations, or simply to please our partners, then we stop growing and our attraction lessens.

Keeping a relationship fresh through change and growth is important, but the authentic expression of both our male and female sides is even more important. It is a man's masculine qualities, when expressed in a way that supports the expression of a woman's female qualities, that excite and awaken her romantic feelings. When women say they want a "Real Man," this is what they are referring to.

The growing expression of a man's female qualities, like love, vulnerability, cooperation, and interdependence, allows him to express his male side in a way that supports a woman more. But unless he combines the expression of these female qualities with the full expression of his male side, with qualities like independence, detachment, confidence, and competence, she may love him, but she will not be attracted to him. In many cases, her love will either shift to something platonic, or she may feel more motherly toward him.

Likewise, it is a woman's female qualities, when expressed in a way that supports the expression of a man's male qualities, that excite and sustain his romantic interest in her. Often when powerful women say they are alone because their power intimidates men, the real reason men are not interested in them is that many powerful women are also suppressing their female qualities.

The growing expression of a woman's male qualities, like independence, assertiveness, confidence, and power, when balanced with her female side, can help a man feel even more successful in their relationship. His support to help her return to her female side after spending her day at work increases her ability to appreciate him, and this increases his sense of success.

But unless she combines the expression of these male qualities with the full expression of her female side, with qualities like love, receptivity, cooperation, and interdependence, he may love her, but he will not be attracted to her. Although he may feel very attracted in the beginning, very quickly the passion will dissipate, because he won't feel she needs him.

A New Appreciation of Our Differences

This new chance to come together in equal relationships that support the full but unique expression of our male and female sides—while appreciating our differences—can help create lasting passion. Even though the newness of a relationship is eventually replaced by the comfort of knowing what to expect, by maintaining and appreciating our natural and authentic differences, we can experience lasting attraction.

In the music world, certain superstars are able to sustain the attraction people feel to their music long after they are a new sensation. This sustained interest and passion for their music is not just from their being new, but from their being different!

What makes a musical artist unforgettable is not just their talent and skill but their own unique expression of that talent and skill. Consider this list of famous musical artists and groups who have sold over 75 million records and whose popularity continues to endure. Notice how unique and different each of their sounds and expressions are:

Luciano Pavarotti	Pink Floyd
The Beatles	Ludwig van Beethoven
Dolly Parton	The Bee Gees
Michael Jackson	Neil Diamond
Diana Ross	Madonna
Sting	Johann Sebastian Bach
Prince	Whitney Houston
Bob Dylan	Queen
Barbra Streisand	ABBA
Wolfgang Amadeus Mozart	U2
The Rolling Stones	Bob Marley
Elton John	Elvis Presley

You recognize these artists as soon as you hear their voice or instruments. They are unique, authentic, and different.

In a similar way, if our relationships can support our own unique expression of our male and female qualities, then we are able to sustain or even reawaken the passion and attraction in our relationships.

Understanding Male and Female Polarity

A big part of what creates and can sustain the attraction in our relationships is our male and female differences. These natural differences between men and women are the physical and hormonal basis of romantic chemistry. Men and women are like magnets: we are attracted to each other because our polarities are different. If we are the same, then when we get too close we will repel each other.

Visualizing the behavior and movements of a magnet can help us to understand our male and female polarity. Opposite poles of a magnet attract each other while similar poles repel each other.

If our male side is the north pole and the female side is the south pole, then when a man is on his male side and a woman in on her female side they will be attracted to each other. It is this attraction that keeps the passion in the relationship alive. But if both partners are stuck on the same side, they will repel each other. As in the diagram below, opposites attract and same poles repel.

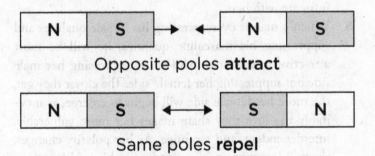

Opposite poles **attract**

Same poles **repel**

This analogy plays out in six ways:

1. When a man is expressing his masculine qualities, he will be most attractive to a woman who is expressing her female qualities. His male side and her female side are opposite poles and will attract each other.

2. When a woman is expressing her feminine qualities, she will be most attracted to a man who is expressing his masculine qualities. Her female side and his male side are opposite poles and will attract each other.

3. When a man is overexpressing his female qualities and suppressing his male side, he will be least attractive to a woman who is expressing her female qualities. The closer they get, the more their female sides will repel each other. They can be great friends, but the passion won't be there.

4. When a woman is overexpressing her male qualities and suppressing her female side, she will be least attractive to a man who is expressing his male qualities. The closer they get, the more their male sides will repel each other. He will appreciate and respect her masculine competence at a distance, and they will be able to work in harmony together, but he will not feel a desire to be romantically intimate with her.

5. When a man is overexpressing his female qualities and suppressing his masculine qualities, he will be most attractive to a woman who is overexpressing her male side but suppressing her female side. The closer they get, the more her female side will begin to emerge, as inevitably the love they share makes her more vulnerable, interdependent, and receptive. As her polarity changes, she will lose respect for or interest in him. Although in the beginning she was attracted to him, she will begin to be repelled.

6. When a woman is overexpressing her male qualities and suppressing her feminine qualities, she will be most attractive to a man who is overexpressing his female side but suppressing his male side. The closer they get, the more her female side will begin to emerge, as inevitably the love they share makes her more vulnerable, interdependent, and receptive. As her polarity changes, he will lose romantic interest in her.

The takeaway from these different examples is that for men and women to feel the attraction to connect, there must be some compatible polarity.

**For passion to last,
there must be a healthy polarity.**

When both partners come home from work on their male sides, it is important to find ways for the man to rebuild his testosterone in order to stay in touch with his male side and for the woman to find ways to return to her female side to restore her estrogen levels.

If a woman continues to suppress her female side, her male partner may feel an automatic tendency to express more of his female qualities. Instead of taking some cave time, he may want to talk, complain, or share. As he moves to his female side and wants to talk, she is further pushed to her male side in an attempt to listen, which increases her stress even more.

To help her return to her receptive and interdependent female side, the man, instead of sharing his feelings, needs to take some time to return to his male side. Then, without feeling a need to be heard in order to feel closer to her, he can listen to her.

When a man listens,
it helps a woman
to return to her female side.

On the other hand, when a woman is too far on her male side, she may not feel the need to talk or share because she is suppressing her female side. Through learning to share her feelings with her partner in a way that he can easily hear, she can come back to her female side while also supporting her partner in returning to his male side.

As we've seen, for most women today, this shift from her testosterone-driven male side to her estrogen-driven female side is not automatic. It is a behavior that must be learned, but once learned, it is one that will help her to find her internal balance. After suppressing her feelings all day at work, sharing her feelings is a powerful way for her to reconnect with her female side.

Sustaining Polarity in Intimate Relationships

In an intimate and loving relationship, when a woman is too far on her male side it can push a man too far to his female side. This can make him feel more passive, needy, emotionally sensitive, or demanding. In a similar way, a man who goes too far to his female side can easily push a woman too far to her male side.

This effect is clearly illustrated with magnets when you attempt to push together two north or south poles.

Two north poles or two south poles will repel each other, but adding pressure in an attempt to connect the poles will cause one of the magnets to spin to the other polarity.

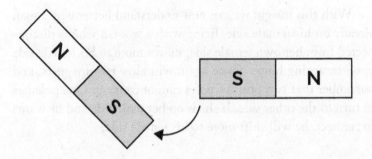

This illustrates how men on their female side can push women to their male side or women on their male side can push men to their female side.

On a positive note, when a woman is on her female side, by receiving the man's support in some way, she pushes him to his male side. Likewise, a man on his male side supports a woman moving back to her female side. This tendency particularly shows up in intimate relationships, where there is naturally a greater push to connect.

In most relationships today, when the woman is more on her male side, it is the man who wants to connect more, while the woman feels too busy to do so. When a man pushes to get close to her, it then pushes him further to his female side.

Sometimes a woman on her male side will attempt to connect with a man by getting him to open up and talk about his feelings. When this is the case, he will be pushed further to his female side and eventually display the side effects of his imbalance.

The closer we are to our partners, the bigger the effect we have on them. After a while, to feel more in balance within ourselves, if our partner's polarity is pushing our own in an unhealthy direction, we may simply suppress the urge to connect. This is often what is happening when couples stop choosing to spend romantic time together or lose interest in sex.

With this insight we can now understand better why a man already on his female side, living with a woman who is disconnected from her own female side, moves more to his female side upon returning home. Once again, visualize two magnets, and remember that two positive poles cannot connect. One pole has to turn to the other side. If she is on her male side and he wants to connect, he will shift more to his female side.

**If she is on her male side,
he may shift to his female side in order to connect.**

The problem with this automatic tendency to switch sides is that, if we continue to suppress our male or female side, our attraction toward each other decreases and our hormones go further out of balance. When he moves too far to his female side, his testosterone goes down, and when she remains stuck on her male side, her estrogen goes down.

Additionally, the more she sees him as a problem to be solved in addition to all her other problems that need to be solved, the more she becomes locked in to her male side. In response, he becomes locked in to resisting her attempts to change him through her complaints. As he resists her, she tends to resist back, and their problems get worse.

What you resist in your partner will persist.

By understanding how to come back into balance within ourselves, we have the power to let go of resistance and instead apply new communication skills to bring out the best of our partners.

This insight is essential because when a woman suppresses and becomes disconnected from the receptive and loving qualities of her female side, her ability to appreciate a man decreases. Likewise, when a man suppresses his male side, his long-term ability to appreciate his partner decreases as well. He eventually becomes more concerned with his feelings than hers and becomes easily angered or makes petty demands.

When on his female side, he may temporarily express more love, affection, and caring, but inevitably he will feel resentful. Without the support of his independent male side, he will become too needy and feel like he is giving more than he is getting. But if he comes back to his male side, his neediness decreases and he can become less demanding. By leaving his judgments behind, he can be less critical and instead be more understanding of what she needs from him.

Role Reversal in Marriage

In my seminars, when I describe common male behaviors, attitudes, and reactions, some women have always said they felt they must be from Mars and not Venus. But this reverse experience is more common today than it was twenty-five years ago, when I published *Men Are from Mars, Women Are from Venus*, because women now have greater permission and opportunities to access and express their male side. Some of these women even say their husbands are from Venus.

For example, I say that "women commonly talk more than men in their intimate relationships" and "men commonly talk more than women at work," but not all men and women today will agree because that is not their experience. I say men go to their cave to lower their stress, but many modern men either do not, or they may be taking cave time without noticing it, by pursuing a hobby, reading the paper, praying, meditating, or watching sports.

**Not all men and women today relate
to the traditional male and female differences
that emerge in a Role Mate relationship.**

However, men on a biological hormonal level are still from Mars and women on a biological hormonal level are still from Venus. If we look a little deeper, we can see that when these men and women do not support their unique biological hormonal needs, they become more stressed. Eventually they lose their attraction to their partner and the passion is gone.

When a woman is more on her male side, she will often talk less at home than she does at work. This is often because when she does talk, her partner interrupts with solutions. But if she were to talk more about her feelings with her partner at home and he were to listen more, it would stimulate more female hormones in her that could more effectively lower her stress.

**When a woman is more on her male side, she will
often talk less at home than she does at work.**

When a man is more on his female side, he will tend to talk more both at work and at home. His talking at work, however, will be more to share his feelings than to solve problems, and at home he will continue to talk more about his feelings and problems than his partner does. Talking more about his feelings both at work and at home will not lower his stress, however, and he may even alienate his coworkers and his female partner. He would more effectively lower his stress by talking less and taking more time to listen to his partner.

Men and women both generally talk at work to solve problems (expressing our male side) and at home to create connection and intimacy (expressing our female side). When a woman is more on her male side, she will talk less at home, but that doesn't mean she doesn't have a female side that would greatly benefit from learning to talk more about her feelings at home, because her body is still from Venus. Likewise, when a man is more on his female side, he will talk more at home, but that doesn't mean he doesn't have a male side that would greatly benefit from learning to talk less and listen more, because his body is still from Mars.

For a woman, talking about feelings is one of the most powerful ways to return to her female side and rebuild the female hormones that lower her stress.

For a man, one of the best ways for him to cope with stress is to stop talking so much and take some cave time to let his body produce the male hormone that lowers his stress.

When a man is expressing his female side, he will talk more and end up feeling more stressed.

When we are doing something that takes us out of balance, it is easiest to let momentum keep us moving further out of balance. To come back into balance takes the awareness that we are out of balance and the wisdom to know how to restore it.

For men, giving up talking too much initially can be like giving up an addiction. It is not easy, in the same way eating just one potato chip or cookie is not easy. One may temporarily go through withdrawal symptoms. Likewise, it is hard for women who do too much to stop and learn to relax. It takes both willpower and wisdom. Without this insight, a woman is not able to fully feel the love in her heart.

Why Can't I Fall in Love?

When women are too far on their male side, they may wonder why they can't fall in love or feel attracted to a man.

Stephanie was forty years old and had dated many men, but she could never fall in love. The men she attracted were clearly not the ones for her.

She said, "I don't know why, but I am just not excited or turned on by the men I meet. We have a nice time but no one feels special. I can't seem to find the one."

Stephanie is not alone. Women often ask, "Where can I find my Soul Mate?"

My answer: "He is definitely out there, but to find him or to be found, you have to stop wondering where he is. The right question is not '*Where* is my Soul Mate?' but '*How* can I meet the right man for me?'"

The right question is not "*Where* is my Soul Mate?" but "*How* can I meet the right partner for me?"

Until a woman is embracing her female side in balance with her male side, she will not attract or be attracted to the right man for her. If she is too far on her male side, she will either attract or be attracted to men who are too far on their female side and who "need her" to care for them rather than wanting to care for her.

On the other hand, she may also be attracted to men who overexpress their male side and suppress their female side. Their strong masculine qualities may clash with her masculine qualities and push her to her more feminine side. While a hyper-masculine man may make her "feel like a woman," because he is suppressing his own female side, he tends to dominate and is unwilling to cooperate and compromise. He will not support her need to express her male independent side and instead demands that she be dependent on him and obedient to his wishes.

Learning to balance our male and female sides in a relationship is the first step to attracting the right person. It is the "how" when it comes to successful dating.

This insight is not only true for women but for men as well. Until a man learns to maintain his hormonal balance in a relationship, while he may feel strong attraction to a woman in the beginning, it will quickly dissipate.

When a man moves too far to his female side, he will pick women too far on their male side. Because he is more on his female side, he can come on really strong in a romantic way and be very generous in the beginning. But eventually, he will need to withdraw to return to his own masculine side. If he doesn't pull away when he needs to, he will tend to become overly needy, demanding, and critical.

Men who are too far on their male side often have no problems starting relationships, but they have a greater difficulty making a commitment because they cannot sustain the passion. When the attraction is gone, they move on. The basic ideas in *Beyond Mars and Venus* will help them to understand a modern woman's needs so that they can maintain the passion more successfully. When they learn to support their partner's female side, her increased appreciation can restore his passion as well.

The same is true for women who are too far on their female side, although that is less common today. With a greater understanding from men, these women can rebalance their hormones and get the love and support they need to grow in love.

Finding Balance Is Not Easy

Particularly now that both men and women have greater access to and permission to express their male and female sides, women can more easily go to their male side and men can more easily go to their female side, losing their attraction for each other as a result. Without this insight, both women and men will have no idea why they are growing apart. Yet even with this new insight, it is still not easy!

Martha and Tom are an example of a couple who, when they came to my weekend relationship seminar, were beyond Mars and Venus but did not yet have the insight and skills to meet their new needs. Martha is the CEO of a clothing manufacturer and runs a big international company. Like many women these days, she spends all day on her male side. While she is successful financially, she has difficulty relaxing at home and enjoying her life and relationship. She takes antidepressants, has a low libido, and uses prescription drugs to sleep at night.

In counseling, Martha said, "After listening to you, I feel like I am from Mars. You say women talk more in their relationships. But when I get home, I have too much to do. I don't have time to talk about my feelings, nor do I want to."

In this example, Martha, like many women today, is clearly too much on her male side at home, and this not only increases her stress but also makes her less attracted and attractive to her partner. She needs to come back into balance by identifying and then expressing her female side. This will effectively stimulate her female hormones and help restore the passion in her marriage, as well as lower the stress hormones that are keeping her up at night.

The problem is that it doesn't feel natural for her to talk about her feelings or feel vulnerable. Her whole life, she has been proud of being assertive, confident, and independent. For her, feelings or needing help are signs of weakness.

When she is on her male side, she just wants to detach from her feelings and get things done. To do the opposite of what she wants and instead do what she needs to do to find balance takes a dramatic act of will. And as with any new skill it takes practice; she may not feel better immediately.

Martha's husband, Tom, is a real estate agent. His job is not nearly as demanding or financially lucrative as Martha's. As a result, he works part time so that his schedule is flexible enough to take on more of the family and homemaking responsibilities.

When Martha comes home, Tom can't wait to go to his cave by spending time with his friends playing basketball or going to the movies. Unlike some men who have more female qualities, he is definitely in touch with his need to swing back to his male side.

But Martha resents that he doesn't want to spend more time with her when she gets home. As she said during their session, "I resent that I am the major breadwinner but when I come home, he gets to go off and have fun."

In response, Tom said, "I have spent all day taking care of shopping, cleaning, and driving the kids everywhere. You have been gone all day. When you come home, you don't appreciate all that I do. I need some time for myself."

Tom's need to get away is even greater because, like many men who make less money than their partner and who care for the home, he doesn't feel she appreciates all that he does. When she comes home, she tends to focus on what *more* needs to be done rather than what he *has* done. When Martha returns home, she is not on her female side, so she cannot access her feminine ability to appreciate, celebrate, and be happy with what Tom has done.

> ### When women are the major breadwinners, men often feel unappreciated for the work they do at home.

In this example, Tom can support his wife and even lower his own stress by doing the opposite of what he feels like doing. Instead of immediately taking his cave time, he can first take some time to support his wife to return to her female side. By remembering that men and women are different and then understanding our different hormonal needs to support those differences, we can better sustain our feelings of attraction.

Men Are Still from Mars, Women Are Still from Venus

As modern men and women shift from having separate and different roles to suddenly sharing the same roles, particularly in the work world, our differences become less obvious. The old stereotypes of what men and women are good at or interested in have ceased to apply. Some women are great at math and some men are terrible at it. Some men are interested in opera and fashion while some women are interested in hunting and sports.

Our old stereotypes developed because our traditional roles suppressed men's female characteristics and suppressed women's male characteristics. In going beyond our traditional male and female roles, we can now more easily access our male and female sides. Every man (whether he is aware of it or not) is now more in touch with his female side and every women is more in touch with her male side. With this change, the line between the sexes has become blurred.

But even with this new freedom to express all parts of who we are, a man expressing his female side is still a man and very different from a woman expressing her female side. A woman expressing her male side is still a woman and very different from a man expressing his male side. We are still different because, biologically, we are not the same.

A man expressing his female side is very different from a woman expressing her female side.

When we forget this difference, as can be easy to do given the way lines between men and women have blurred, it becomes harder to discern our unique and different needs for support. As a result, men and women do not get the unique emotional support they need.

With more women expressing their male side, the male hormones their bodies produce can suppress their female hormones, and this can kill the passion. But when men are not supportive of a woman's need to express her male side, it can actually lower his male hormones and increase his female hormones, and this can kill the passion as well.

By first accepting that men and women are different biologically, we can begin to understand new ways to support women in staying connected to their female side while they are also expressing more of their male qualities. Likewise, we can learn new ways to support men in staying connected to their male side: as a man expresses more of the loving, caring, and cooperative qualities of his female side, it can be challenging for him to stay fully connected to his male side. Supporting our hormonal differences is the basis of sustaining attraction, but the first step is recognizing and accepting that men and women really are different in many significant ways.

Our inability to sustain our unique and different hormonal balance within our relationships not only kills the passion but also prevents couples from growing in love. It increases disappointment and dissatisfaction in our lives and also amplifies the unique challenges men and women confront in our complex, fast-paced world.

For each of the following problems, certainly there are many other contributing factors, but fundamentally these outer problems in society are a reflection of our unique and different male and female challenges. Our traditional roles have dropped away, but we have not gained a new understanding of our different male and female needs to find balance—and the gap between our problems widens.

1. *Ninety percent more men than women end up in jail, and more men than women die in accidents.* Being more testosterone driven, men take more risks than women. Men's higher testosterone levels give them faster reaction times. While this means they can easily act without first thinking or feeling, it also makes them more likely to act without considering the potential consequences.

2. *Four times more men than women complete suicide, while almost twice as many women than men attempt suicide.* Women are much more likely to talk about feelings of suicide while men tend to follow through and do it. Being more estrogen driven, women want to talk when under stress more than men do; men, being more testosterone driven, tend to take immediate action when life is too painful. Instead of seeking therapy to end stress, men end their lives. Ninety percent of people who seek out counseling are women.

3. *More women file for divorce, while more men are addicted to online porn.* Being more estrogen driven, women are more relational; their new expectations from personal relationships are leading to greater disappointment, which then

leads to divorce. Being more testosterone driven, men are more vulnerable to sexual addiction to mask the pain of their unmet new needs for increased physical intimacy and lasting passion.

4. *More men are alcoholics and drug addicts, while more women take antidepressants and sleeping pills.* Being more independent, more men seek to medicate their pain on their own by drinking too much or taking addictive drugs, while more women seek the help of doctors and the drugs they prescribe to suppress or escape their pain.

5. *Nearly half as many men as women are graduating from high school and college, and more female college graduates are finding they can't find a suitable male partner or do not want a partner at all.* Because men and women are fundamentally different, when children of divorce do not have access to their fathers, girls strive to be overly independent because they have no successful experience depending on a man, while boys lose the motivation to work hard to provide for a family because they have no role model of a man succeeding in making his mother happy. Being testosterone driven, men are primarily motivated by the confidence that they can make a difference. Without having seen a confident father making his mother happy and providing for his family, boys are less motivated to do what it takes to achieve success, including continuing their education.

6. *Women are nearly twice as likely to need sick leave from work, while men are much more likely to be workaholics.* Because most areas of the work world outside the home are testosterone producing, women take home more stress, which can increase susceptibility to illness. Men are more vulnerable to overworking, especially if they don't feel successful in their personal lives, because higher testosterone levels produced by longer working hours, in the short term, help them reduce stress.

Reflecting on these obvious differences, as determined by national statistics, does little to directly improve our personal relationships. But it does emphasize how different our challenges and vulnerabilities are. By teaching men and women to get the unique support they require, these problems can eventually be solved. Ultimately, all real solutions must come from a place of love. As couples learn to sustain the love and passion they feel at home, then together men and women can overcome these different gender challenges.

Without new insight for supporting our differences in our personal relationships, we cannot reverse the rising tide of global social problems. With more men and women going beyond the traditional roles of Mars and Venus by accessing both their male and female sides, it is more important than ever to remember that we are different, that we have different needs, and that we require different kinds of support.

As we go beyond traditional Mars/Venus roles, it is even more important that we remember how men and women are different.

If men and women really were the same, then at a time when there is more freedom for women to behave like men and men to connect with their female side, you would expect the global male and female challenges in the previous list to have decreased. Instead, they have increased.

The Norwegian Paradox

Norway, the most affluent and oil-rich country in the world per capita, is proud of being more gender equal than anywhere else in the world, but couples there also complain they have lost the passion. Divorce is common and more singles are not getting married. Men and women at work and at home are expected to play very similar roles and behave in a gender-blind fashion. It is considered culturally inappropriate to suggest that men and women are different, except in regard to obvious physical differences.

This sometimes makes the Mars/Venus ideas a challenge to present in Norway. When doing an interview there on national TV with the prime minister, we discussed the idea of cave time—that men, unlike women, needed time alone to regenerate their testosterone. He refused to admit that he took cave time or that men and women were different. He believed that was an outdated, sexist idea.

I pointed out to him that he walked his dog for twenty to thirty minutes at the end of every workday before he joined his wife and family for dinner. That was his cave time, and by taking it, he was unknowingly making the male anti-stress hormones, so that when he returned home he could be more relaxed and present for his family. The TV show cut that example from the program.

If men and women really were the same, you would think that, in Norway's environment of greater equality and thus greater choice, there would be roughly equal numbers of men and women in every field. This, however, is not the case. Surprisingly, in a country where experts believe men and women are the same and equal representation in government jobs is mandated, more women in the private sector choose to take on traditional female jobs while more men choose to take on traditional male jobs.

For example, women still dominate the caring professions such as kindergarten and secondary school education, cleaning, and nursing, while more men still work as building and construction workers, drivers, technicians, and engineers.

In Norway, with greater gender equality, more women still choose the traditional female jobs and more men choose the traditional male jobs.

This has been called the Norwegian Paradox. With greater social and economic freedom to choose their preferred work free from Role Mate limitations, more women choose traditional female jobs and more men choose traditional male jobs. This same shift is slowly occurring in America, as men are becoming greatly outnumbered in the publishing, teaching, and medical industries, which have more to do with communication, education, and nurturing the sick.

One has to wonder why more women in particular, with the freedom to choose a masculine or feminine profession, are not choosing to take on traditional male jobs and why more men are not choosing to take on traditional female jobs.

Compare this to India, where men and women are expected to play traditional roles in the home, and women until recently have been extremely limited in their ability to join the traditionally male workforce. There we see something very different occurring: women eagerly taking on male jobs. Given the opportunity to take on masculine work, they have jumped at the chance to break free from the suppression of their masculine side.

In India, with new freedom, more women are expressing their male side.

In India, for example, roughly one-third of engineers are women. In Norway that number hovers around 20 percent, despite significant government efforts to increase it. In India, 52 percent of primary school educators are men; in Norway only 25 percent are. Why?

With greater freedom to choose, why are more women choosing traditional female jobs? Why, in traditional societies, are women rushing to embrace traditionally male jobs?

The answer is *balance*. Women in Norway have no permission to express their female side at home, just as men are not supported in expressing their male sides. Because they do not embrace their differences at home, women choose traditionally female jobs and men choose traditionally male jobs to find some balance in their lives. If women cannot express their female side at home, at least at work they can. The same is true for men and the expression of their male side.

In India, the reverse is true. Women don't have permission to express their male side at home and so are aggressively embracing traditionally male jobs. Similarly, many men are embracing female jobs, often to the consternation of government leaders. In at least one Indian state, men's access to the nursing program has been shut down because officials felt too many men were interested in pursuing a career in that field.

Both of these examples demonstrate why, while leaving behind our traditional roles, we must also learn to appreciate and respect our differences.

Norway and Sweden are two of the most progressive countries when it comes to equal rights for women, and we can learn a lot from their strengths and mistakes. In these countries, while women and men are free to choose traditional male and female jobs at work, they are expected to behave the same way at home.

Everything must be "equal." They must participate equally in all activities as if gender does not exist.

But while men are more willing to express their female side by becoming more nurturing at home, they are missing both the insight and cultural support or permission to get the unique support they need to first rebuild their male hormones after a day of work. Likewise, women are proud to have jobs and contribute to their families financially, but do not have the insight, cultural support, or permission to get the support they need to return to their female side.

Gender Equality Does Not Mean Gender Blindness

The kind of gender equality commonly promoted in Norway and Sweden is actually gender blindness. At home, it causes men to suppress their male side and women to suppress their female side.

This denial of our differences is not real equality. Equality does not mean sameness. It means equally respecting our differences and holding them in a positive light. All people are different; each of us has a unique blend of male and female characteristics. To expect everyone to conform to one standard is the opposite of respect.

If we hold the perspective that we should all be the same, we cannot feel compassion for one another's different vulnerabilities and needs, nor can we appreciate each other's efforts to do our best. There can be no real gender equality until we can learn to understand, accept, appreciate, and respect our unique differences. With this insight it becomes crystal clear that gender blindness defeats gender equality.

Not only is believing men and women are the same false and bad for working relationships, it also makes our romantic relationships more difficult. In my experience teaching gender differences in Norway and Sweden over the past thirty years, the common belief that women and men are not different kills the passion in their relationships. Men and women become like roommates, with few romantic feelings. Divorce rates in Norway (44 percent) and Sweden (47 percent) are among the highest in the world.

Gender blindness defeats gender equality.

By denying our natural differences, we lose access to our automatic feelings of chemistry and attraction. Chemistry is not something that we "figure out" or choose to create. You cannot just decide to feel attracted to or turned on by someone. It is an automatic hormonal reaction created in response to different but complementary levels of male and female hormones along with complementary differences in one's genes, which are communicated through pheromones, by way of smell, touch, or kiss.

**Physical chemistry is an automatic
hormonal reaction created in response
to different but complementary levels
of male and female hormones.**

We cannot sustain our feelings of attraction or physical chemistry if we are required by society to suppress our authentic male and female qualities. On a very basic level, when a man's testosterone levels drop because he is suppressing his male side or generating too much estrogen through overexpressing his female side, a woman eventually becomes less sexually attracted to him. Likewise, when a woman suppresses her female side and overexpresses her male side in a relationship, over time a man will lose his feelings of attraction for and interest in her. It is all too common for married couples to lose their passion and physical attraction for each other because they are suppressing their authentic male and female qualities, which in turn suppresses their male and female hormones.

By denying our natural differences, we lose access to our automatic feelings of chemistry and attraction.

In traditional Role Mate relationships, when passion was lost it was for different reasons. Because women had to suppress their male side while men had to suppress their female side to fit society's limiting male and female roles, couples could not grow in their personal self-expression.

But in modern Soul Mate relationships, unlike in Role Mate relationships, when the passion is lost, couples are dissatisfied because they intuitively feel more is possible. And more *is* possible. But to get it, we must first learn to embrace our differences while simultaneously supporting the free expression of both our male and female sides.

It is only by embracing our differences, while letting go of limiting male and female stereotypes and roles, that we can sustain passion in our relationships.

It is only by embracing our differences that we can sustain passion in our relationships.

The chapters that follow introduce behavioral insights and techniques for getting your hormones in balance. It's vital to keep in mind that the behaviors I recommend aren't just psychological; they create important physical responses in the body that improve our well-being. This deeper understanding of how to use our behavior to affect our hormones provides the foundation to keep the passion alive and create a successful Soul Mate relationship.

5

TESTOSTERONE
IS FROM MARS

When I first wrote *Men Are from Mars, Women Are from Venus*, the major challenge in most relationships was learning how to accept and understand our common gender differences in order to improve communication and restore the romance. While readers found these insights were incredibly helpful then and still will today, now the bigger challenge is to balance the expression of our male and female sides to lower our stress. How we relate to each other at home can either decrease our ability to cope with stress or be a major tool through which we can achieve this balance and relieve stress.

**Our biggest challenge today has to do
with balancing the expression
of our male and female sides.**

As women become decision makers and leaders, they express more masculine qualities like problem solving, detachment, and independence. This freedom to express their male side is valuable and important, but without the support they need to return to their female side for balance, their stress levels rise, along with feelings of dissatisfaction about their partner or their life in general.

In a similar way, as men express more of their female side both at work and at home, their stress levels rise. At work, many men are expressing more female qualities like cooperation, nurturing, and interdependence. Likewise, workplaces over the past fifty years have dramatically integrated a wide range of feminine qualities: team building, to create more cooperation and interdependence; better communication skills, to be more nurturing and supportive of the customer; improved working conditions and more flexible working hours, to be more nurturing of workers; as well as greater inclusiveness, respect, and appreciation for women's contributions.

The more men express their female side at work, the better the workplace becomes for all of us, but without the insight and support to return to his male side, his stress levels will rise and he will have less to give to his relationship at home. Unable to find balance, he begins to feel more dissatisfaction with his partner or his life in general.

**Men are expressing more of their female side
both at work and at home
and their stress levels are rising.**

Men are further tapping into their female side at home, by attempting to provide more love and support for their partners than their fathers did. Even more significant are the increasing numbers of fathers who are more involved in parenting at home. His extra support, particularly with so many women working outside the home, helps to reduce the pressure and feeling of being overwhelmed so many women feel when they return home. But while this nurturing time is valuable and important to a man, his wife, and their children, it also lowers his testosterone levels.

With this greater expression of their female sides, men also have a greater need to find balance. Without this balance, their energy levels drop and feelings of dissatisfaction and stress gradually increase. In traditional Role Mate relationships, to recover from a stressful day at work, most men would take some time to lower their stress by reading the newspaper or watching TV. They would relax, have a drink, and forget the problems of their day. But in our complex modern world, if both men and women are to find balance, his taking this time to relax is not enough. New communication skills are required that support his male side, while simultaneously helping his partner return to her female side.

When a woman returns home from work, she needs a new kind of support to reconnect with her female side to lower her stress levels and be happy. Likewise, a man also needs a new kind of support to reconnect with his male side to lower his stress and be happy. With new Mars/Venus insights, both their needs can be fulfilled.

Our Different Hormones That Lower Stress

One of the easiest ways to understand and discuss the differences between men and women, as well as learn how to balance our male and female sides, is to understand how our reactions to stress are hormonally different. We have already touched on this difference, but now let's explore a little deeper.

Every couple of years, it is big news in the media when some study reveals that men and women are not that different, with headlines like "The Myth of Mars and Venus" or "Men Are Not from Mars." These studies are quite misleading because they merely point out that men can develop female characteristics and vice versa. Such reports support the notion that every man and woman has a male and female side, but they also ignore the fact that our hormones are dramatically different and directly affect our moods, behaviors, and health in countless ways.

As we've discussed, when a man's testosterone levels significantly drop or his female hormones go too high, or when a woman's estrogen and other female hormone levels are too low or high, stress levels go up. A man requires at least ten times more testosterone than a healthy woman to experience health and well-being. On the other hand, a woman requires at least ten times more estrogen than a healthy man to experience health and well-being. This striking difference is universal for all men and women.

The Big Difference Between Men and Women
Men: Ten times more testosterone.
Women: Ten times more estrogen.

Throughout *Beyond Mars and Venus* we will return to this basic hormonal difference again and again. It helps to remind us that our differences are very real despite how similar we may sometimes appear.

In fact, understanding this difference gives us the needed insight to make conscious behavior and attitude changes to support our hormonal balance. Balancing our hormones through specific changes grants us new power to lower our stress levels and increase our capacity to express our full potential at work and at home.

**Our behavior and emotional changes
are always reflected in our hormones.**

The Effect of Stress on the Brain

Our bodies, both male and female, respond to stress by releasing a hormone called cortisol. When we feel defensive, unloved, or threatened, cortisol floods our brains, activating the fight-or-flight center and redirecting blood flow from the front part of our brains, which houses our wisdom and compassion, to the back part of our brains, which reacts automatically according to programming from childhood and our most primitive instincts.

For both men and women, cortisol and its effects prevent us from accessing our higher potential for loving. But what lowers our cortisol is different depending on our sex. For men, increasing testosterone decreases cortisol levels; for women, balancing the hormones she produces, especially estrogen and progesterone, decreases her cortisol levels.

Testosterone and Aggression

Testosterone replacement for men is in the news a lot today because healthy testosterone levels have been linked to a man's youthfulness, health, weight loss, energy, focus, memory, mood, strength, and libido. You name it—if it is good for men, then it is connected to healthy testosterone levels.

People used to think that too much testosterone was responsible for male aggression and anger. In the last decade it was finally discovered that the opposite is true. Men tend to become aggressive when their *estrogen* levels surge out of balance.

Men tend to become aggressive when their estrogen levels surge out of balance.

For men, testosterone is crucial for regulating stress, because testosterone is what keeps their cortisol levels in check. When a man is stressed, tired, or even depressed, it's generally because his testosterone levels are too low. If his estrogen is too high, he will be more emotional and prone to feelings of anger, defensiveness, and aggression.

If a man's estrogen is too high, he will be more emotional and prone to feelings of anger, defensiveness, and aggression.

Testosterone is important for the authentic expression of both a man's male and female sides. If testosterone is too high it can suppress his access to his female side; if it is too low it can suppress his access to his male qualities.

When testosterone is too low, if a man doesn't shift gears and take time to nurture and express his masculine side, then his female side becomes overexpressed in some dysfunctional manner, and eventually his male side will become suppressed.

If a man doesn't sustain healthy testosterone, then his female side will be overexpressed in some dysfunctional manner.

When a man is facing a threat or challenge, his automatic first reaction is an increase in testosterone. However, if he loses confidence in his ability to meet that threat, then his cortisol levels increase and an enzyme called aromatase is released, causing his testosterone to convert into estrogen. From an evolutionary perspective, this increase in estrogen gives him greater access to his feelings of anger or fear, which increase his willingness to either fight or, as a last attempt to survive, flee.

But with his rising testosterone converting into estrogen and activating his female side, his access to his masculine side gradually decreases. He loses his masculine quality of detachment or independence and eventually becomes overly controlling, demanding, emotional, sensitive, submissive, or needy.

Anger and Defensiveness

The number one problem in relationships today is a man's tendency to express his anger through arguing with his partner. This eventually creates a lack of emotional safety in the relationship. When a woman doesn't feel safe, rather than feel trusting and vulnerable, she toughens up and closes her heart. She is unable to make the sufficient female hormones needed to open her heart with feelings of love and passion.

A man does not realize how destructive expressing his anger can be. After all, many in the field of psychology are still encouraging men to feel and express their anger, rather than learning to feel it but then transform it back into love, patience, understanding, generosity, and kindness.

**When a man expresses anger
to his partner about his partner,
she will toughen up and close her heart.**

Feeling one's anger and not suppressing it is a good thing, but expressing anger and hurt in words or actions toward your partner is a very bad thing. Throughout history, when men became angry, people have died or were punished. Men don't realize the effect their anger has on women because when women are angry, a man usually just sleeps alone on a couch.

**When men get angry, people die.
When women get angry,
a man just sleeps alone on the couch.**

For thousands of years, women have suppressed their authentic feelings in the presence of men to prevent men from getting angry. A woman was expected to agree with her man, follow his lead, and always be happy. While this certainly prevented men from getting angry, it also prevented women from expressing their authentic selves.

To create true equality in relationships between men and women, men must learn to manage their anger and defensiveness. (In later chapters, we will also explore how women can communicate in new ways to support a man in managing his anger. It is a new skill for women to authentically express themselves without triggering a man's defensiveness.)

If a woman is to gradually express her authentic self in a personal relationship, she needs to feel that it is safe for her to express her feelings. When a man can exercise his male side to detach, rather than respond from his female side with angry emotions, a woman feels assured that she is safe and that he will not leave or hurt her because of something she said or did that upset him.

The role of men throughout history has been to make women safe, and today it is needed more than ever, just with a different twist. In the past men protected women from physical danger; today women need men to create emotional safety so that they can express themselves and their feelings authentically.

This does not mean that a man should suppress his anger. Not expressing is not the same as suppressing. The biggest problem in relationships is not whether a man feels angry but that he expresses it to his partner. (In later chapters we will explore how a man can feel his anger and let it go simply by temporarily not talking about his anger to his partner and instead coming back to his male side to rebuild his testosterone.)

**The biggest problem in relationships
is not whether a man feels angry
but that he expresses it to his partner.**

Most men don't realize that in loving relationships expressing anger always makes things worse. When a man expresses anger directly to his partner, it not only creates defensiveness in her but it continues to increase his stress levels, pushing him further out of balance. On a biological level, when he is angry, his testosterone is converting into estrogen; his male hormones are converting into female hormones. By instead learning to quiet the mind and rebuild his testosterone he can return to his male side and feel cool, calm, and collected, which then allows him to open his heart and express his love rather than anger.

By applying new listening skills, a man can eventually build his confidence that his listening to a woman without getting angry actually helps her to return to her most loving and appreciative self. This new confidence can prevent him from becoming defensive or overly emotional because his testosterone is then not converted into estrogen, and he can instead patiently listen with authentic interest and empathy.

Anger Is Not Masculine

Anger and defensiveness are the most common consequences of the suppression of a man's male side and the overexpression of his female side. We tend to think of an angry man as being very masculine because he appears powerful; he uses the threat of violence or other aggression to intimidate and control others. However, his need to express power over others is really his inability to feel powerful within himself. Rather than change himself to get what he wants, which would be an expression of the masculine qualities of accountability and competence, he attempts to change or control others. When he is angry, he tries to look powerful, which is a male quality, but in reality his female hormones (estrogen) are surging.

**When a man is angry, he tries to look powerful,
which is a male quality,
but in reality his female hormones are surging.**

Here are a few examples of how the suppression of a man's male qualities can lead to the dysfunctional overexpression of his female side:

- When he loses the cool of his masculine side, the hot characteristic of his female side becomes overheated. He literally heats up and can turn red with rage.
- When he disconnects from the *independent* characteristic of his masculine side, the characteristic of *interdependence* on his female side becomes overexpressed and he becomes needy and demanding. Nothing is good enough for him.

- When he disconnects from the *confidence* of his male side, then the *trusting* nature of his feminine side becomes overexpressed. His felt needs and emotional sensitivities are converted into unrealistic expectations. When these expectations are not met, he eventually feels exaggerated feelings of hurt and injustice. He feels an out-of-proportion sense of entitlement and demand for respect that can erupt into anger.

- When he disconnects from his *analytical* male side, the *intuitive* female side becomes overexpressed. Silently listening without reacting is one of the most masculine things a person can do. Now, rather than seeking to understand and validate another's point of view through listening, he is too quick to believe his feelings are facts. Overcome by his feelings and the need to be right, he is quick to become angry and defensive.

- When he disconnects from his *accountable* male side, which lets him own his mistakes and apologize, the *responsive* characteristic of his female side is overexpressed. In an attempt to quickly solve the problem, he discounts or minimizes it. He might say, "It is not a big deal" or "Don't worry about it" or "You are just making a big deal out of nothing!" If he is still expected to apologize despite this, he will get angry and defensive.

The list could go on and on. What is important is to recognize the pattern: when a man's testosterone is low, different aspects of his male side become overshadowed by the overexpressed characteristics of his female side. This imbalance then encourages a wide range of automatic reactions and behaviors that are usually inappropriate to the situation, irrational, or dysfunctional and that do not help him achieve his goals.

Male Stress Symptoms

The steady production of testosterone is linked to a man's well-being. When a man is confronted with external stressors, eventually his testosterone levels become depleted. They become even more depleted when different aspects of his male side become overshadowed by overexpressed characteristics of his female side. When his testosterone is low or his estrogen is too high, he is more vulnerable to a wide range of male stress symptoms.

These are some of the most common symptoms of chronic stress in a man. Quite often they unfold in the following order over time, unless he is unable to find a way to return to his masculine side.

1. Low motivation
2. Apathy
3. Rigidity or stubbornness
4. Grumpiness
5. Anger and irritability
6. Resistance to change
7. Low libido with his wife (more likely to be addicted to porn)
8. Moodiness
9. Anxiety
10. Despair
11. Aggression

Certainly there are other potential symptoms, but these are the most common. When any of these symptoms are present, it is a warning sign that a man needs to temporarily back off from activities that stimulate his female side, and instead focus on activities that will stimulate the production of his male hormones.

Common Testosterone-Producing Activities

Driving a car
Making decisions
Effort and hard work
Solving problems (rather than complaining)
Working on projects
Being efficient
Providing selfless service
Making a difference
Sacrificing for a noble cause
Prayer, meditation, or silence
Fasting
Learning and developing skills
Making money
Taking risks
Facing challenges with confidence
Success
Winning
Competition
Sports
Physical exercise (like running)
Physical intimacy
Romance
Listening
Researching
Joking or making light of problems with other men

Because modern men are moving more in the direction of greater authenticity, their greatest challenge is to stay connected to their male side as they embrace and express more of their female qualities.

When Men Suppress
Their Female Side

In the past, it was more common for men to suppress their female side and overexpress their male side. This tendency is less common in the modern world, but it does still happen, particularly in second- and third-world countries.

Most men are not aware of how different they are from men of previous generations. Simply supporting his wife in having a job outside the home is an expression of a man's interdependent female side. In traditional relationships, women were dependent on men for their financial support and men were much more independent and not dependent in their role as providers. As she expresses more of her independent side, he becomes more interdependent.

Yet men can still revert to their historical imbalance. When men suppress their female side and as a result overexpress their male side, it can create a different kind of stress that causes him to become overly independent and detached, decreasing his need for emotional intimacy.

**With high testosterone and low estrogen,
a man has less need for emotional intimacy.**

The overexpression of his masculine side results in a kind of narcissism that makes him incapable of feeling empathy for others. This overexpression of his male side may be moderate or more extreme.

When this overexpression is moderate, men are simply more self-centered and less aware of the needs of others. They can be well meaning but behave like a bull in a china shop, unknowingly breaking everything in their path. They lack the sensitivity or empathy to be more considerate of others. To various degrees they are disconnected from the qualities of their female side like vulnerability, interdependence, and nurturing.

These men are best described as "macho." UrbanDictionary. com defines macho as a "male who cannot 'lose face' in front of women. Most macho men have the emotional range of a teaspoon and have enough empathy to fill the ink tube in a pen." A more standard definition is a man who has a strong or exaggerated sense of power or who feels he has the right to dominate and control others.

When the overexpression of the male side is extreme, a man becomes a sociopath who only cares about himself and has little capacity to think beyond his own needs to consider and care about the needs of others. He has completely suppressed his female-feeling side. Throughout history, these men have often assumed the most powerful positions of leadership or become criminals because they are devoid of conscience and not held back by the fear of hurting others. They simply do not care about others. Because they are disconnected from their female side, they will hurt, cheat, steal, and kill without remorse.

**When a man's male side
is overexpressed to the extreme,
he will hurt, steal, and kill without remorse.**

Rebuilding Testosterone
to Lower Stress

Engaging in male activities like the ones listed earlier generates testosterone, but the internal stress a man experiences in response to the external stress from his daily challenges uses that testosterone up. This is why, after a stressful day, he will need to restore his testosterone levels. In addition, if his job requires him to express more of his female side, his testosterone levels will drop and he will need to rebuild testosterone levels then, as well.

These four basic scenarios show how testosterone is created and depleted over the course of the day:

1. To the degree he is challenged to express his male qualities, a man will make more testosterone at the same pace he uses it up. At the end of the day, he will not need to rebuild his testosterone levels because he only uses up what he continues to make.

2. To the degree he faces external stressors while also expressing his male qualities like confidence and competence, he uses up more testosterone than he is making. For example, when I am driving, I have plenty of confidence, but if I am faced with the external stressors of traffic jams I will use up more testosterone than I am making. This means I will use up part of my reserves and therefore need to rebuild my testosterone levels at the end of the day.

3. To the degree a man faces external stressors without feeling his male qualities like confidence and competence, his cortisol will increase and his testosterone will begin converting to estrogen. Using the car example again, if I am driving and I hit traffic that slows me down when I am already late to an important meeting, I will use up much more testosterone than I am making. This means I will have an even greater need to rebuild my testosterone levels at the end of the day.

4. To the degree that a man expresses his female qualities during the day and does not express his male qualities, his estrogen levels will rise too high and his testosterone levels will drop. I can experience this drop when I am

spending all day Saturday taking care of my grandchildren, which expresses my nurturing female side more than my detached, competent, and confident male side. This means that at the end of the day, after they leave, I have the most urgent need to rebuild my testosterone levels.

Men Go to Their Cave

To rebuild his testosterone levels, a man needs to temporarily detach from his female side and take some time to return to his male side. I call this cave time. "Cave time" is a term I used in *Men Are from Mars, Women Are from Venus.* This insight has helped millions of women to correctly interpret their husbands' need for time alone. At times when he is in his cave, she recognizes it is his way to recover from stress. With this insight she doesn't take his behavior personally, feel a need to interrupt his time, or attempt to connect with him during it.

I borrowed the term from a particular American Indian tradition. When a bride married her husband, her mother told her that after marriage, at the end of the day, a man would withdraw into his cave. At those times, don't go in his cave or you will be burned by his dragon. She was referring of course to a man's anger.

"Don't go into a man's cave or you will be burned by his dragon."

When a man doesn't take the time he needs to rebuild his testosterone, he will unknowingly sabotage his ability to feel selfless, generous, and lovingly patient. Unless he is able to rebuild his testosterone, he can easily become irritable, more selfish or demanding, and less attentive overall to his family or his partner.

During cave time, a man temporarily disconnects from any estrogen-producing nurturing activities and focuses on activities that can stimulate his testosterone production.

During cave time, a man temporarily disconnects from any estrogen-producing activities to rebuild his testosterone levels.

As long as these activities are done in a very low-stress context, he will be rebuilding his testosterone reserves, and will have more energy to give to his relationship, family, and the next day's work. For cave-time activities to rebuild his testosterone, they must be in a stress-free context.

For cave-time activities to rebuild his testosterone, they must be in a stress-free context.

For example, driving is a testosterone-stimulating activity. If a man is driving in traffic when he is late, this external stress will deplete his reserves. However, if he likes to drive and he is not feeling a sense of urgency or frustration, he will make more testosterone while driving than he is using up. In this stress-free context, driving while listening to some great music can be cave time.

Activities that produce testosterone will assist a man in rebuilding his testosterone only as long as he is able to sustain feelings of confidence or competence. In each activity, to the degree that he is challenged, his body will make more testosterone. However, if he also becomes stressed, he will use up this increased testosterone.

When a man is challenged but also stressed, he will use up his testosterone.

For example, one way a man can rebuild his testosterone levels is by watching a football game, which activates his competitive and problem-solving male side. But if he has bet a lot of money on the outcome, watching the game can cause more stress and use up the testosterone he is producing rather than restore its levels. Similarly, if he is watching a game to forget his problems but his wife disapproves of his actions, the feeling that he is letting her down can prevent him from rebuilding his testosterone levels. In both cases, he will feel the need to take more cave time than he otherwise would have.

Generally, with twenty to thirty minutes of testosterone-stimulating activities in a relaxed, stress-free context, a man can rebuild a sufficient level of testosterone. However, if he experienced greater external stresses during his day or his estrogen levels are too high for another reason, he will need more cave time to rebuild his testosterone. In addition, a man who has more masculine qualities will require more cave time than one who has fewer masculine qualities.

If You Don't Use It, You Lose It

You can see how crucial it is for men to have stress-free cave time to rebuild and generate healthy levels of testosterone. What fewer people realize is that a man has to first use up the testosterone he produced previously, through work and challenge, before successfully replenishing it—if he doesn't, he loses his ability to make more of it. After facing challenges that deplete his testosterone levels, if a man can take some to time to express his male qualities in a relaxed context without stress, his body automatically reacts to rebuild his testosterone.

A dramatic example of this is well known to weight lifters. When weight lifters challenge their bodies through exercise, it depletes their testosterone. To rebuild it they need to take time to relax. This means weight lifting one day and then giving their muscles plenty of rest by taking one or two days off. This gives the body a chance to generate more testosterone to rebuild and increase muscle mass.

Likewise, if a man just works hard all day but doesn't balance his work with relaxation, his body becomes depleted of testosterone. However, if he just relaxes without first using his testosterone up, his body does not make more testosterone. Both action and rest are required.

In fact, over time, if he does not use up the testosterone his body produces, his body begins to shut down the production of testosterone altogether. This is often what happens when men retire and their testosterone levels suddenly drop. The average man in America at fifty years old has half the testosterone levels he had as a younger man. In indigenous tribes, in contrast, healthy men at ninety years old have the testosterone levels of a young man. My own levels at sixty-five are higher than they were when I was a young man.

A man's ability to make testosterone will also drop if he takes steroids to compensate for low testosterone. Steroids are a synthetic form of testosterone. They can build his muscle mass, increase his low libido, and make him feel like Superman, but there are side effects.

The average man in America at fifty years old has half the testosterone levels he had as a younger man.

After taking testosterone replacement or steroids, because his body no longer needs to make testosterone, a man's testicles begin to atrophy and literally shrink. After years of steroid use, even with the natural solutions I explore in my health blogs at MarsVenus.com to raise a man's testosterone, it may take many months to years to restore normal testosterone production.

Testosterone replacement temporarily makes a man feel young again, but there are side effects.

How Women Can Support Men

The support of a loving partner can go a long way to boost a man's testosterone. Likewise, a lack of support from his partner can do a lot to knock it down.

Let's look at the twelve basic qualities of a man's male side and discover how a woman's love and support can help increase his testosterone levels.

What a Man Needs to Express His Male Side
Increase His Testosterone

Characteristics of His Male Side	The Support He Needs That She Can Provide	The Benefits Received
1. Independent	He needs her to not give him unsolicited advice.	He feels trusted to make his own decisions and can also take credit for his successes. He then feels appreciated for what he has done on his own and wants to spend more time with her.
2. Detached	He needs to be able to take cave time without her disapproval.	He gets space and time to mull over his challenges and not talk about his feelings or thoughts. He can then access his clarity and understanding, which leads to greater compassion for her.

3. Problem solver	He needs her to remind him that when she is stressed, the problem she needs solved is her need to talk; she needs him to listen, not give solutions.	With a greater understanding of her needs, he is more motivated to help her. He can be more relaxed when she is talking about her problems, and she feels more supported when she does.
4. Tough	He needs to be admired for his sacrifices and hard work.	He can access his inner power and courage, and she is free to express herself without fear of offending him or hurting his feelings.
5. Competitive	He needs his effort to do his best to be appreciated even when he fails. He needs his successes to be a cause for joyful celebration.	He is much more willing to appreciate the strengths of others and even ask for help when he needs it.

6. Analytical	He needs to hear supportive comments about his analytical thought process, like, "That makes sense," "Good idea," and "You're right."	He is much more interested in what she has to say and more willing to admit his mistakes.
7. Powerful	He needs to be asked for his help and celebrated for his support.	He gets to feel like her hero. When he is needed, he feels a greater sense of meaning in his life and has more energy to support her.
8. Assertive	He needs to be able to express his dreams or when he is proud of something without being corrected or edited with concerns. Be careful not to "rain on his parade"!	He will feel much more supported, trusted, and appreciated. This makes him more supportive, caring, and respectful of her feelings and needs.

9. Competent	He needs to be appreciated for doing little things to make her day better.	He feels successful in his relationship and is able to access more love, respect, patience, and appreciation for his partner.
10. Confident	He needs her to accept him rather than expressing complaints or judgment.	He is confident that he can make her happy and becomes a more patient listener, allowing him to understand her better.
11. Accountable	He needs his mistakes minimized, and his apologies accepted and appreciated. No one wants to say they are sorry and then be told why they should feel bad.	He apologizes for mistakes and strives to be a better partner.

12. Goal-oriented	He needs to be able to plan things. She should let him know various options that she would like and then let him plan and deliver.	He can take credit and she can feel cared for. When it is his plan, he is more focused and motivated to please his partner.

In short, when his hormones are in balance, not only is he happier, but he has the motivation and energy to be a better partner.

The same is true for her. In the next chapter we will explore in great depth the importance for women to sustain healthy estrogen levels to be happy, healthy, and loving.

6

ESTROGEN
IS FROM VENUS

During the last twenty years, more and more women have turned to estrogen hormone replacement to relieve menopausal symptoms. Some researchers claim that estrogen replacement can not only stop menopausal hot flashes but also support positive moods, increase energy, and reduce anxiety. Hormone replacement for women has become common because of the harm decreased levels of estrogen can cause.

In women, decreased estrogen has been linked to osteoporosis, low energy, lack of concentration, mood swings, depression, poor memory, infertility, low libido, and anxiety.

With rising testosterone levels and declining estrogen levels, women's risk of dementia has outpaced men's. More than two-thirds of Americans with Alzheimer's disease are women. One out of six women over sixty-five have Alzheimer's disease, compared with only one out of eleven men. Research also reveals that when women's estrogen levels are too low, they are more vulnerable to heart disease, diabetes, and cancer.

However, taking hormones is not always the answer. A worldwide debate is raging today regarding the harmful side effects of taking hormones versus their possible benefits. While some studies say taking hormones increases a woman's risk of breast cancer, others claim that it can reduce the risk. Some experts claim bioidentical hormones, which are made from plant chemicals, are safer, while synthetic or animal-derived hormones are not. (We'll discuss this more in the next chapter.)

**When women's estrogen levels are too low,
their risk of disease is higher,
but taking hormones is not always the answer.**

What is completely overlooked in this debate is a woman's potential to create the right balance of hormones without taking hormones. Through a good diet, regular and moderate exercise, and, most important, changing her behavior and applying new relationship skills, a woman can restore healthy estrogen levels appropriate for her age.

**By applying new relationship skills,
a woman can restore healthy estrogen levels
appropriate for her age.**

Hormones at Menopause

It is normal for a woman's hormone levels to drop at menopause, but if she is not stressed, her adrenal glands will usually supply the right balance of hormones so that she does not need hormone replacement therapy.

Yet because so many women today are imbalanced toward their male side, without sufficient levels of the female hormones, they experience chronic stress levels in their body. This eventually leads to fatigue of the adrenal glands, which are the primary source of female hormones for women during and after menopause.

Without sufficient female hormones, women experience chronic stress in their body, which leads to adrenal fatigue and further hormonal deficiency.

During menopause, if a woman's adrenals are fatigued, she will not be able to make enough estrogen and so experiences a host of common menopausal symptoms like hot flashes, anger, resentment, insomnia, vaginal dryness, low libido, and low energy, along with increased vulnerability to the many diseases previously mentioned.

As more and more younger women express their masculine side without finding balance by also expressing their female side, they, too, experience a host of female stress symptoms associated with hormonal imbalance. The most common complaints are mood swings, PMS, painful periods, depression, lack of sustained passion or attraction, inability to enjoy time alone or take time for herself, and (most common) feeling overwhelmed with too much to do and not enough time.

Taking hormones can sometimes relieve both younger and menopausal women's symptoms, but it doesn't treat the causes, which are adrenal fatigue and hormonal deficiency. When taking hormones for symptomatic relief, the dose also has to be perfect, otherwise there are side effects—and the body's hormonal needs are always changing. In addition, when you take a hormone, your body stops making them, as we saw with men and testosterone in the last chapter.

Just as sufficient testosterone is important for men, sufficient estrogen is important for the balanced expression of a woman's female and male sides. If her estrogen is too low, it can suppress access to her female qualities, which will lead her to overexpress her masculine side. If her estrogen is too high, although this is not as common, then her male qualities will be suppressed. This imbalance also increases her stress levels.

Estrogen is not the only hormone whose function is vital to lowering a woman's stress levels. There is another hormone, one that is rarely mentioned in discussions of whether a woman should or should not get hormone replacement. This hormone assists a woman's body in making the perfect balance of estrogen for her. The hormone is called oxytocin, and by learning to make more of it on her own through shifts in her thinking and behavior, a woman holds the key to naturally increase her estrogen levels . . . with no negative side effects.

Oxytocin, the Love Hormone

During the last fifteen years, new research has shown that experiences and activities that increase the hormone oxytocin will reduce stress in women. This research has been a remarkable breakthrough. It has helped us to understand a major reason why, biologically, men and women have different emotional needs in relationships.

In both men and women, oxytocin is associated with love, affection, trust, and safety, but increasing oxytocin levels affect men and women differently. Oxytocin lowers testosterone in men and women. For a man, this is fine if his testosterone is very high, but if it is low, oxytocin will make him sleepy or even increase his stress levels. This is why men are not as instinctively motivated to engage in oxytocin-producing activities as women are.

**The hormone oxytocin is associated
with love, affection, trust, and safety,
but it affects men and women differently!**

Women need oxytocin to have an orgasm, but high oxytocin in a man can decrease his libido. Research shows that when a man gets married or has children, as his oxytocin levels rise because he feels greater love for his wife and family, his testosterone levels drop along with his libido. This is why it is common for couples to have less sex after many years of marriage (although with new relationship skills, a man can increase his testosterone and sustain his libido in marriage as his oxytocin levels also increase).

Oxytocin lowers a woman's stress hormones but it cannot lower her stress on its own; it needs estrogen's help. Oxytocin has a special relationship with estrogen. When a woman has low estrogen, oxytocin is rendered virtually powerless to lower her stress levels. But oxytocin's stress-lowering effects become increasingly powerful as women's estrogen levels rise. This is why it is so important for women to balance the expression of their male side at work with their female side at home. By choosing to express her female qualities in her personal life, estrogen levels can rise and oxytocin can more effectively lower her stress.

**Oxytocin's stress-lowering effects
become increasingly powerful
as women's estrogen levels rise.**

With greater oxytocin, a woman's testosterone drops, allowing her estrogen to rise. This increase in estrogen, as mentioned before, increases oxytocin's ability to lower her stress. This is particularly important for women today because expressing their male qualities during the workday increases testosterone and, because testosterone opposes the production of estrogen, the testosterone produced at work decreases her estrogen levels. Fortunately, oxytocin stimulation reduces her high testosterone to allow estrogen-producing activities to bring her estrogen levels back into balance.

Women and Touch

We'll talk about more ways to stimulate oxytocin in chapter eight, but one of the major ones is touch. Because touch is a major oxytocin producer, compounding the ability of estrogen to lower stress in women, women are far more affected by touch than men. The same is true of other major oxytocin producers like affection and attention.

One of the most common complaints from women that I hear in counseling sessions is that their husbands are not attentive or affectionate enough. Why is this so common? It's because women require more touch, attention, and affection to produce the oxytocin they need to cope with stress.

I first realized this difference over thirty years ago, when I would hear women in counseling complain, "My husband only touches me when he wants sex."

Before I understood women better, I quietly thought, "What's wrong with that?"

Gradually, I came to understand how important nonsexual touch and hugs were to women. Unless a woman is in the mood for sex, sexual touch is a turnoff. This is because nonsexual touch, hugs, and affection generate much more oxytocin than sexual touch. Once her oxytocin levels increase, she is able to return to her female side and increase her estrogen. This increased estrogen, paired with oxytocin, allows her to fully enjoy more sexual touch.

However, as more women become disconnected from their female side, because their estrogen levels are low, oxytocin doesn't lower their stress and so they don't miss being touched. When this happens, it is the male partners who often complain that their wives are not affectionate or attentive enough. When a woman has low estrogen levels, a man's needs for affection and attention, which become greater as his estrogen levels rise, can be a turnoff.

The relationship between oxytocin and estrogen also explains why women respond to the same touch differently at different times of the month. When her estrogen is high during ovulation, even a slight touch can have a strong beneficial effect on her stress levels, but when estrogen is low during menstruation, touch has much less of a beneficial effect.

When a woman's estrogen levels are highest, this is when she needs touch and attention the most. After menopause, when a woman no longer ovulates, her estrogen function will tend to peak around the full moon and drop to its lowest point around the new moon. Research reveals that melatonin levels in the brain for both men and women decrease by 30 percent around the full moon; a similar decrease happens at ovulation, and in women this increases estrogen function.

In the last few years, more research in women's hormones has revealed that certain social behaviors that stimulate the female hormone progesterone can also lower a woman's stress levels, but only during the twelve to fourteen days after ovulation, before her period. In later chapters we will explore in greater detail the different behaviors that increase her progesterone, oxytocin, and estrogen levels, as well as the best times of the month to increase each. Understanding these hormone shifts can help both men and women understand a woman's tendency to have different emotional responses at different times in her hormonal cycle.

Why Men Think Women Are More Emotional

Every experience, from looking at a beautiful sunset to closing a business deal, evokes a unique biological reaction. When a woman experiences the moderate external stress of facing a threat or challenge, her first biological reaction is an increase in estrogen. This rise in estrogen increases blood flow to the limbic system, the emotional center of the brain.

Men often think women are overly emotional because a man's automatic reaction to moderate external stress is very different than a woman's. At times of moderate external stress, a man's brain is wired to detach from his emotions. As his testosterone levels rise in response, blood flow in his brain is diverted from his emotional center. His first reaction to moderate stress is therefore to detach.

By contrast, a woman's first reaction is to feel a stronger emotional reaction. This increased emotional response to moderate external stress is not an overreaction, but an appropriate reaction that increases her intuitive awareness so that she is able to properly prioritize the problem as well as recognize the support she has available to help solve it. A man's detached reaction is not a sign that he doesn't care or have a heart, but rather a way to step back and analyze a problem so that he can prioritize its importance and then consider how to solve it.

These different gender-based reactions are basically hardwired into the brain. They are automatic. This is why when women resist their automatic emotional reactions by not sharing their feelings they end up creating more internal stress by suppressing their female side, and when men resist their automatic nonemotional reactions by immediately talking about their feelings they end up creating more internal stress by suppressing their male side.

A woman's increased emotional response is not an overreaction but an appropriate reaction that increases her intuitive intelligence.

This distinction also helps us to understand why men commonly interrupt a woman when she is talking about a problem. This interruption generally occurs in an intimate relationship when a woman is not looking to solve a problem but instead is talking in order to feel better or closer to her partner.

When confronted with a problem, a man wants to solve it while a woman often wants to talk about it first. For women, talking and then feeling heard and understood stimulates oxytocin, which allows her estrogen levels to rise and her stress to decrease. Through expressing her feelings, she is able to return to her female side, which balances her hormones and lowers her stress levels. In this way she is better able to cope with life's inevitable external stresses.

When confronted with a problem, a man wants to solve it while a woman often wants to talk about it first.

For a man, thinking about a solution raises his testosterone and lowers his stress. If he cannot immediately do anything about the problem, his solution is then to forget it until he can do something. This is why it can be difficult at first for men to learn to listen to a woman talking about a problem.

When a woman is upset about something, men either want to suggest a solution (which is why they interrupt) or encourage her to forget it, and while she is talking about it, they can do neither. But there's another reason men often interrupt women when they are upset and talking about a problem: they incorrectly interpret her strong emotional reaction to moderate external stress. A man wrongly assumes that if a woman is getting upset then it is because she can't solve her problems on her own. He interprets her stronger emotional response as an urgent need for help, and then tries to give it.

When Men Have Stronger Emotions Than Women

When I point out that women have stronger emotional reactions to stress, this sometimes doesn't ring true for women for two reasons. First, if they are too far on their male side, they may not have enough estrogen to feel their emotions and so their reactions to external stress may not be very emotional.

Second, almost all women have experienced a man becoming very emotional, particularly when he is really upset. When a man is threatened by a situation, as long as he is confident, he will not get emotional. However, when he is not confident and doesn't know what to do, his testosterone turns to estrogen, his stress increases, and then he can become very emotional.

Men do become very emotional when they have a big upset.

With moderate stress, men detach, but if the external stress is greater, he can be more emotional than any woman. When a woman is really upset and she feels that she cannot get the support she needs, she has the opposite reaction and becomes more detached. She suppresses her female trusting and vulnerable side because she doesn't feel safe. She raises the sword of her independent male side. As she puts up walls around her heart to protect herself, her testosterone rises and her estrogen levels drop. By suppressing her emotional female side, she becomes very detached, cold, and self-protective. By separating from her female side, she cannot be hurt but she also cannot let love in; she is safe but she is alone.

At times of great upset men become more emotional and women become less.

**At times of great upset,
men become more emotional
and women become detached.**

This insight is so important because often men misinterpret what a woman needs when she shows her emotions. They think if a woman is emotional then she is confronting a huge problem that she cannot solve. They think this because when men become upset, it is because they don't know what to do to solve a problem. When he discovers that the problem she is emotional about is not huge, he misinterprets her reaction as an overreaction, because under moderate stress he doesn't have an emotional response. He concludes that she is getting upset over nothing because he would only get upset if the problem were really big and he didn't know what to do.

Having said this, it is also true that both men and women can and do emotionally overreact to situations. When our internal stress builds up, then inevitably we will overreact. Instead of momentarily feeling frustrated in response to moderate stress, we feel angry or resentful; instead of momentarily feeling disappointed, we feel sad, hurt, or depressed; instead of momentarily feeling our concerns, we feel afraid, scared, or anxious, or we shut down.

If these negative emotions are not transformed, we begin to close our hearts; we lose our natural ability to grow in love, compassion, and wisdom.

The Tend-and-Befriend Response

In psychological terms, a woman's first reaction to stress is to express one or more of her female qualities like interdependence, trust, emotionality, or nurturing. Instead of reacting with a fight-or-flight response, as a man would, her first instinct has been labeled by researchers as the "tend-and-befriend response." Tending refers to caring for or nurturing those who may need her help and befriending refers to seeking out another person to give and receive support. On a biological level, this response releases oxytocin and increases her estrogen, lowering her stress.

One of the most powerful ways a woman can increase her oxytocin is by sharing her feelings. Sharing her feelings, as long as a woman is not seeking a solution, will increase her estrogen and lower her stress. However, if she is seeking a solution or expressing her feelings to change her partner, then her testosterone will increase and her estrogen will decrease. Instead of lowering her stress, talking about her feelings will only drain her or make him feel bad.

Many women too far on their male side are completely unaware of their inner feminine potential to lower stress and

feel really good by simply sharing the feelings they have to suppress during their workday or even at home in their personal
relationships.

**When a woman shares feelings, positive or negative,
as long as she is not doing so to seek a solution,
it will increase her estrogen and lower her stress.**

In the workplace, when it is her job to solve a problem, it
stimulates higher testosterone levels and so she also reacts to
moderate external stress by disconnecting from her emotional
center to come up with quick solutions. Talking through her
feelings about the problems of her day, without looking for
solutions, is kind of a therapy for women to come back to their
female side after being on their male side all day. It has a restor-
ative effect similar to a man taking cave time.

But when a woman is facing a threat or challenge and
doesn't feel supported, she loses her ability to access her feminine side. Estrogen-producing qualities like trust, interdependence, and nurturing become suppressed. As her estrogen levels
begin to drop, her testosterone levels increase. This imbalance
brings out her male side, to solve the problem herself, but suppresses her female receptive side, which recognizes the value of
seeking help.

With testosterone levels rising, if her female side is suppressed, she becomes overly independent, detached, and goal
oriented. She has difficulty asking for help. Asking for help
expresses our female vulnerability and receptivity. It is common knowledge in the medical field that women are much more
diligent than men in asking for doctors' help. When men suppress their female side, they resist asking for help. For example,
when driving, men tend to avoid asking for help in the form of

directions. Likewise, when women suppress their female side, they also resist asking for help.

Quite often in relationships, when a woman with more female qualities is too far on her male side, she will not directly ask a man for support. Instead she will expect him to be a "mind reader" and offer his support automatically. This is frustrating for her because she thinks he should have offered assistance, and now believes he's unwilling to help. She does not instinctively recognize a man's tendency to wait until he is asked for help rather than offer his help unasked. On the other hand, when a woman is more on her male side or has more male qualities, while she may not take the lack of offer to help so personally, she instead decides it is just easier to do it herself than to ask. It is true that women can do it all, but when they do, they don't sleep well at night because they are so overwhelmed and stressed.

Women can do it all, but when they do, they don't sleep well at night because they are so overwhelmed and stressed.

The most common consequence of the suppression of a woman's female side and the overexpression of her male side is feeling overwhelmed. We tend to think of a woman who is feeling overwhelmed as being very feminine because she is trying so hard to please everyone, but actually at those times her male hormone, testosterone, is surging.

When a woman suppresses different qualities of her female side, the outcome is always increased stress, which most commonly shows up today as a "time famine." Women become overwhelmed with too much to do, feeling like there is not enough time. Here are a few examples of how and why this happens:

- When she loses the *emotional warmth* of her feminine side, the *cool detachment* of her male side becomes overly icy. Rather than slowing down to relax and enjoy her life by connecting with her nurturing feminine feelings of love, receptivity, and vulnerability, she becomes detached and disconnected from her feelings. As a result she becomes overly task oriented, primarily focused on solving problems. She then becomes distressed and overwhelmed.

- When she disconnects from the *interdependent* characteristic of her feminine side, the characteristic of *independence* on her male side becomes overexpressed and she becomes a martyr. She has to do everything on her own; she resists support, and no support she is offered is good enough.

- When she disconnects from the *trusting nature* of her female side, then the *confident nature* of her male side becomes overexpressed. She feels like she is the only who can get the job done right. She rejects others' help, then resents that she has to "do it all."

- When she disconnects from her *vulnerable side* and stops sharing how she feels, she then overexpresses her male quality of *being tough* by ignoring her own needs. She listens to the needs of others, but her own go at the bottom of her never-ending to-do list.

The list could go on and on. What is important is to recognize the pattern: when a woman's testosterone is higher than her estrogen, different aspects of her female side become overshadowed by overexpressed characteristics of her male side. This imbalance then encourages a wide range of automatic reactions and behaviors that are usually inappropriate to the situation and prevent her from achieving her goals.

Female Stress Symptoms

In a woman, the always-changing balance of female hormones during her menstrual cycle is directly linked to her well-being. Her body has the wisdom to balance her estrogen, progesterone, oxytocin, and testosterone when she is able to embrace her female side and then get the support she needs to fully express her male and female sides in balance.

As we've seen, a woman's hormones go out of balance when different aspects of her female side become overshadowed by overexpressed characteristics of her male side. When this happens, she becomes more vulnerable to a wide range of stress symptoms.

These are ten of the most common symptoms of chronic stress in women. Quite often they unfold in the following order over time, unless she is able to find a way to return to her female side to find hormonal balance:

1. Feeling overwhelmed
2. Looping negative thoughts
3. Exhaustion
4. Difficulty sleeping
5. Resentment
6. Dissatisfaction
7. Low libido
8. Mental rigidity
9. Resistance to change
10. Depression

Certainly there are other potential symptoms, but these are the ones that are most common in women when the overexpression of her male side suppresses her female side.

When Estrogen Goes Too High

On the other hand, when a woman's freedom to express her male side is restricted, aspects of her female side can become overexpressed. This creates different stress symptoms. With the suppression of her male side, she may feel so emotional and vulnerable that she becomes indecisive, manipulative, passive-aggressive, or anxious.

In previous generations, the rules of society prevented women in various ways from freely expressing the qualities of their male side. The imbalance this created was commonly referred to as *hysteria*.

Hysteria was a once-common medical diagnosis reserved exclusively for women that medical science no longer recognizes. Its symptoms were said to include fainting, nervousness, sexual desire, insomnia, irritability, loss of appetite, and a "tendency to cause trouble." In extreme cases, a woman would be forced to enter an insane asylum.

The medical treatment for hysteria in Europe and then in America up until 1952 was having a woman rest more, thereby protecting her from serious responsibilities. Ironically this suppression of her male side only made the problem worse. She was stressed primarily because she was not permitted the freedom to express her male side. A better solution to balance her hormones and relieve this condition of high estrogen levels and no testosterone would have been to support her in expressing her male side.

Certainly not all women were diagnosed with hysteria, but it was reported to be common. As many as one in four women were reported to suffer from it, which was enough for men to form the inaccurate conclusion that women were the weaker sex.

It is not femininity that creates weakness but the suppression of our male side. On the other hand, it is the suppression of our female side and the overexpression of our male side that creates evil and corruption in the world.

It is not femininity that creates weakness but the suppression of our male side.

Historically, one treatment did actually relieve symptoms of hysteria: masturbating a woman twice a week. Descriptions of this treatment appear all the way back to the first century A.D. A woman would visit her doctor or nurse twice a week to be masturbated. This could temporarily relieve her symptoms because the act of masturbating a woman in a clinical and nonromantic setting does temporarily increase testosterone and lower high estrogen.

For a woman who was suppressing her male side, this nonromantic, clinical masturbation therapy could help her find relief by balancing out her high estrogen with testosterone. What we now know is that she could have received the same benefit by having a job or a lifestyle that supported the expression of her male side.

One might wonder, in that case, why women didn't just masturbate themselves for relief. Certainly some did so privately, but throughout the last two thousand years, women were shamed by society for pleasuring themselves and even enjoying sex.

This insight that masturbation increases testosterone is particularly important to know because it may help women whose testosterone levels are too high. Those whose main challenge is coming back to their female side need to know that masturbating may only further boost their testosterone levels. By focusing instead on oxytocin-stimulating behaviors, women can more effectively find hormonal balance and relieve stress. Also, having her partner lovingly stimulate her during sex can increase her oxytocin and estrogen in ways that solo masturbation does not.

How Oxytocin Lowers a Woman's Stress

When a woman is stressed from too much testosterone and the temporary suppression of her female side, her body produces an excess of the stress hormone cortisol that prevents her from accessing her higher loving potential. In women but not men, oxytocin has been proven to lower cortisol levels. What testosterone does to lower stress for men, oxytocin does for women.

When modern women are stressed, oxytocin lowers their stress as measured by decreasing cortisol levels.

As mentioned, women in relationships often tell me their husbands have stopped being affectionate. Touching, hugs, and cuddling are big oxytocin producers. If a man comes home with low testosterone, the last thing he feels an urge to do is become affectionate. Doing so lowers his testosterone further. But by taking some time to rebuild his testosterone levels, he is then able to become more affectionate, particularly when he understands how important it is to his partner.

Cuddling in bed before going to sleep helps men and women in different ways. For women, the oxytocin produced from cuddling helps to lower their stress so they can forget their problems and worries and then fall asleep. For men, the oxytocin makes them sleepy. However, for most men, *too much* cuddling will increase his stress, and then he can't sleep unless he gently pulls away.

Cuddling in bed before going to sleep helps men and women in different ways.

Certain kinds of support like affection, attention, caring, understanding, and respect increase her oxytocin levels, lowering her stress and allowing her to give love more freely and in a balanced way.

In the beginning of relationships, women's oxytocin levels increase dramatically. As a result, she will tend to invest a lot of time, consideration, and energy in the relationship. Often, she gives too much—more than she is getting. This giving is the pure expression of her female side and causes her estrogen levels to rise too high. This imbalance increases her stress levels.

Because women now have greater opportunity and social permission to express their male side, when her estrogen goes too high from giving too much, she can increase her testosterone levels to lower her estrogen.

But when her testosterone goes too high, oxytocin is necessary to restore normal estrogen production and help her find balance. Oxytocin lowers her testosterone so her estrogen can rise to the correct level for her, lowering her stress.

How Men Can Support Women

Women produce oxytocin when they are receiving or anticipating the support they need to express their female side and increase their estrogen. Oxytocin motivates a woman to give more support and is produced when a woman anticipates getting the support she needs or because she has already received the support she needs.

When a woman is looking forward to a romantic date, she feels more feminine and loving. She gives more of herself in the anticipation of receiving her partner's attention. And when a woman receives loving affection or empathy from her partner, she then wants to reciprocate.

Let's look at the twelve basic qualities of a woman's female side and discover how her partner can provide the support necessary for her to freely express her female side.

What a Woman Needs to Increase Her Oxytocin and Estrogen and Express Her Female Side

Characteristics of Her Female Side	The Support She Needs That He Can Provide	The Benefits Received
1. Interdependent	She needs hugs and affection.	She is reassured that she is not alone and has backup. She feels safe to love and is able to better appreciate his support.
2. Emotional	She needs to be listened to without having her feelings judged.	She feels understood and validated.

3. Nurturer	She needs extra time and support so that she can support the needs of others to grow and thrive.	She is better able to support the needs of others, including her partner.
4. Vulnerable	She needs her feelings to be considered respectfully and not dismissed or met with anger or conflict.	She feels safe to feel her feelings and becomes more in touch with her needs, allowing her to experience joy and gratitude.
5. Cooperative	She needs her wishes and needs to be understood and respected.	When he sacrifices for her, she is willing to sacrifice for him. She helps find win–win solutions and is willing to compromise.
6. Intuitive	She needs to be acknowledged for her intuitive insights.	Her intuition can increase both her and her partner's success.

7. Loving	She needs to feel her needs are known and are made a priority.	She is able to love freely. When a woman loves, she is happy and he will always feel more successful.
8. Receptive	She needs him to have a caring attitude.	She is able to trust that he will do his best for her and has more to give.
9. Sincere	She needs him to restrain himself from expressing complaints or judgments, and try to recognize that she is always doing her best to be a loving partner.	She is able to access more of her inner potential to love. He becomes more forgiving of her shortcomings as well as his own.
10. Trusting	She needs him to be considerate of her and make an effort to take a time-out when he is angry or defensive.	She feels safe in his presence and can grow in trust that he will not hurt her. This increases her ability to love and accept him the way he is.

11. Responsive	She needs him not to blame her or demand apologies.	When she doesn't feel his disapproval or blame, then she is less inclined to hold on to her feelings of blame and disapproval. She does not have to defend herself, and can more freely respond to his needs.
12. Relationship-oriented	She needs him to not neglect or minimize her need for time together.	She is able to get her needs met without shame and freely gives him her love and affection. He gets to connect with his own female side, which can easily become suppressed in his quest for success. They can grow together in love rather than apart.

In later chapters we'll explore many powerful oxytocin producers, but overall, the most powerful support a man can give a woman to stimulate oxytocin, lower her testosterone, and increase her estrogen is good communication, which primarily involves him listening more and saying less.

Why Talk Therapy Works

In counseling, when a woman shares her feelings and complaints about her husband with me, it helps to lower her stress and is therapeutic for her because I am simply listening and she is not blaming me for her problems. She is not trying to change me, nor is she expecting me to change in any way. She is sharing her feelings to feel understood as well as to understand her own feelings better.

When she shares the same feelings and complaints with her partner, her intent is not just to be heard. She wants him to change. This makes him feel criticized and defensive or moves him into problem-solver mode. She doesn't get to feel heard without resistance as she does with a therapist.

Only once a woman is fully heard does her stress go down. And then, once she has been heard, if she still needs his help to solve a problem, it is ideal for her to approach him at another time with her heart open, and make a clear request for his support.

Men need to remember that listening is not just the first step in solving a problem. When a woman is stressed, it is also a solution. Without having to "do" anything, he can be the hero.

Women need to remember that complaining to her partner about him never works. By learning to meet her need to be heard by sharing problems that are not about him, she can discover her power to bring out the best in a man. As he listens more without feeling defensive, he automatically becomes more empathetic, compassionate, and motivated to help her. With practice he discovers that without him saying anything or doing anything, she moves from feeling upset to feeling good just by freely sharing her feelings. This makes it much easier for him to listen and understand her different sensitivities and needs.

When a woman complains without this insight, in most cases it doesn't bring them closer and he is unable to listen. Because she is sharing her feelings to motivate him to change, she is coming from her male side. Her male side talks to solve problems while her female side talks to get closer and connect. Talking to solve a problem brings her back to her male side at a time when she is stressed and needs to move to her female side.

In counseling, she feels better after sharing because she is not trying to change me, nor do I have any need to defend myself or correct her. As she feels heard, she comes back to her female side and, as a result, feels better. She feels safe and supported in expressing her female side and that promotes hormone balance in her body.

It is challenging at first for women to talk about feelings to their partner without complaining. I call this process the Venus Talk.

A woman I once explained this process to said to me, "If I am not supposed to complain to solve problems or talk about our relationship, then what is there to talk about?"

With practice, there is always plenty to talk about. Women have a world of feelings and emotional reactions that get dismissed or suppressed during the day. To return to her vulnerable, emotional female side, she needs to shine a light inside and express what is there. Unless she takes the time to look, she will not even know these feelings exist. Instead she will just feel stressed, with an urgent list of problems that need to be solved.

Practicing the Venus Talk

The Venus Talk is a specific formula for sharing and not complaining. Its specific purpose is not to solve any problems, but instead to help her return to her female side and him to his male side.

There is nothing wrong with a woman discussing and solving problems together with her partner at another time when she is not feeling stressed. And there is nothing wrong with a man sharing his feelings or offering to help solve his partner's problems when she is wanting his advice.

The Venus Talk is a specific tool to help solve a much bigger and more general problem that looms over our lives: it is done to help the woman come back to her female side and help the man feel greater empathy for her, and help both lower their stress levels.

A Venus Talk is simple, and anyone can learn to do it:

1. She talks, he listens.
2. She shares but does not complain about him. (She only talks about the stress at her job or activities that have nothing to do with him.)
3. He doesn't try to fix or correct her while she becomes completely transparent about the feelings, thoughts, and emotions that are giving rise to her stress.
4. After a maximum of eight minutes of sharing negative feelings, even if she has more to say, she takes a couple of minutes to share her positive feelings and thank him. Then she goes in for a three- to six-second hug. (In the beginning, when women have been suppressing their female side most of their life, they can only come up with two minutes of sharing. That is fine, but the goal is ten minutes.)
5. After the hug, they don't talk but instead they immediately take some time apart. This frees him from his urge to offer solutions. It also frees her to notice how good it feels to be heard without interruptions or arguments.

Sharing with her partner any thoughts, feelings, emotions, wishes, and wants that she held back from expressing at work for fear of being inappropriate, misunderstood, or rejected will bring her back to her female side. On an emotional level she is getting naked in front of her partner. Not only will she feel more feminine, but he will also feel more masculine.

A woman's sharing feelings is like becoming emotionally naked in front of her partner.

The easiest way to be completely transparent and share feelings with your partner is to talk about problems that have nothing to do with your partner. This makes it clear you are not expecting him to change in some way or take action to solve the problem you are talking about.

I suggest a three- to six-second hug in step 4 because most of the time, couples will hug but only briefly. By counting to three or six it helps a man to remember to relax into the hug. If a woman is shedding a few tears, then it should always be at least a six-second hug.

Here are some examples of how a woman can share feelings versus complain. Take a moment to reflect on how much easier it would be for the man to listen and feel compassion for his partner when she is sharing feelings that are not about him.

Also notice how much more you can connect to the woman's feelings when she shares an emotion and doesn't just describe what is upsetting to her.

Good: Talking About What Is Upsetting Her
1. Today, I was late to the office. There is so much traffic these days and just too many people.
2. Once again the computers went down in the office. I couldn't finish my work.
3. I talked with Johnny's teacher and he is not finishing his projects. He is not doing his homework.
4. Today, we had to redo all the payroll checks. I completely forgot to approve the new changes.
5. There is so much to do and I don't have a chance to catch up on paying the bills.
6. I don't spend enough time creating new products. I spend too much time with all of the financial spreadsheets.

Better: Sharing Feelings
1. Today, I was late to the office. *I feel frustrated* that there is so much traffic these days. There are just too many people.
2. Once again the computers went down in the office. *I feel disappointed* that I couldn't finish my work.
3. I talked with Johnny's teacher and he is not finishing his projects. *I feel concerned* that Johnny is not doing his homework.
4. Today, we had to redo all of the payroll checks. *I feel embarrassed* that I completely forgot to approve the new changes.
5. *I wish* that there was not so much to do and I had a chance to catch up on paying the bills.
6. *I want* to spend more time creating new products and less time with all of the financial spreadsheets.

Not Good: Complaining

1. Today, you didn't answer your phone when I called. I feel frustrated when you don't answer your phone. I need to feel I can get you when I need you.
2. Did you call Richard to fix the computers? I have asked you three times. I feel disappointed that you keep forgetting.
3. I talked with Johnny's teacher today. I feel concerned that you are letting him watch too much TV and he is not finishing his projects.
4. This house is a mess. We are having the Browns over for dinner tonight and we need to clean it up. It is so embarrassing. I was so stressed that I forgot to redo the payroll changes.
5. I wish you could remember to turn off the lights when you leave a room. I have others things to do. There are bills to pay.
6. I want you to stop leaving your jackets around the house and put them in the closet. I don't have enough time to pick up after you.

When a woman is stressed, she can share the vulnerable feelings that she suppressed during the day to pull herself back to her female side. Complaining about her partner will only make him defensive and lock her into her male side.

Sharing Feelings Is Different from Complaining

The Venus Talk is simple to describe but can be difficult for a woman to do if she is locked into her male side. Most women on their male side have great difficulty connecting with and then sharing their more vulnerable feelings. Men may also find it difficult because most men have difficulty listening with empathy to a woman's feelings and not interrupting with solutions.

If a woman cooperates by opening up and sharing her feelings while her partner only listens, he will return to his male side and she will return to her female side. Most people do not realize that silently listening brings a man back to his male side, while sharing feelings brings a woman back to her female side.

Listening connects us to our male side and sharing feelings connects us to our female side.

But it is nearly impossible for a man to give this new kind of support if a woman does not recognize that she needs his help to return to her female side. If she is not willing to cooperate, he is powerless to help her. Listening to a woman's feelings will only work for a man if a woman's feelings of stress, frustration, and disappointment are about her day at work and not about him. If she complains about him in any way, it will just shut him down.

The research is very clear on this point: when men feel successful, their testosterone levels go up. For example, when a man watches a sporting event, his testosterone rises if his team wins; if they lose, it falls. Likewise, when a woman appreciates a man's support, his testosterone goes up.

When a man feels successful, his testosterone goes up.

To appreciate his support, a woman first needs to recognize that she needs his help to return to her female side. When women are stressed or overwhelmed by doing too much, the last thing they think they need to do is share their feelings, unless sharing feelings can solve some problem. But sharing feelings with the intent to solve a problem—for example, to get her partner to change in some way or otherwise take action—is not sharing. Instead, it is complaining. Sharing increases estrogen and lowers a woman's stress, but complaining increases her testosterone and doesn't lower her stress.

**Sharing feelings to solve a problem
is no longer sharing; it is complaining.**

When a woman is more on her male side, she and her partner must both understand the reasoning for as well as the importance of sharing in a Venus Talk. Without this new insight, a busy woman will resist talking because she has too much to do. Her partner will resist listening because he will want to return to his cave.

In a Venus Talk, a man can listen without interrupting with solutions because he clearly understands that by listening and not offering solutions, he is solving her most important problem: she needs his help to return to her female side. Although he is not actively doing something for her by silently listening, he is actually providing the solution she needs most.

By doing something in a short amount of time that actually works to make his partner happier, even before returning to his cave, a man's sense of success will begin to increase his testosterone. And because he feels more appreciated by her, his need for cave time to rebuild his testosterone will be less.

After my seminar, one strong woman had this to say:

"Once I learned that talking about my feelings, without try-ing to solve my problems, would stimulate more female hor-mones, I tried it and it worked.

"It took an act of will but I did it. Just like going to the gym. I don't always want to do it but it is good for me. I was surprised that just asking Tom to just listen and not try to solve my problems actually felt good.

"I don't think I had ever talked for ten minutes straight without being interrupted. I began to soften. Now when I get home I can relax more. My sense of urgency to do more is much less. We are also feeling much closer!"

These insights have worked for thousands of men and women and they can work for you. By understanding our new male and female needs based on our hormonal differences, men can learn to be more supportive of women as well as awaken her feelings of romantic attraction. Likewise, women can apply their new skills to open their partner's heart and sustain his attraction to her.

When a man can sustain higher testosterone levels, at least ten times more than his partner's, and a woman can sustain higher estrogen levels, at least ten time more than her partner's, these dif-ferences create the attraction that can sustain a lifetime of passion.

A Man Can Only Help

As both men and women apply insights that support our biolog-ical differences to lower stress, we become free to express both our male and females side at times when we are not stressed. We are all responsible for our own happiness, but a loving relation-ship can go a long way to help.

Understanding a woman's need for support to help her cope with stress is not enough on its own to create a Soul Mate relationship. A man can create the safety for a woman to find happiness, but he alone cannot make her happy. A woman's hormonal needs in order to be happy and fulfilled go far beyond what any man alone can provide.

Unlike a man who particularly requires a job or some other testosterone-producing activity outside the relationship to sustain his hormonal balance, a woman requires a rich social life as well as plenty of time to do the things that she loves to do.

7

THE RISKS OF TAKING HORMONES

Hormones are very powerful substances. Even minute quantities or small fluctuations produce profound effects in our bodies. Different hormones have very specific and limited functions, and understanding these varied, complementary functions explains why we get so stressed and "out of whack" when they are not properly balanced.

Most people would agree that our moods are affected by many factors, including our social relationships, physical environment, diet, exercise, and daily sleep patterns, just to name a few. But a deeper reality is that those same factors significantly affect our hormones, which regulate our brain's response system, and thereby determine our moods, including our stress levels, mental clarity, and memory.

Our hormones are the most potent chemical signals affecting the brain, male or female. Changes in our hormones regulate the production of brain neurotransmitters like dopamine, serotonin, and GABA.

Our different hormones regulate our brain's response system, and thereby determine our moods.

Dopamine is responsible for feelings of pleasure, motivation, interest, and focus. Serotonin produces feelings of optimism, gratitude, and appreciation. GABA produces feelings of happiness, euphoria, and love. Declining levels and imbalances of estrogen, testosterone, and progesterone have profound effects on the balance and production of brain chemicals. An imbalance in brain chemicals gives rise to depression, anxiety, and all of the other symptoms of chronic stress. (I explore how balancing these brain chemicals through diet, cleansing, and extra nutrition can improve relationships in my book *Staying Focused in a Hyper World*.)

Just as millions of men are now encouraged to take testosterone to correct hormone imbalance, millions of women are prescribed female hormones to regulate their moods, energy levels, and well-being. This social experiment, which some consider to be a miraculous breakthrough for health and happiness, may actually be a major contributor to social and relationship breakdown.

Taking hormones is just like taking any drug: in some cases there are immediate benefits, but these benefits are just from the relief of symptoms and do not address their underlying causes. If the underlying causes are not addressed, the condition only gets worse and other systems begin to break down in the body.

By learning to express and not suppress her male and female sides, women can address the underlying cause of hormonal imbalance by adjusting their attitudes, beliefs, and behaviors to support their bodies in producing the right balance of hormones.

By learning to make her own hormones, she may not need to take them at all.

> **By learning to stimulate the production
> of her own hormones,
> a woman may not need to take them.**

The Problem with Taking Hormones

While some women have received great benefits from taking hormones, for others it can be a nightmare, especially if they are unable to achieve the correct balance. Some studies have shown that hormone replacement can increase the risk of developing uterine cancer, breast cancer, heart disease, stroke, and blood clots.

> **While some women have received great benefits
> from taking hormones,
> for others it can be a nightmare.**

Taking hormones, particularly the synthetic ones, has side effects. In particular, many experts believe that when you take hormones over time, your body gradually loses its ability to make them. This is why holistic doctors will only prescribe hormone replacement as a last resort after first recommending a program of good diet, exercise, and extra mineral, vitamin, and herbal support. If that fails, only then do they recommend taking hormones. Usually a holistic doctor will prescribe only bioidentical hormones because they believe they are less toxic when compared to synthetic hormones.

One of the main reasons women today take hormones is not to regain lost hormonal balance, but as contraception. "The Pill" is a blend of synthetic hormones that interrupt a woman's natural hormonal cycle to prevent ovulation, and today it's taken by over half of women of reproductive age.

While the Pill has been an incredibly valuable tool in women's liberation, the benefits of putting the ability to prevent pregnancy entirely and affordably under women's control do not negate the seriousness of its side effects. Since it was first introduced in 1960, the rates of cardiac disease, depression, sleeping disorders, breast cancer, osteoporosis, and dementia in women have skyrocketed, increasing at a rate much higher than those of men. Because all of these disorders are directly linked to hormonal imbalance, taking the Pill is certainly a major contributor to this increasing health crisis.

Many women have reported becoming depressed or even suicidal as a side effect of taking the Pill. In 2016, in one of the largest studies to date, researchers at the University of Copenhagen studied the health records of more than a million Danish women aged between fifteen and thirty-four. They found that those on the combined Pill, which contains artificial versions of estrogen and progesterone, were 23 percent more likely to be prescribed an antidepressant than those not on hormonal contraception. For those on the progestin-only Pill, the figure rose to 34 percent. The number was even higher for girls aged between fifteen and nineteen on the combined Pill: they were 80 percent more likely to be on antidepressants.

The Pill is a major contributor to a woman's difficulty in returning to her female side. It contains both estrogen and progesterone. When a woman takes these hormones, her body does not need to make them. When her body doesn't need to make these hormones, she does not feel as deeply her natural instincts, wishes, and needs to engage in progesterone-producing social activities as well as oxytocin- and estrogen-producing nurturing and interdependent relationships.

Taking birth control pills has been linked to depression.

During ovulation, an egg is released from one of the ovaries, and for the next twelve to fourteen days, the corpus luteum in that ovary produces progesterone. Because a woman does not ovulate on the Pill, she is unable to make sufficient levels of the female hormone progesterone.

In the next chapter, we will explore all the different activities that support the production of progesterone during the twelve to fourteen days following ovulation. We will explore as well the many benefits of progesterone. But the most powerful benefit of progesterone, similar to oxytocin, is that it lowers a woman's stress. It calms her mind and increases her ability to appreciate who she is, what she has, and what she can do.

When a woman is on the Pill, it provides her with the extra progesterone her corpus luteum would otherwise produce, but because she does not ovulate and so is not making it herself, she does not feel the same instinctive and automatic motivations that would normally be needed to stimulate the production of progesterone. During the two weeks after ovulation, her rising progesterone levels should motivate her to create social bonding that further stimulates the production of progesterone; this increased progesterone lowers her stress and creates a sense of well-being.

Social bonding occurs when women support the same needs in others that others support in her in a roughly equal give-and-take. (This is different from bonding in intimate sexual relationships, which is called "pair bonding." We will also explore this distinction in greater depth in the next chapter.) For example, playing cards or cooking a meal together is social bonding. When a woman is motivated to create and maintain social relationships outside of work or her intimate partner, the increased fulfillment she experiences from them puts less pressure on other areas of her life.

While the progesterone supplied with the Pill may calm a woman's mind, she may no longer feel the full extent of her need for social bonding. Without this natural motivation to create social bonding, socializing is less fulfilling and as a result she can easily become overly dependent on her relationship for her fulfillment. This neediness makes her more dissatisfied with her partner than she would normally feel, and this dissatisfaction, rather than helping her meet her need for support, tends to push her partner away.

**When a woman takes progesterone,
rather than making it, she no longer feels
the full extent of her need for social bonding.**

When the body is given hormones, they suppress the desires that would normally motivate us to seek out the stimulation needed to make that hormone. When you are hungry and feel your authentic need for food, then you are motivated to eat good food. As a result, you experience being fulfilled from the food. But if you take a diet pill so that you don't feel your need for food, you may not be hungry but you are also not fulfilled. This same thing happens when you take hormones rather than make hormones. Taking something that your body is supposed to make on its own is not only disruptive to the body but to your ability to feel fulfilled as well.

This is also the case with taking antidepressants. Antidepressants may stop us from feeling unhappy, anxious, or depressed but that doesn't mean we automatically feel happy, trusting, and fulfilled. We just stop feeling, and therefore we lose our natural motivation to seek out fulfilling experiences. We lose our ability to appreciate others and the world we live in.

It is no secret that antidepressants inhibit our sex drive. What most people do not know is that when they take an antidepressant, their cortisol levels double as well. We have already discussed that higher cortisol levels not only inhibit our ability to experience love, happiness, and fulfillment, but they also weaken our immune system and make us more vulnerable to things like cancer and heart disease.

In emergencies, antidepressants may give a person the chance to put their life in order by supporting them in setting up positive habits and relationships, but most people become dependent on them. At MarsVenus.com I explore a variety of all-natural solutions to assist people in healing depression without antidepressants.

Balancing Progesterone and Estrogen

A woman's happiness and well-being primarily comes from a balance of loving and appreciating others and herself. Estrogen is, to a great degree, what allows women to appreciate others, while progesterone allows women to appreciate themselves and what they can do for others.

Certainly these two kinds of love are related and interdependent. If I can appreciate what I do, then it is much easier for me to appreciate what you do for me. On the other hand, if I demand perfection from myself, then what my partner can do for me will never be enough. When women cannot make their own progesterone they are much harder on themselves and their partners. Their unrealistic expectations for both themselves and others lead to dissatisfaction.

Estrogen supports women in appreciating others while progesterone allows them to appreciate themselves.

Progesterone's biological function is to regulate estrogen and vice versa. Each prevents levels of the other from rising too high. The psychological effect of both hormones is similar: a woman's ability to love, and be happy with herself and her contributions (progesterone), prevent her from being needy or *too dependent* on others (estrogen). On the other hand, her ability to depend on others to get what she needs (estrogen) prevents her from being *too independent* (progesterone).

When a woman's hormones are out of balance, the needs of others become more important than her own. Feeling stressed and rushed, she is unable to enjoy some of the simple pleasures that can come from things like cooking a meal or spending time with her children. These activities, which used to be nurturing and relaxing, can become unpleasant or boring responsibilities, necessary obligations, or even burdens rather than peaceful moments in generous, selfless service to those she loves.

When a woman's progesterone levels are low, it will always seem to her like she is not getting enough (just as when a man's testosterone levels are low it will always seem to him that he is giving plenty). At those times, when she is giving too much and not getting enough, she will continue to give more, thinking that she will get more.

By looking more to her social life for fulfillment and not her partner, she can give less and get more. By raising her progesterone through more social bonding, and bringing it in balance with her estrogen, she can be simultaneously less demanding and more appreciative of her partner.

The Importance of Feeling Our Needs

As we've discussed, when a woman doesn't make her own progesterone by taking the Pill or hormone replacement, she is no longer fully motivated by her innate need to pursue happiness and fulfillment through social bonding. This same phenomenon occurs when she makes too much testosterone on a stressful workday.

When a woman overexpresses her male qualities and suppresses her female side, her body converts her progesterone into testosterone. The end result is not only higher stress from low levels of progesterone, but also that her need to express her male qualities overshadows her authentic need for more social bonding.

High testosterone in women uses up their progesterone.

When she is unable to feel her authentic needs, she loses a sense of motivation and direction in her life that could bring increasing fulfillment instead of increasing dissatisfaction and stress. Instead, she becomes more vulnerable to what her job, family, and society have to say regarding what she should do with her life.

Ultimately, much of the suffering in both men's and women's lives comes from making what is really not important more important than things that actually are important. So many people on their deathbed regret the time they wasted worrying about money, making money, or complaining about not having enough money instead of creating more love in their lives. They regret the petty complaints and resentments that kept them from giving and receiving more love and support in their lives. Too bad we gain this wisdom on our deathbed and not earlier in our lives when it could do some good.

**People on their deathbed
regret all the time wasted on petty resentments
rather than giving and receiving love.**

It is our inability to feel our true needs that blocks this inner wisdom of what is most important. Our needs determine our priorities and motivations. We eat food because we feel a need to eat, and we fall asleep at night because we feel a need for sleep. We seek to love and be loved by others because we feel a need for love. We want to be successful because we have a need to make a difference. Our basic needs help to guide and motivate us into activities that promote health, happiness, and love.

**Feeling our basic needs in life
helps to guide and motivate us into activities
that promote health, happiness, and love.**

When we eat junk food, then over time we don't feel our healthy need for real food. Eventually, real food doesn't even taste good. When we stay up late watching TV, we lose touch with our need to go to bed at a healthy time and get up with the sun. Eventually, we have to drag ourselves out of bed rather than feeling excited and motivated. In a similar way, when women rely on synthetic progesterone, they disconnect with their need for social bonding. Eventually they become overly independent, which pushes them too far to their masculine side.

In short, taking hormones is a social experiment with unconfirmed long-term consequences and should never be done lightly.

Choosing to take hormones is always a woman's choice. I certainly do not recommend hormone replacement, but if a woman chooses to get hormone replacement therapy or take birth control pills (rather than using other, non-hormonal forms of birth control), she should be diligent in taking extra time away from work and her intimate partner to create a rich social life, along with taking plenty of time for herself to do the things that she loves to do.

If you are taking hormones on the advice of your doctor, seek medical advice before discontinuing use. If your doctor is resistant to alternate methods of treating hormonal imbalance, try a more holistic doctor. Even after getting a hysterectomy, there are natural ways to support a woman's body in achieving hormone balance. Neither a hysterectomy nor menopause will prevent a woman's adrenal glands from making the hormones she needs as long as she also gets the extra nutritional support her body needs.

Taking hormones is a social experiment
with unconfirmed side effects
and should never be done lightly.

Avoiding Hormone Disrupters

There is another way that our hormones can become unbalanced, and that is from known hormone disruptors. These disruptors are synthetic chemicals commonly found in our air, water, and food. These toxic chemicals "bind with" or activate estrogen receptors in the body the same way synthetic estrogen does. External exposure to these estrogen-mimicking chemicals lowers progesterone levels in women and testosterone in men.

BPA and phthalates in plastics are major hormone disrupters, as are pesticides in nonorganic foods. The worst of nonorganic foods are called GMOs. These GMO foods are genetically modified to be resistant to glyphosate, a powerful herbicide used to kill weeds and grasses that compete with crops. Most GMO foods have been treated with glyphosates. These glyphosates remain in the food and, when eaten, kill the beneficial bacteria in your gut.

These beneficial bacteria are necessary not only to digest your food but also to make the amino acid precursors required by the brain to make feel-good neurotransmitters like dopamine, GABA, and serotonin. Brain neurotransmitters and hormones are interdependent. The balance of our hormones stimulates the production of neurotransmitters and these same neurotransmitters directly affect our hormone balance. In addition, when we cannot fully digest our foods, inflammation occurs in the gut. This inflammation increases cortisol levels, which in turn inhibits the production of beneficial hormones.

Nonorganic wheat products, although not GMO, are also grown in soil that is sprayed with glyphosate, which may help explain why over 10 percent of Americans now consider themselves to be "gluten intolerant." Bread, which was once nourishing to most people, is now toxic to many.

In my own experience of helping children and adults with ADHD symptoms, autism, anxiety, and depression, taking bread and other gluten products out of their diet has eliminated many digestive, mood, and energy complaints. Common symptoms eliminated or lessened by a gluten-free diet are bloating, weight gain, diarrhea, fatigue, nausea, migraines, brain fog, irritability, mood swings, depression, achiness, joint inflammation, enlarged blood cells, vertigo, and acne.

Hormone disruptors even affect those of us who do not ingest them directly. Pesticides, along with the hormones in birth control pills, can now be found in unfiltered tap water. The breast milk of mothers who do not eat organic foods has measurable trace levels of estrogen-mimicking pesticides.

Pesticides along with the hormones of birth control pills can now be found in unfiltered tap water.

These hormone disrupters also affect the normal process of sexual maturity in children. The increase in estrogen-mimicking pesticides in some parts of America causes boys to take two years longer to reach puberty and girls to start puberty two years earlier.

With so many hormone disrupters in our lives today, it is even more important that we use our relationships as a way to fully express our authentic male and female qualities and come back into hormonal balance when we are stressed.

Vitamins, Minerals, Herbs, and Super Foods for Additional Hormonal Support

Prescribed drugs and hormones hijack and control different functions in the body regardless of changing behaviors. That is why they have side effects. Natural nutritional support is not a quick fix but rather makes positive behavior and lifestyle changes more effective in balancing your hormones.

There are many natural solutions to assist you in restoring your hormonal balance. Here are a few:

- The mineral lithium orotate, combined with the cofactors calcium, magnesium, zinc, and potassium in low, nontoxic doses is sold over the counter and can help increase oxytocin.
- The herb chasteberry can help increase progesterone in women and, by increasing dopamine in men, can also support testosterone production.
- Short fasting protocols can help to remove hormone disruptors from the body to restore testosterone and estrogen hormone balance.
- The herb tongkat ali or the super food maca can help to increase testosterone for both men and women.

- Swiss-made Bravo yogurt with forty-two strains of probiotics can, if eaten over three months, help restore the gut micro-biome to dramatically improve digestion and support optimal brain function. This directly lowers stress, allowing the body to make more hormones.

You can learn more about nutritional hormonal support and find my recommendations—for both men and women—in my health blogs at MarsVenus.com.

The Symptoms of PMS

Hormonal imbalance in women reveals itself in a variety of ways throughout the month: through chronically high stress levels, fatigue, depression, anxiety, sleeplessness, and dissatis-faction. But the classic condition of this imbalance is PMS, or premenstrual syndrome. This condition is generally described as a noticeable physical and emotional tension a few days before menstruation, which disappears once menstruation begins. While PMS is very common in women today, it doesn't have to be. By learning to keep their hormones balanced, women can avoid most if not all PMS symptoms.

For some women, the time leading up to their periods can be debilitating, seriously affecting their ability to cope with daily life. Dr. Katharina Dalton, who pioneered the treatment of PMS over forty years ago, reports that approximately half of all women's suicide attempts are made during the four days just prior to menstruation and the first four days of menstruation.

PMS typically involves a combination of intense tiredness, irritability, and depression, which is easily aggravated by any other stress. During this time, many women become weepy, have difficulty making decisions, and quickly snap at those around them.

With PMS, many women temporarily become weepy, have difficulty making decisions, and quickly snap at those around them.

An understanding that PMS is the result of hormonal imbalance can help men be more patient, understanding, and nondefensive at this time. Without this insight, a man will tend to take it personally and become defensive, critical, or angry, which only makes her symptoms worse.

Women often resist discussions about PMS because many times PMS is used to suggest women are inferior to men and cannot be trusted or depended on at those times. This, however, is completely inaccurate. With the right support in her personal life to balance her hormones, she will be able to function in a consistent and competent manner in both her work and home lives. Just as women have unique vulnerabilities and emotional challenges, so do men. These challenges just show up differently. For example, while more women experience depression, more men have serious addiction problems that impair their ability to function.

While more women experience depression, more men have serious addiction problems that impair their ability to function.

With clear insight for expressing and not suppressing her male and female sides at different times of the month, a woman can discover her inner power to determine her responses to life's challenges. Certainly outer stresses can trigger hormonal imbalance, but it is up to her to then restore balance so that she can cope with energy, optimism, and love. Outer stresses and the challenges in our relationships do not have to control our moods.

Outer stresses and the challenges in our relationships do not have to control our moods.

In the next chapter, we look in more detail at the four key hormones affecting women's stress and moods, and the insights a woman can use to keep her hormones balanced as they naturally change throughout the month.

8

WOMEN, HORMONES, AND HAPPINESS

There are four key hormones that assist a woman in managing her stress to increase her happiness: oxytocin, estrogen, progesterone, and testosterone. Let's look closer at each one of these, how they affect her stress, and how to increase their production to support healthy hormonal balance. With this new insight for creating hormonal balance, both men and women can experience greater peace of mind, love, happiness, and fulfillment.

Oxytocin and Estrogen

Oxytocin is the most important hormone in helping women lower stress. It is produced when a woman receives or anticipates receiving the support she needs to express her female side.

Volumes of research and several books over the last fifteen years have discussed oxytocin's many benefits. It is known to have the following effects:

- Increases feelings of love, trust, and attachment
- Amplifies emotional memories
- Facilitates childbirth by creating contractions
- Promotes the letdown of milk into the nipples during breastfeeding
- Boosts sexual arousal and responsiveness to increase women's ability to have an orgasm
- Reduces addictive cravings
- Increases eye contact
- Triggers protective instincts
- Improves sleep
- Increases her sense of generosity

Working with estrogen, oxytocin also lowers a woman's stress. When a woman suppresses her female side, her testosterone goes too high, along with her stress hormones. Oxytocin lowers her high testosterone and allows her estrogen to rise, which supports the expression of her female side.

Oxytocin lowers a woman's high testosterone and increases her estrogen to support the expression of her female side.

Estrogen is the primary female sex hormone and is responsible for regulating the female reproductive system. It promotes the development and maintenance of female bodily characteristics. A woman's estrogen levels are supposed to change throughout the month. In approximate terms they gradually rise during the first ten to twelve days after her period, peak around ovulation, and then drop over the next twelve to fourteen days.

When a woman is expressing the qualities of her female side, her estrogen levels rise, and the higher her estrogen levels, the more she expresses the qualities of her female side. These qualities, which we listed in chapter three, include interdependence, emotional responsiveness, vulnerability, cooperation, intuition, and nurturing. When her estrogen is too low, she will go too far to her male side, which is tougher and more independent, detached, competitive, analytical, and powerful.

**When a woman is expressing
the qualities of her female side,
her estrogen levels rise.**

In the second part of her cycle (the approximately twelve days after ovulation), if her estrogen is too high, her progesterone levels will become too low and she will become overly needy in her intimate relationships. This is often called estrogen dominance, and can cause decreased sex drive, irregular menstrual periods, bloating, breast swelling and tenderness, headaches, mood swings, irritability, and depression.

For some women, when their estrogen is too high in the second part of their cycle, they can swing too far to their male side to lower their estrogen. While this brings some relief of symptoms, it may perpetuate higher stress because increasing testosterone can use up the progesterone she needs in the second part of her cycle to lower her stress.

Pair Bonding, Oxytocin, and Estrogen

Throughout her cycle, the optimum, healthy balance of her hormones is continuously changing. Supporting the free expression of both her male and female sides allows her body to do its job and keep these hormones in balance. Any symptoms of stress are indications that she is suppressing her male or female side and that her hormones have gone out of balance.

Both oxytocin and estrogen are increased during what researchers call "pair bonding." Pair bonding, in this context, describes when a woman gives one kind of support but in return gets another kind of support that helps her to access and express her female side. In a traditional Role Mate relationship, for example, where the man was the provider and the woman was the homemaker, when a man provided financial support and safety it allowed his wife to freely express the many qualities of her female side. In return, she cared for their children and provided him with her love, admiration, and appreciation.

Pair bonding is when a woman gives one kind of support but in return gets another kind of support.

Pair bonding is not limited to intimate relationships. In a classroom, a woman pays tuition but in return she learns something she did not know before. During a checkup with her doctor, she receives important advice and information she needs and depends on while she pays for her doctor's time and expertise. In a beauty parlor, her stylist washes and cuts her hair and in return is paid for that service. In each of these examples, the support a woman gives is different than the support she receives. (The support a woman receives in pair bonding is more personal but the support the teacher, doctor, or stylist gives and gets is their work, and so stimulates testosterone rather than oxytocin and estrogen.)

Pair bonding in a romantic relationship is much more personal and therefore is a more powerful stimulator of oxytocin and estrogen. When a man is in a romantic, loving relationship, he is also pair bonding. Because this pair bonding increases his oxytocin and estrogen levels, also, he must be careful to make sure he is fulfilling his specific emotional needs that increase his testosterone as well, as discussed in chapter five.

For a woman, pair bonding also requires that she receive the specific support she needs to bring forth her female side. This pair bonding is in contrast to social bonding, in which she gets the support she needs to express her male side along with her female side, and which stimulates the production of progesterone. (In a work setting she gets the support she needs to express more of her male side than her female side.)

Here are two common examples of pair bonds and how they raise women's oxytocin and estrogen levels:

- In a Role Mate relationship, a woman's oxytocin and estrogen increase when she depends on a man's financial support. Her nurturing female side emerges to support his needs at home as he supports her needs for survival and security.

- In a Soul Mate relationship, a woman's oxytocin and estrogen increase when she depends on a man's more personal emotional support. When he demonstrates caring, understanding, and respect through his listening and romantic affection, her nurturing female side emerges to support him with feelings of appreciation, trust, and acceptance.

But this oxytocin- and estrogen-producing pair bonding is not limited to a Role Mate or Soul Mate relationship. Whenever a woman is not getting the pair bonding she needs in her intimate relationship, she can find it in her other pair-bonding relationships. Here are a few examples:

- With a child, because a child gives her unconditional love while she expresses her feminine nurturing qualities in return
- With her pet, because a loving pet, like a child, can pull forth her nurturing maternal instincts
- With her parents or family members, if she feels she can share her challenges and they will listen with compassion and respect
- Depending on her spiritual beliefs, with God when she can freely open her heart in prayer or in praise
- With a religious or spiritual authority, if she feels safe discussing her mistakes and sharing openly
- With her counselor or coach when they emotionally support her in times of stress or during challenges in her life or relationships
- With a teacher, guru, or spiritual guide who inspires in her higher feelings of love and motivation to be her best
- With her doctor, body worker, or health consultant, when she is depending on their guidance or services for her health or survival
- With her boss at work, if she feels that they personally support her, or if her paycheck is responsible for her security and survival
- With her lawyer, when she is depending on their protection to defend her or protect her rights
- With her financial planner or consultant, when they are helping her protect her finances and save for her future
- With any construction worker or "handyman," when they help her with roofing, plumbing, and equipment problems around the house

- With a house cleaner, whose work allows her to attend to other responsibilities
- With a computer consultant, who helps fix her computer so she can finish her work or connect with friends

Reviewing this list can help remind a woman that she should never make a man (or any single pair bond) the main meal of oxytocin in her life. Her Soul Mate should just be dessert.

Forty Ways to Increase Oxytocin and Estrogen

Although every woman needs pair bonding to balance her hormones, every woman will have her own preferences as to what pair-bonding experiences work best for her. Below is a list of forty possible activities that will produce estrogen and oxytocin as long as they are activities that she enjoys.

Each of these activities will produce different degrees of oxytocin and estrogen depending on the support she gets. The oxytocin produced is in response to getting the support she needs to express her female side. The estrogen produced comes from expressing her female side. If she is already producing lots of estrogen by expressing her female side in other ways, then engaging the activities in this list will not be as important. These activities particularly help women to return to their female side, which is most important in the first ten days after her period.

Oxytocin is produced in response to getting the support she needs to express her female side. Estrogen is produced in response to expressing her female side.

In each of these pair-bonding examples, a woman is either receiving a particular kind of support for her female side to emerge, or she is doing something to express her female side with the anticipation of receiving support in return. The anticipation of receiving support produces just as much oxytocin and estrogen as actually receiving that support.

Many of the activities in this list could also lead to social bonding if she is doing them with a friend. The difference is the kind of hormone produced: with a friend, she would be making a combination of progesterone, oxytocin, and estrogen, whereas with a romantic partner, or with a doctor, stylist, or other professional, she would be primarily making oxytocin and estrogen.

Receiving Support from Others

1. Talking about problems
2. Talking about relationships
3. Hugging
4. Expressing feelings and feeling heard
5. Getting her hair cut
6. Getting a pedicure
7. Getting a massage
8. Cooperating
9. Collaborating
10. Receiving compliments
11. Receiving help
12. Having plenty of time to do the things she wants to do
13. Getting extra support to take time for herself
14. Feeling safe
15. Prayer
16. Expressing gratitude
17. Going out on dates
18. Romance

19. Being touched in a nonsexual way
20. Receiving affection
21. Receiving attention to her feelings and needs
22. Receiving apologies
23. Getting flowers
24. Receiving unsolicited help or support
25. Receiving notes or greeting cards
26. Attending concerts or social or cultural events
27. Receiving reassurance
28. Feeling seen
29. Feeling respected or honored
30. Feeling loved

Anticipating Support from Others

1. Asking lots of questions on a date, because she anticipates that a man will be more interested in her (*note*: men will actually be more interested if she asks fewer questions and talks more; see my book *Mars and Venus on a Date*)
2. Shopping, because she anticipates having new purchases to impress, please, or support others
3. Buying or wearing shoes or other accessories, because she anticipates receiving increased attention, status, and interest from others
4. Putting on makeup that will make her look younger and flawless, because she anticipates attracting favorable attention as well as protection from critical scrutiny
5. Getting dressed up in a way that makes her feel special and beautiful, because she anticipates she will be seen and adored
6. Wearing sexy lingerie that makes her feel more desirable, because she anticipates that her partner will be more attracted to her

7. Giving gifts, because she anticipates that others will include her and appreciate her more

8. Helping others, because she anticipates that she will be included and valued in her community and later supported if and when she needs it

9. Cooking dinner or any other nurturing activity for her partner, because she anticipates that when he comes out of his cave he will give her more attention and affection as well as do things for her that she doesn't want to do (more about this in chapter nine)

10. Caring for her children, because she anticipates receiving extra support from her partner and unconditional love from her children

Men may also like or enjoy the above activities, which increase their estrogen and oxytocin levels, too. The difference between men and women is that, while these activities may feel good to him, they do not lower his stress. Too much oxytocin and estrogen can actually lower his testosterone and decrease his energy and sense of aliveness, thus increasing his stress.

However, when he successfully provides the support a women needs to experience pair bonding, the fact that he has helped to increase her happiness will stimulate his testosterone and lower his stress. With higher testosterone from the anticipated success of her increased happiness, he can also enjoy the higher level of oxytocin that also gets produced in his body without increasing his stress. Here are a few examples:

- I am not thrilled about going to an art show, but if it makes my wife happy, then that success increases my testosterone levels and my happiness.

- I may not need a hug to lower my stress, but when I give my wife a hug because she needs the oxytocin, my success in providing the right support for her increases my testosterone and my stress goes down. I also get to enjoy the increase in bonding from the release of oxytocin.

- I would be happier staying home and watching TV in the evening, but if going out to a social or cultural event or some other romantic date makes her happy, then it increases my testosterone and my stress goes down.

Without the surge in testosterone from making her happy, the surge in oxytocin during these activities would normally just lower a man's testosterone, making him bored or tiring him out. However, when a man knows that he is fulfilling an important need for his partner, it can give him energy and lower his stress. He feels successful particularly if she verbalizes her appreciation, which further increases his testosterone and lowers his stress.

Estrogen, Oxytocin, and Workplace Stress

Anything a woman wants to do or enjoys doing that expresses her female qualities, when done without time pressure, raises her oxytocin and reduces her stress. Just having plenty of time and not being rushed, as long as she is being allowed to express any of her female qualities, increases her oxytocin levels and supports the increase of estrogen. When she feels pressured by not having enough time, her testosterone levels increase, which lowers her estrogen.

Feeling rushed in all areas of her life is the number one condition that contributes to a woman feeling stressed and overwhelmed. Here are twelve examples of how feeling rushed or setting up her day with too much to do overexpresses a woman's male side while inhibiting her ability to access and express her female qualities.

Common Examples of Ways Women Feel Rushed and Overwhelmed	Resulting Change in Male/Female Qualities
1. Not enough time to depend on help from others	Increased independence (male) Decreased interdependence (female)
2. Not enough time to share her feelings	Increased detachment (male) Decreased emotionality (female)
3. Not enough time to support her husband and family	Increased problem-solving (male) Decreased nurturing (female)
4. Not enough time to open up and ask for help	Increased toughness (male) Decreased vulnerability (female)
5. Not enough time to work together with others	Increased competition (male) Decreased cooperation (female)
6. Not enough time to explore her feelings before making decisions	Increased analysis (male) Decreased intuition (female)
7. Not enough time to consider the feelings and needs of others	Increased power (male) Decreased love (female)

8. Not enough time to relax and receive support	Increased assertiveness (male) Decreased receptiveness (female)
9. Not enough time to ask for help or recognize the support she has	Increased competence (male) Decreased virtue (female)
10. Not enough time to patiently depend on the support of others	Increased confidence in herself (male) Decreased trust in others (female)
11. Not enough time to receive more support	Increased accountability (male) Decreased responsiveness (female)
12. Not enough time for her personal life	Increased goal orientation (male) Decreased relationship orientation (female)

When a woman does something that she doesn't want to do but has to, her testosterone levels rise, her estrogen levels begin to drop, and she is unable to make oxytocin. Certainly we all have to do things we don't want to do, but unlike men, who thrive with increased testosterone, women become more stressed when testosterone levels are too great.

In reviewing these lists of estrogen and oxytocin producers, it becomes clear that the workplace is not the ideal place for women to increase oxytocin, nor does it need to be. As women work in greater numbers, workplaces are slowly becoming more supportive of women's needs, but in the meantime a woman can most effectively manage stress at work by having a personal life outside of work that meets her oxytocin and estrogen needs.

More and more experts talk about the importance of work–life balance, but unless we understand the importance of oxytocin and estrogen, work–life balance is unattainable. It just becomes another thing to put on her never-ending to-do list.

Without an understanding of oxytocin, achieving work–life balance becomes another burden.

A woman can, however, make oxytocin during her workday if she anticipates a future oxytocin- and estrogen-producing event. If she expects to return home to a personal life rich in oxytocin- and estrogen-producing activities, then her stress levels will remain lower throughout her workday.

When she is looking forward to a romantic date, for days in advance she will make lots of oxytocin and estrogen. When she anticipates that her husband or a friend will be interested in hearing her day's frustrations, disappointments, and concerns, her oxytocin and estrogen levels will be high even before she goes home.

Anticipating an oxytocin-producing event actually produces oxytocin in advance.

Research studies over the past decade reveal that women who work outside the home for money are often more stressed at home than they are at work. In stress research done by Frankenhaeuser and Lunberg in 1999, they found similar stress levels in men and women at work, but women's stress levels remained elevated after work. For women and not men, stress exposure at work spilled over into non-work situations.

Women with high stress levels at work tend to have high stress levels after work, and women who work overtime have even higher stress levels in the evening at home and over the weekend. However, the stress levels of men who worked overtime did not increase compared to men who didn't work overtime.

Women with high stress levels at work tend to have high stress levels after work.

One of the benefits of testosterone for both men and women is an increased ability to postpone gratification. It is only when a man loses confidence that he can achieve a desired outcome that his higher testosterone makes him more impulsive. Men's higher testosterone levels let them more easily endure the hardships and stress of heavy labor or dangerous jobs. Knowing that they will be rewarded later lets a man temporarily detach from any discomfort or distress they may feel in the moment.

While working all day in a testosterone-stimulating environment, a woman is also able to cope with stress by postponing gratification. For a man the gratification he seeks is some quality cave time and a happy wife, both of which support the expression of his male side; the gratification a woman needs is a personal life that supports the expression of her female side. If she doesn't get the support she needs to lower her stress when she gets home, then her stress levels go up further.

While higher stress levels in women at home are more common today, this does not have to be the case. By understanding how to increase oxytocin and estrogen to decrease her stress, a woman can be more productive at work and also happier at home.

Progesterone

Progesterone, like estrogen, plays important roles in a woman's menstrual cycle and maintaining the early stages of pregnancy. As we've discussed, progesterone is produced after ovulation and counterbalances estrogen levels in the second half of the menstrual cycle (twelve to fourteen days after ovulation) while playing a major role in reducing stress.

Progesterone opposes estrogen to maintain the correct balance of hormones to maintain the body's ability to get pregnant. This important hormone also has a major effect on mood. Estrogen excites the brain and progesterone calms the brain. While both are required in the second half of a woman's cycle, progesterone needs to be higher, otherwise her stress symptoms will increase.

**Estrogen excites the brain
and progesterone calms the brain.**

Progesterone is responsible for caring and friendly behavior. Research reveals that it is produced when we experience "social bonding," which we discussed briefly in chapter seven; levels of progesterone increase when women have close, harmonious, and friendly social interactions with other women or men who are "just friends."

As we've seen, there is a minor but significant difference between social and pair bonding. Social bonding produces progesterone, and pair bonding produces estrogen and oxytocin. The same situation could produce progesterone or estrogen, and could be considered social bonding or pair bonding, depending on whether the activity is primarily supporting the expression of both her male and female sides (social bonding) or just her female side (pair bonding).

For example, if she were participating in a group activity like a yoga or aerobics class, the social bonding with the other class members would increase her progesterone, but if she looked to the leader of the class for special instruction or support, that pair-bonding experience would generate oxytocin and estrogen.

Progesterone is also produced when a woman takes time to nurture her own needs for fun, happiness, love, and pleasure. Basically, anytime a woman primarily depends on herself for her fulfillment during a non-stress-producing activity, progesterone is produced.

Here are two lists of common progesterone-stimulating activities:

Social Bonding with Others

1. Playing cards or board games
2. Sports or other team activities
3. Singing together in a group
4. Group yoga or other classes
5. Making a meal together with others
6. Spending time with a parent or family member who thinks or feels in a similar manner
7. Sharing in a women's support group or other meetings of people who share the same experiences
8. Getting involved in a fund-raiser for her children's school or other charity events.
9. Sitting together and sharing with friends at a party or a girls' night out
10. Attending a concert and dancing with friends

Self-Nurturing Activities

1. Going on a (healthy) diet or working out to improve her health
2. Taking time to learn a new skill
3. Reading a book she really wants to read
4. Making a new recipe she's been meaning to try
5. Creating time to organize or clean her home
6. Taking time to journal her thoughts, emotions, and feelings
7. Practicing meditation
8. Reading books or watching TV shows or movies where she relates to the characters
9. Gardening
10. Exercising or walking in nature
11. Taking a candlelit bubble bath
12. Listening to great music and dancing alone

What social bonding and self-nurturing have in common is that they are activities she does for her own personal benefit without sacrifice for others.

Any of these activities are particularly helpful in the second part of her cycle, when she needs to have more progesterone than estrogen to lower her stress hormones. During the first part of her cycle (ten to twelve days after her period), her body requires only low doses of progesterone. At this time, oxytocin and estrogen are the most important hormones for her happiness and well-being. Progesterone-producing social-bonding activities are not as important during this part of her cycle. While social bonding can produce some oxytocin and estrogen to the degree that she feels supported to express more of her female side, it does not produce as much as pair bonding.

**Progesterone is primarily produced
when she can express her male side
while also accessing her female side.**

During the second part of her cycle, when progesterone production is most important, if she is giving more than she is getting, then progesterone is not produced. Often women are stressed in their relationships because they are not taking enough time for themselves or other social-bonding experiences. They blame their partners and get stuck feeling resentful from expecting more. Understanding the importance of Me Time and social bonding frees a woman from overdepending on her partner.

Particularly in the second part of her cycle, whenever a woman begins to feel resentful it is generally a sign she needs to back off from looking to her partner for more (through pair bonding) and instead take time to make more of the progesterone (through social bonding) that will be more effective at lowering her stress. While her partner can help her make estrogen and oxytocin, as we've seen, it is primarily up to her to make progesterone.

**When a woman feels resentful,
she needs to back off
from looking to her partner for more
and instead take time to make progesterone.**

During the second part of her cycle, a man's support has less power to lower her stress or make her happy. But while he can't make her happy, his presence, attention, and affection can support her in making herself happy by helping her get the time she needs for social bonding. Without this insight, however, he can do a lot to interfere with her happiness. If he tries to change her mood by giving advice or explaining to her why she should be happy, he just makes her feel worse.

Testosterone

Although men have at least ten times more testosterone than women, it is still an important hormone for women. Just as progesterone prevents estrogen levels from rising too high in the second part of her cycle, testosterone is required to oppose the rise of her estrogen levels in the first part of her cycle.

A woman's testosterone and estrogen levels are like a seesaw. When one goes up, the other goes down. Ideally her estrogen should always be much higher than her testosterone. When her testosterone is too high, her stress levels rise and she cannot ovulate or mentally relax.

**A woman's testosterone and estrogen levels
are like a seesaw.
When one goes up, the other goes down.**

In the second part of her cycle, when progesterone is the main stress-reducing hormone, too much testosterone can lower her progesterone. As mentioned, a woman's body uses up her progesterone to make testosterone. More testosterone is produced in situations where she is required to express her male qualities and temporarily suppress her female side. This increased testosterone helps her meet her daily challenges without additional stress—as long as she can look forward to having the opportunity to express her female side later in the day or in the near future, as we've seen.

Testosterone is produced when a woman is expressing her male side, particularly in an impersonal work setting, while progesterone is produced when she is expressing both her male and female side in a more personal setting. Here are few examples of situations that increase testosterone but not progesterone:

- When a woman is working for money and serving people who are not necessarily her friends or family. She is solving problems but not necessarily nurturing.

- When a woman is in a leadership role where it is up to her alone to make decisions and she is not sharing her sense of accountability with others.

- When a woman's well-being is dependent on competing with others as opposed to cooperation.

- When a woman is not able to make choices based on her feelings, preferences, and intuition but must follow specific job requirements, rules, or instructions.

- When a woman faces a deadline and must postpone her own wishes and wants until the goal is achieved.

- When a woman must deny her own personal needs to achieve an urgent requirement of her job.

- When a woman must ignore her conscience because the end justifies the means (i.e., be willing to kill a person to protect her country).

- When a woman's job is completely technical or impersonal problem solving and doesn't require any love, intuition, or nurturing.

- When a woman feels she doesn't have enough time or support to achieve her goal of doing a really good job (e.g., even being a parent, responsible for the well-being of her children, will stimulate testosterone and not estrogen if she feels alone or that she does not have backup or help).

The situations described in each of these examples increase testosterone for a man or a woman. But unlike for men, who need testosterone to lower their stress, for women even a small surge in testosterone can increase her stress, unless it is tempered by oxytocin.

A Woman's Monthly Cycle

By understanding a woman's monthly hormonal cycle, both women and men can better understand her needs and how they change along with her hormone levels.

To help visualize a healthy and stress-free woman's changing hormones during her monthly cycle, refer to the chart below.

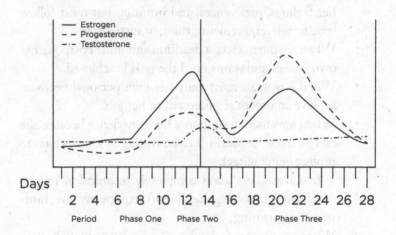

Here is an overview of what a healthy, stress-free woman needs at different times during an average twenty-eight-day cycle to best cope with stress:

- During the five days of her period, when all her hormones are low, she needs him to not make any demands on her. She needs more quiet, self-nurturing, or social bonding time.
- During the next five days, when estrogen is lower but rising, she is best able to express both her male and female sides together and delay gratification. Her greatest need at this time is the opportunity to express her male side in the work world, but in a cooperative and collaborative context that supports her female side as well. At this time she is more creative and independent and has a greater need to feel appreciated and admired for what she can do and accomplish.
- During the next five days, around her time of ovulation when her estrogen levels double, she has the greatest need for pair bonding. This is the best time for her to go out on a romantic date or share her more vulnerable feelings with someone who knows how to listen. This is when a man has the greatest power to make a difference in how she feels.
- During the last twelve to fourteen days of her cycle, she primarily needs social bonding. A man can make the biggest differences by supporting her needs for more social bonding, with or without him, as they arise.

Both men and women are encouraged to get a calendar to chart out these phases so that they can better support each other.

Note: The best time to *plan* a romantic date or get away is during the *first* five days after her period, but the best time to *go on* the date is some time during the *second* five days after her period.

As I mentioned in chapter six, research shows that after menopause, even though a women's ovaries no longer make female hormones, her adrenal gland keeps making them. She still continues to cycle as before, but the hormonal swings are not as pronounced and more flexible. Because of this, as a general guideline, when a woman is no longer having her period, she can consider the time of the new moon to be equivalent to the start of her period and the full moon to be equivalent to ovulation.

9

YOU TIME, WE TIME, AND ME TIME

I n an online, women-only course that my grown daughter, Lauren Gray, teaches, she reveals how women can sustain feelings of peace, love, happiness, and fulfillment during the many natural hormonal changes that occur monthly in a woman's body. The key is to optimally balance You Time (work bonding), We Time (pair bonding), and Me Time (social bonding and self-nurturing). The challenge is that as she moves through her menstrual cycle, this optimum balance continuously changes.

Understanding a woman's different hormonal needs during her menstrual phases is important for both women and men. It gives women new power to motivate a man to provide the romance, good communication, and help she needs to find happiness. And it gives men greater confidence in their relationships because they finally understand their partner's changing moods, feelings, reactions, and needs.

Without this insight, men often complain they can't figure their wives out. What he says or does one day works great; the next day, it doesn't. This is because with each change in a woman's hormonal cycle, her needs in a relationship change as well.

Sometimes she needs a man's love and attention more than at others. She couldn't care less if he ignores her at one point, but feels hurt at another. At certain times he has the power to make her much happier, but at others he can only support her as she makes herself happy.

As we explore this phenomenon in great depth, keep in mind that the timing of her hormonal changes is approximate. While on average the span between the first day of one period and the first day of the next period is twenty-eight days, it varies from month to month and between women.

A New Understanding of Women's Hormonal Changes

During her cycle, a woman's optimum hormonal balance continuously changes. When external stress disrupts these changes, her internal stress increases and her hormones go out of balance.

When external stress disrupts a woman's monthly hormonal changes, her internal stress increases.

With this new insight into restoring her natural hormonal balance, a woman can lower her internal stress response. But this insight also reveals particular relationship activities, attitudes, and behaviors that can best support her hormonal balance at different times in her monthly cycle. It helps men to know the best times for romance and sex and when he can best support her by creating a safe space for her to find and create her own happiness.

This fresh insight helps free men from thinking their job is to make a woman happy all the time, and frees women to most effectively find their own support by being themselves and pursuing their own happiness. A man's role in relationships has always been and still is to provide safety for his partner, but now that safety is not physical. Instead, it is the safety she needs to follow her heart and find her happiness. As adults we are all responsible for our own happiness, but we can certainly help each other in that process by acting with love.

A man's role in relationships has always been and still is to provide safety for a woman to find her happiness.

Looking at a woman's hormonal changes during her cycle reveals the best times of the month for a woman to apply different hormone-stimulating behaviors—You Time, We Time, and Me Time—to lower her stress. These broad distinctions can be summarized as follows:

1. During **You Time** a woman is engaging in work bonding. She is at work outside the home, or at home parenting her children. She is making testosterone along with estrogen as she expresses more of her male qualities with the support of her female side for the benefit of others.

    You Time (and the testosterone it naturally produces) has the greatest power to restore a woman's hormonal balance and lower her stress *in the five days after her period.*

    For clarity and easy reference, we will refer to this five-day period, when she is naturally making testosterone and her estrogen levels are rising, as the first phase in her cycle. For women during and after menopause, these five days start about four days after the new moon.

2. During **We Time** a woman is engaging in pair bonding. She is increasing her oxytocin, which lowers her testosterone (if it is too high) and increases her estrogen, as she expresses her female qualities and gives one kind of support to get back another kind.

   During days six through ten after her period, around the time of ovulation, a woman's production of We Time hormones is at its highest. Her estrogen level naturally peaks in this phase, doubling in comparison to any other time in her cycle. Her oxytocin will also rise to its highest level, depending on the support she gets.

   Over these five days, increasing her oxytocin has the greatest power to balance her hormones and lower her stress. This five-day window is when a man's romantic overtures and efforts have the biggest impact. She is very vulnerable and needs his emotional and caring support the most at this time.

   For clarity and easy reference, we will refer to this five-day period, when her estrogen and oxytocin peak, as the second phase in her cycle. For women during and after menopause, this is the five days around the full moon.

3. During **Me Time** a woman is engaging in either social bonding or self-nurturing activities. Whether she's spending Me Time on her own or with others, she is expressing her male and female qualities. She is doing what she wants, without sacrifice. Both Me Time activities—social bonding and self-nurturing—increase her progesterone, which in turn lowers her estrogen level if it is too high.

If her testosterone levels have been depleted during You Time, she will need more self-nurturing activities during Me Time. Like a man's cave time, self-nurturing activities, besides increasing progesterone, help a woman restore testosterone, which will increase her libido and energy.

If her estrogen levels go too high during We Time because she is giving more than she is getting back, social bonding during Me Time can increase her progesterone enough to lower her estrogen. This surge of progesterone will calm her mind, lower her stress, and increase her positive feelings.

During the twelve to fourteen days before her period (after the second phase of her cycle), Me Time and the progesterone it produces have the greatest power to balance her hormones and lower her stress. The activities of Me Time can also be very supportive during the three to five days of her period.

For clarity and easy reference, we will refer to these twelve to fourteen days before her period and the three to five days of her period as the third phase in her cycle. These sixteen to eighteen days of her third phase are when her body requires more progesterone than estrogen and very low levels of testosterone to best cope with stress. For women during and after menopause, Me Time is most effective from a couple of days after the full moon until five days after the new moon, about eighteen days in all.

Understanding the particular hormones stimulated in each of these three phases can help a woman every day. When she spends her day in You Time during the first phase, she is often quite positive and happy. Her needs and fulfillment at work are more important than her personal needs at home. But then, in the second phase, her need for pair bonding becomes more important to remain fulfilled. During the third phase, she can certainly enjoy time spent pair bonding, but if she is stressed, then to lower her internal stress she needs more Me Time.

During Me Time in the third phase of her cycle, a woman needs to make time for social bonding and some time for self-nurturing. Me Time is essential for a woman to keep her heart open and experience fulfillment in her life and her intimate relationship. During this third phase she may think she needs more from her partner, but it is up to her, not her partner, to access her inner fulfillment.

The Importance of We Time

It is during the second phase that a woman most needs the pair-bonding activities of We Time. When her needs are met at this time, it can have a lasting positive impact for the rest of her cycle. At other times in her cycle, her partner's support through We Time is still needed, as it can still assist her in finding her happiness through You Time and Me Time, but during this five-day love window is when a man's affection, touch, romantic actions, good communication, compassion, and help can have the biggest and most positive and lasting influence.

Her positive response to the support a man provides during this window has the most positive influence on him as well. It is at this time, when she needs his support the most, that he can be her hero. During this second phase, when she is most connected to her female side due to higher estrogen levels, she can feel her vulnerable and most loving appreciation of his support. If he misses this window, their connection during the third phase will be diminished or compromised.

If couples don't pair-bond in the second phase, their connection during the third phase will be lesser.

When men and women don't understand the importance of her hormonal needs for We Time during the second phase, they find themselves fighting the most in these five days. As a woman's estrogen levels are naturally doubling, if she doesn't get the emotional support she needs to express her feminine side, this suppression of her authentic self increases her stress hormones, which in turn increase her testosterone levels and defensiveness. Depending on her unique temperament, she may experience a variety of negative reactions. Here are a few:

What She Feels When Neglected during the Love Window	What She Thinks When Neglected during the Love Window
Hurt	"He doesn't love me anymore."
Angry	"I feel left out, invisible, unappreciated, and taken for granted."
Resentful	"I give more in this relationship than I am getting."
Numb	"I am not in the mood for romance or sex."

In a very real sense, when her stress increases because of this hormonal imbalance, she will experience a kind of temporary amnesia, "forgetting" all the good things he has done for her in the past, and instead remembering his mistakes.

When her stress hormones are higher, she will temporarily forget all the good things he has done for her.

The bottom line is that during these five days a woman is most open to her partner's influence. If she gets what she needs she is happiest, and if she doesn't she is not.

It is only when our hearts are fully open that we can be affected by our partners. If we are hurt, angry, defensive, or disappointed, our hearts remain closed, and nothing our partner can do will make us happier. However, if we are open to our partner's efforts, we can experience the heights of pleasure and happiness.

In the five-day love window of his partner's second phase, a man can make a happy woman much happier. But even if she is not happy, this is the time when his support can most help her find her happiness. In addition, if he neglects her, he can make her much more unhappy. This is when she needs his emotional support the most, and if she does not get that support during these five days, then for the next eighteen days she will feel something is missing in her relationship and either want more or feel a growing sense of resentment. However, when her We Time needs are met during this five-day window of time, then she doesn't need pair bonding as much during the rest of her cycle.

During her five-day love window, a man can make a happy woman much happier.

In contrast, during the first and third phases of her cycle, he cannot make her happier, but he can provide the safety and support for her to freely express herself to find and feel happiness, appreciation, and fulfillment.

This insight helps to free men from the illusion that they are responsible for making a woman happy. Freedom from the false idea that we can make our partners happy takes a lot of the blaming and complaining out of a relationship and lets love grow.

If a man can stay detached from feeling responsible for his partner's happiness, then when she is not happy in response to the many stresses in her life, he doesn't take it too personally. He doesn't feel like he needs to "fix" her or explain why she should be happier. Without this need to control her feelings, he doesn't get upset when she is upset or doesn't want his advice.

Instead, he can use his new understanding of women's different hormonal needs to listen more and create the safety, detached compassion, and caring interest that will let her freely express herself.

From You Time to Me Time

In working with thousands of women, Lauren Gray has observed that because women spend so much of the day in You Time at work, they need more Me Time to restore the high testosterone levels produced and used up at work. Similar to a man's need for cave time, when a woman expresses her male side in the more impersonal work world, she, too, needs the opportunity to rebuild her testosterone.

I completely missed this idea in *Men Are from Mars, Women Are from Venus*, even though women had been saying to me for years, "I have too much to do and no time for me. I am too exhausted to relax and enjoy my life."

**When a woman expresses her male side
in the work world, she, too,
needs the opportunity to rebuild her testosterone.**

As mentioned, the self-nurturing aspect of Me Time is best for rebuilding testosterone. A woman's body makes testosterone out of progesterone. The time spent self-nurturing during Me Time rebuilds a woman's supply of progesterone so that she can make more testosterone from that extra progesterone whenever she needs it.

It is progesterone that provides a biological basis to support her libido. While oxytocin and estrogen increase her ability to respond and enjoy sex, progesterone, and the testosterone from progesterone, are what increase her desire for sexual pleasure and help her to fully enjoy sexual experiences.

**The self-nurturing aspect of Me Time
is best for rebuilding testosterone.**

By shifting from simultaneously making and then using up testosterone in You Time to making an abundance of progesterone in Me Time, a woman can rebuild her testosterone levels. But making this shift from You Time to Me Time is easier said than done. That is why so many millions of women have difficulty prioritizing Me Time, and why many of those that do take Me Time do not fully relax and enjoy that time.

When a woman is unable to recharge her hormones with Me Time, she will have a greater tendency to stay stuck in You Time, thinking only of other people's needs and not her own. In addition, because she remembers the happiness she felt previously due to her partner's support during We Time, when she is stressed she will often blame her unhappiness on perceived neglect from her partner rather than take the necessary steps to experience the inner fulfillment and happiness that comes from Me Time.

Although women today instinctively know they should take more time for self-nurturing, doing so often feels like an impossible challenge. They are overwhelmed with that never-ending to-do list and their own needs are always at the bottom of the list.

This is because, as Lauren points out in her teaching, women need We Time to shift from You Time to Me Time.

It is nearly impossible biologically for a woman to shift from producing more testosterone (You Time) to suddenly making progesterone (Me Time) without a surge in oxytocin. If a woman's testosterone levels are too high from You Time, it blocks her ability to make progesterone in Me Time. The oxytocin produced by We Time lowers her testosterone and allows her to then more easily make the progesterone she needs to enjoy her Me Time.

It is even more challenging for a woman to shift into Me Time if she is stressed from her workday. When a woman is stressed, her body uses up its existing progesterone to make the stress hormone cortisol. As long as she remains stressed, cortisol is being produced, and as long as cortisol is being produced, she will be unable to make the progesterone needed for her to benefit from taking Me Time. Even if she tries to take Me Time, it is not fulfilling.

Women Need We Time to Shift from You Time to Me Time

It was Lauren's insight that We Time is needed for women to transition from You Time to Me Time that then inspired me to write this book. This understanding is not only important for women but for men as well. Every man wants the woman in his life to be happy, and understanding a woman's need for We Time to shift into Me Time is the key.

Every man wants the woman in his life to be happy, and We Time is the key.

Expecting a man to know what a woman needs is unrealistic, but so is expecting a woman to create We Time or fully benefit from Me Time without new relationship skills and insights.

In addition to discussing the many new ideas and discoveries in this book for hormone balance, Lauren teaches women during her eight-week program to master the art of creating We Time in their relationships through doing less and motivating men to create more romance, communicate better, and help around the house. She also helps women discover the patterns and limited beliefs that prevent them from putting into practice what they have learned. After reading this book, finding a coach, friend, or support group to assist in putting these new insights into practice can be immensely helpful. These revelations will help you create the relationship of your dreams, but they only work when you carry them out.

The Power of Oxytocin

Of all the female hormones, oxytocin is the most important for a woman to make to keep her other hormones in balance. During all three phases of a woman's cycle, she needs to stimulate oxytocin to different degrees and for different reasons. In phase one, oxytocin feels really good, but it is not so important in lowering her stress levels. In the five days of phase two, she needs oxytocin stimulation the most, not only to lower stress but also to experience maximum fulfillment that will support her for the rest of her cycle. In phase three, oxytocin will help her to transition from You Time to the Me Time she needs to lower her stress, even though it does not have the same powerful influence on her happiness that it did during phase two.

For increased clarity, let's explore these distinctions in oxytocin's effects during different phases a little more.

Phase One: Stimulating oxytocin during the first phase is generally not as important. It is in this first phase that her body most needs to make testosterone through her work as her estrogen levels gradually begin to rise.

You can directly associate a woman's need for pair bonding with her rising estrogen levels. When her body's natural cycle requires more estrogen, she needs more pair bonding. In this first phase, her estrogen levels are rising slowly, so she has less need for pair bonding. In addition, she has less need for Me Time during this first phase, as her body does not make more progesterone.

Although she has less need for oxytocin at this time, if external stresses trigger her internal stress hormones, then some pair bonding to increase oxytocin will help lower her excess testosterone and support the production of estrogen to lower her stress.

Phase Two: In the second phase, during her five-day love window, oxytocin is most important to sustain and balance her testosterone production while allowing her estrogen levels to peak. With this support, her passions can swell up in waves. Her potential to open her heart and connect with pleasure in her body and senses is amplified.

To be fulfilled, she needs more We Time and not Me Time or You Time; to sustain her rising estrogen levels during this time, she needs more oxytocin. Without enough oxytocin, she can be easily upset, but with enough oxytocin, she is more easily pleased.

> **Without enough oxytocin,**
> **a woman can be easily upset,**
> **but with enough oxytocin,**
> **she is more easily pleased.**

Oxytocin is generally increased in short bursts. Little expressions of love, attention, empathy, and understanding can create a series of these bursts. The three- to six-second hug I suggest at the end of the Venus Talk, for example, will create a burst of oxytocin. A longer hug may feel good to her but it doesn't produce any additional oxytocin, unless she has been missing a hug for a long time.

Though it is most important during the second phase of her cycle, a little oxytocin support is certainly good every day of the month. I will generally give my wife four hugs a day every day of the month: one when we get up, one when we depart for work, one when we return from work, and one before bed. These physical expressions of love make a big difference for a woman to feel loved and connected.

In her second phase, increasing oxytocin helps a woman shift gears from feeling overwhelmed with obligations and responsibilities to temporarily turning off her never-ending to-do list and feeling relaxed, peaceful, happy, loving, and fulfilled. She can shift from being in her head to being in her heart and body. She no longer feels the compulsion to do and do and do. Instead she can take a deep, relaxing breath and simply rest in her being.

As one woman I spoke with said, "When I feel this safe, I can turn off the world and just be."

The oxytocin produced from pair bonding in this second phase gives her the ability to more fully enjoy the sensuality of food, art, music, touch, movement, dance, and sex than at any other time of the month. It is during this phase that she can most easily climax, as long as she gets the right support to stimulate many small bursts of oxytocin. Research has shown that for a woman to have a climax, her oxytocin levels need to be very high.

**Research has shown that
for a woman to have a climax,
her oxytocin levels need to be very high.**

The second phase is the best time for a couple to enjoy a romantic date, but they should schedule the date in phase one so that she is already looking forward to their special time together in phase two.

The whole point of foreplay in the bedroom is that, because of her sensitivity to touch, it stimulates oxytocin release, which in turn increases her orgasm potential. But before a woman can fully enjoy the sexual touch of foreplay, her levels of oxytocin and estrogen must both already be high. Nonsexual touch, along with romance outside the bedroom, increases her oxytocin so that inside the bedroom she can more fully enjoy sexual touch. (I explore this dynamic in much greater detail in my book *Mars and Venus in the Bedroom*.)

**Nonsexual touch outside the bedroom
helps a woman to increase oxytocin
to enjoy sexual touch in the bedroom.**

A woman needs lots of short bursts of oxytocin before sex to increase her pleasure and responsiveness. After sex, she needs extra cuddling to rebuild her oxytocin, which is released and depleted when having an orgasm.

Phase Three: In the third phase, oxytocin is just as important to a woman's sense of fulfillment but only in a few, short bursts. During the third phase, a woman requires more progesterone, less estrogen, and almost no testosterone to lower her stress hormones.

If a woman's testosterone levels are too high, which is her common response to the external stresses of her work, all it takes is a few short bursts of oxytocin to lower her testosterone enough for the hormonal stimulation of Me Time to help her body make the progesterone it needs most during this phase.

Oxytocin always feels good to her because it is the love and safety hormone, but in the third phase it isn't enough to reduce her stress. All it can do is momentarily lower her testosterone and stress hormones enough that she can more easily shift to Me Time to begin making the progesterone that *will* lower her stress levels. This increased progesterone not only calms her mind but also increases her ability to enjoy both self-nurturing activities and social bonding.

To make this transition from You Time to Me Time in her third phase, she only needs a few short bursts of oxytocin. At this time, if she depends too much on the support of pair bonding to feel good, the increased oxytocin will cause her estrogen levels to rise too high, which will lower her progesterone levels.

**Too much oxytocin
in the third phase of her cycle
can raise her estrogen levels too high.**

During the third phase, a woman's body needs her progesterone levels to be higher than her estrogen levels. In this phase, if estrogen is higher than progesterone it can create a host of negative symptoms often referred to as "estrogen dominance." These symptoms include decreased sex drive, irregular or abnormal menstrual periods, bloating, breast swelling and tenderness, headaches, irritability, depression, and mood swings.

If a woman in her third phase doesn't focus on the self-nurturing or social bonding of Me Time to stimulate more progesterone but instead focuses on more pair bonding to create more oxytocin, it can raise her estrogen higher than her progesterone and cause the uncomfortable symptoms of estrogen dominance.

In addition, with higher estrogen, instead of feeling satisfied with her partner's support, she just wants more and more. This estrogen stimulation feels good, but does not lower her stress.

The best way for a woman to know if she is spending too much time in We Time and not enough time in Me Time is to check in with her feelings. If she is feeling good and not stressed, then her hormones are balanced, but in her third phase, if she is stressed or feeling unhappy with her partner, or experiencing resentment, pettiness, or neediness, she most likely needs more Me Time and not We Time.

Taming the Mind and Opening the Heart with Oxytocin

In practical terms, a woman can avoid too much oxytocin if she listens to the warning signs of estrogen dominance. Whenever a woman notices that her mind is filled with negative thoughts and feelings that keep looping in her brain, it is a warning sign that she needs to balance her hormones by shifting from You Time into Me Time.

However, some women resist taking the necessary steps to take Me Time, because in opening their hearts through pair bonding, they often begin to feel the negative emotions that they have been ignoring to avoid feeling upset. Women who pride themselves in being strong may, as they open up while producing oxytocin during pair bonding, suddenly experience their resistance to being so vulnerable.

With the temporary increase of estrogen from increasing oxytocin levels, a woman begins to feel more. If she has been suppressing her emotions, she will briefly feel them on their way out as she pair-bonds. When you are feeling more, you can't easily suppress what you are really feeling. This is why a woman might briefly cry at the time of orgasm or when looking at a beautiful sunset. Both experiences involve a surge of oxytocin and estrogen.

When you are feeling more, you can't easily suppress what you are really feeling.

Without understanding how to let go of these suppressed emotions and feelings as they come up, her only option is to continue avoiding them by eating a snack, turning on the TV, reading Facebook, or otherwise distracting herself. Most women don't know or have not experienced that by simply putting into words and then sharing with her partner her frustrations, concerns, and disappointments from her day, along with her wishes and wants, as well as what she appreciates and is grateful for, as she would in a Venus Talk, she can actually feel much better.

In most cases, she has not experienced this because she has not felt safe previously to share her feelings, because, as we have mentioned, men will usually interrupt with solutions, and unless men are trained to listen in a new way, they may think she is overreacting or just being negative. The irony is that when a woman can't share her feelings, to various degrees she eventually becomes more negative in her thinking and feeling. Unable to share her suppressed feelings, she becomes powerless to let go of looping negative thoughts and concerns, and even as she continues trying to be a loving partner, her resentments continue to build up.

By suppressing her negative emotions, a woman becomes powerless to let go of looping negative thoughts.

Nearly every woman I have ever counseled in my office or in front of a group in a seminar will, within a few minutes of being asked specific questions about her emotions, begin to tear up. When a woman feels safe enough to return to her female side with the intention to look inside, all of her suppressed and then past-repressed feelings automatically begin to emerge, to be briefly felt on their way out.

One of the reasons some women stay so busy is to avoid pair bonding in their relationships and thus avoid feeling the emotions that they are suppressing during their day. By staying busy expressing her male side, a woman does not have to confront the emotions of her vulnerable female side. Without insight on how to deal with the buildup of negative emotions, she may easily become addicted to staying on her male side. Venus Talks are so important because they can help her to bring up those feelings and let them go through sharing.

Because it lets her avoid feeling the buildup of negative emotions, a woman can become addicted to staying on her male side.

Avoiding her emotions also prevents her from feeling orgasmic in the bedroom with her partner. She may love him, but if she has to suppress her feelings, then she cannot fully open her heart to access her feelings of love and surrender and then have a real orgasm. She may experience some waves of pleasure but not a real, full-blown, ecstatic orgasm.

Many women have never had an orgasm with a partner. Often this is because a man has not taken enough time in foreplay to generate enough oxytocin, but the other reason is that she has repressed feelings inside that she has not shared or resolved with love, understanding, and forgiveness.

By turning off her ability to feel her negative emotions, she gradually loses her ability to feel positive emotions as well. Despite loving her partner dearly, she may no longer have the same capacity to feel that love. Certainly, if she is suppressing her feelings, she can still feel some pleasure, but eventually she loses her desire to have sex. For many women, having sex starts to feel more like work or an obligation.

When his partner stops enjoying sex, a man will eventually lose interest in having sex with her. He may still continue to have sex as a necessary release of tension but not as an ecstatic union of two souls being completely vulnerable and fully feeling their love and devotion to each other. If he stops having sex altogether, he may take care of his needs in other ways (for example, through online porn) because his wife no longer turns him on.

When a man is unable to open his heart to his wife in sex, he can easily begin to disconnect from his ability to fully feel his love for his partner. Certainly he may love her, but he is unable to feel that love. As result, to feel his connection with her he may move too far to his female side and disconnect from his male side. This commonly happens to men as they get older if they stop having sex. Great sex with the woman he loves is a powerful testosterone stimulator that keeps a man young and healthy.

Releasing the Negative Emotions Oxytocin Brings Up

When a woman's suppressed negative emotions come up as a result of pair bonding, she has the opportunity to deal with those emotions in a healthy way. By holding in mind the intention to release her negative thoughts and emotions as they come up, she will be able to briefly feel those thoughts and emotions and then let them go. (If she does not feel safe expressing her feelings to her partner, she can perform this process by writing in a journal, praying, or talking to a friend, coach, or therapist.)

Through feeling and releasing her negative emotions, her positive feelings can shine forth like the sun's warm rays when the clouds open up on an overcast day. The sunshine of her love is always there inside; the clouds of her suppressed negative emotions just cover it up. Without plenty of oxytocin, it is much harder for her to feel and then let go of these negative thoughts and feelings.

Here are twelve examples of the defensive reactions that may come up during pair bonding when she is stressed and hormonally out of balance. The second column lists the underlying emotions associated with those stress reactions, and the third column lists the positive feelings that can emerge if she looks for them after exploring a few of her underlying negative emotions.

Automatic Stress Reaction	Underlying Emotion (to Be Felt and Released with Forgiveness)	Positive Feeling That Can Emerge
Annoyance	Angry	Peace
Pickiness	Sad	Love
Pettiness	Afraid	Happiness
Being demanding	Sorry	Fulfillment
Judgment	Frustrated	Patience
Criticism	Disappointed	Persistence
Opposition	Concerned	Compassion
Being argumen-tative	Embarrassed	Humility
Irritation	Mad	Caring
Resentment	Hurt	Appreciation
Jealousy	Scared	Gratitude
Disapproval	Ashamed	Innocence

When you feel a negative emotion, looking a little deeper often allows you to discover another emotion or two resting just below conscious awareness. Feeling these emotions and then putting them into words is primarily what helps you to let them go, as long as you commit to the intention to let them go in order to feel the love and other positive feelings in your heart. Sharing your feelings with another makes this process much more powerful as long as you feel safe.

For example, if you are frustrated, after feeling that frustration for a few minutes, giving it words, and then asking yourself why you are frustrated and what you wanted that you did not get, will usually reveal a deeper emotion. At this point you will generally begin to feel some disappointment, hurt, sadness, and/or fear. By feeling the underlying emotions that are linked with your negative stress reactions, as long as they are felt with a willingness to let them go with forgiveness, you are then able move beyond your defense reactions and replace them with feelings of love and appreciation. (I have written three different books on this process: *What You Feel, You Can Heal*; *How to Get What You Want and Want What You Have*; and *Mars and Venus Starting Over*.)

A final note about automatic stress reactions and pair bonding: If a woman is feeling automatic stress reactions like resentment and disapproval during her five-day love window, she will not feel like receiving her partner's support. If this is the case, her first move should be to shift gears into (nonromantic) pair-bonding activities with someone other than her partner. This can lower her stress enough so that she will be open to initiating pair-bonding activities with her partner. Having a Venus Talk or planning a date together will then "help him help her" by creating more oxytocin. This will help to open her heart to him again.

Relaxing after a Day of Work

So many women report that they have difficulty making the shift at the end of the workday from thinking about everyone else's needs to thinking about their own needs. Studies show that women much more than men tend to ruminate about problems from their workday or complaints they have about their partner, children, or life in general.

When a woman is feeling overwhelmed, it is difficult for her to come back to expressing her female side so that she can relax. If she has been expressing her male side a lot, she first needs a burst of oxytocin from We Time to temporarily turn off testosterone production. Then she can more easily relax by choosing to take Me Time or, if she is no longer feeling stressed, simply stay in We Time.

The hormonal stimulation of We Time helps women to transition from You Time at work to enjoying Me Time at home.

If women were not working in a testosterone-stimulating job during the day, it might be easier to shift back to Me Time, but in the long run, they would be suppressing their male side. This suppression would lead to increased stress in the long term. Unable to express both her male and female sides, a woman would eventually lose her sense of passion, in life and with her partner.

Unable to express both her male and female sides, a woman eventually loses her ability to feel passion with her partner.

How much pair bonding a woman needs to increase her oxytocin depends on what phase she is in and how stressful her day was. She might need just a three-second hug or she might need a ten-minute Venus Talk or to plan a romantic date.

During phase three, if she is stressed, as we have already discussed, then too much pair bonding will have the opposite effect from the one she wants. Because oxytocin increases her estrogen, too much pair bonding can actually suppress her progesterone at the very time when her body needs more of it.

For some women, more We Time instead of Me Time in phase three may cause her to feel needy for more, because she thinks that she needs We Time rather than recognizing that she needs Me Time. Wanting more We Time in her third phase is a warning sign that she actually needs more Me Time. Other women with more male qualities, instead of seeking too much We Time, will ignore it all together. They stay stuck in You Time when they get home and attempt to do everything by themselves. In either case, the social bonding or self-nurturing of Me Time will help a woman to find balance.

To a certain extent in phase three, whenever a woman is feeling dissatisfied or stressed, she needs to first create some pair bonding through We Time and then move into Me Time social bonding or self-nurturing activities. Holding on to blame or complaining about her partner, in her mind or out loud, will only continue to increase her cortisol levels, using up her progesterone and inhibiting her ability to enjoy Me Time.

Wanting More and Motivating Men

A woman wanting more We Time but really needing Me Time can prevent a man from coming out of his cave. Men are motivated to come out of their cave when they feel they are needed and that the support they can provide will help women find their happiness.

**When a woman wants more We Time
when she really needs Me Time,
it prevents a man from coming out of his cave.**

Women often complain that men don't help enough around the house. Certainly, a woman who goes to work full time, but also feels responsible for raising the children and creating a beautiful home, will need more help around the house. But to lower her stress, her more important need during the third phase of her cycle is not a cleaner house but a burst of oxytocin to then help her take some Me Time.

Unless she is able to shift from You Time to Me Time, no amount of extra domestic support from her partner will lower her stress or make her happy, and the more he experiences that his domestic efforts to help her do not make her happy, the less he is willing to help. If he continues to help but doesn't feel his efforts have increased her happiness, then his testosterone will drop, his estrogen will increase, and he will either resent her or lose his attraction to her. They will live together in a clean house with no sex!

**When a woman prioritizes a man's domestic help
over her emotional needs to balance her hormones,
they will have a clean house and no sex!**

These new insights can help a woman motivate her partner to participate more in the routine responsibilities of cooking, cleaning, shopping, and nurturing the children. If she normally cooks dinner or does more of the housework, but occasionally needs him to do these so she can continue to be stressed out by doing other things, he will have less energy and motivation to help. But if she can clearly identify and ask for the support that will help her to feel happy, then he will be much more motivated to come out of his cave and give more.

A man is always more motivated when he experiences that his efforts to support her lead to her increased happiness.

For example, it is much more motivating to a man when a woman says, "Would you make dinner tonight? I am so tired I just want to relax and take a bath. It would feel so good." Recognizing that he can do something that will contribute to her happiness motivates him.

It is much less motivating when she says, "Would you make dinner tonight? I did it last night. I still have more work to do online and the house is a mess." In this case, his help is presented as a way for her to continue to "do more" and stay overwhelmed. His natural reaction is to say, "Relax, you don't have to work all the time. And so what if the house is a mess. We can clean it up tomorrow. Who are we trying to impress?" As a result, he is not motivated to do more.

A man helping around the house is certainly important, but much more important is a woman's need for a burst of oxytocin to help her relax and enjoy her Me Time. By learning to balance her hormones through Me Time, during this third phase of her cycle she can lower her stress and feel happy and relaxed no matter how clean the house is. When a woman is successful in taking her Me Time in the third phase, she can stay relaxed and happy even if the floor is sticky, the laundry is piling up, the dishes are dirty, and there are only leftovers to eat because there is no time to go shopping or make dinner.

Getting more of a man's help for the routine responsibilities of creating a home may be very exciting at first but very quickly it will become routine. Particularly during the eighteen days of phrase three of her cycle, it is his emotional support that stimulates short bursts of oxytocin in her body and her ability to take Me Time to increase her progesterone that will keep her stress down. When women want a divorce, it is much less about a messy house and much more about a man's lack of emotional support.

When women want a divorce, it has much more to do with a lack of emotional support than a messy house.

After all, what woman picks a man to marry these days because he is a good cook or house cleaner? Certainly those are added bonuses, but she picks a man because she anticipates he will be able to give her the love, romance, and emotional support she needs to be happy. A woman today most needs a man to provide the emotional support and safety for her to discover and express her authentic self, and not only be a dishwasher.

Men and Me Time

Unlike women, men are able to easily move directly from You Time at work to Me Time (cave time) at home. Once a man has rebuilt his male hormones through Me Time, with the right support, he is then able to come out of his cave to enjoy We Time or support her in taking her own Me Time. But without these new insights and relationship skills, men often stay stuck in their caves just as women stay stuck feeling dissatisfied and overwhelmed.

This is compounded by the higher stress we are experiencing today. The more stress a man is experiencing, the more likely he is to get stuck in his cave and never come out. But the new insights for creating a Soul Mate relationship can motivate him to come out of his cave for more We Time.

Some men, however, return home and don't take cave time. They will either continue working online or they will immediately shift into helping their wives with the immediate problems of running a household. In the first case, he stays on his male side and eventually burns out because he is not rebuilding his testosterone levels. In the second case, he burns out even more because he is moving to his female nurturing side when his body needs cave time to rebuild his testosterone.

As a woman's stress levels increase at home, caring men who haven't had this vital insight into our biological hormonal differences try to help out "equally" but only end up burning out, feeling overwhelmed and exhausted just like her. Because her to-do list is never ending, the more he does for her, the more things she will take on to do. Just as he needs to take Me Time, for most of the month she does, too!

He can still help her to cope with stress, but first he needs to get his cave time; then, when he comes out, he can provide the support she needs to effectively lower her stress.

A man's need for cave time to rebuild his testosterone after work presents a clear challenge for modern relationships. At the end of the day, women need We Time just when men need Me Time. Fortunately, with a clear understanding of what it takes to create the pair bonding of We Time, a woman can create the burst of oxytocin she needs to shift from You Time to Me Time, while still giving her partner the space he needs.

Remember from chapter eight that a woman can create pair bonding even while her partner is in his cave by doing something that expresses her female nurturing side. As long as she anticipates receiving his support in return when he comes out of his cave, when she does something that supports him in some nurturing way, her body will produce the oxytocin she needs.

A woman can create the burst of oxytocin she needs to shift from You Time to Me Time while still giving her partner the space he needs.

For example, say he is in his cave reading the news and she is making dinner. If she anticipates receiving his support in return when he comes out of his cave, then, while she is cooking, her body will make a burst of oxytocin to lower her stress.

When he comes out of his cave, she can then ask for his support so she can take her Me Time or create more We Time, depending on her cycle. For more Me Time she might ask him for some particular help around the house or with the children so that she can take a bath, read a book, or spend some time with her friends.

If she needs more quality We Time during the five days around ovulation, she might invite him for a Venus Talk or to sit together and plan a romantic date. Or they might just cuddle while watching a favorite TV show (that she wants to watch). In chapter eleven we will explore a wide range of ways they can create more quality We Time.

By applying and practicing this insight, a man can be in his cave and a woman can be lowering her stress with oxytocin while she is folding laundry or helping the kids with homework because she is anticipating his support when he comes out of the cave. Her new welcoming and encouraging attitude toward her partner visiting his cave ensures that he can easily come out to provide the support she needs.

A man is automatically (and hormonally) more motivated to come out of his cave when he feels that he is needed and he can help his partner take the Me Time or create the We Time she needs to be happier. He is not automatically motivated to come out of his cave when his support doesn't seem to lower her stress or help her to find her happiness. Even worse, if she is unhappy with him, his testosterone levels crash and his normal need for cave time is extended.

A man is more motivated to come out of his cave when he sees he is needed to support her We Time and Me Time.

When she is unable to find her happiness, he becomes less motivated to come out of his cave. On the other hand, the happier she is from fulfilling her needs, the more he wants to come out of his cave and help!

As both men and women clearly understand their new emotional needs for creating a Soul Mate relationship, men are automatically more motivated to come out of their caves. With this new insight a man can easily shift from taking care of his own hormonal needs by rebuilding his testosterone levels to supporting his partner's hormonal needs for the You Time, We Time, and Me Time that will help her find happiness.

What Makes a Man More Attracted to a Woman

Just as it is challenging for women to move from You Time to Me Time, it is also challenging for men to move from cave time to enjoying We Time. His inability to shift gears is like a woman's inability to shift from caring for others to caring for herself.

As discussed, when a woman is overwhelmed, it is nearly impossible for her to suddenly shift from the concerns of You Time to enjoying her Me Time without the help of extra oxytocin to lower her testosterone and increase her estrogen. For this reason, it is useless and unproductive for a man to tell an overwhelmed woman to just relax and forget her concerns. ("Don't worry about it" is a phrase men should just never utter to a woman again.) In a like manner, it is just as unproductive and useless to tell a man what he *should* be doing instead of fulfilling his need to relax in his cave after a day of work.

**A man's inability to shift gears
from Me Time to enjoying We Time
is like a woman's inability to shift
from caring for others to caring for herself.**

While women need a burst of the hormone oxytocin to shift from You Time to Me Time, men need a burst of another hormone, called vasopressin, to shift from cave time to the pair bonding of We Time. Vasopressin in men lowers their estrogen levels and increases their testosterone. This extra surge of testosterone is what motivates a man to come out of his cave and participate more in fulfilling the needs of his wife and children. Without enough vasopressin, it takes a deliberate and exhausting act of will for him to get off the couch.

Vasopressin not only helps a man to transition out of his cave but also is the hormone that causes men to bond with others. It increases his sexual attraction to his partner as well as his motivation to protect her. In women, vasopressin has the opposite effect. Situations that increase her vasopressin actually decrease her interest in sex and are linked to increased anxiety and greater motivation to protect herself or become defensive.

Vasopressin is the hormone in men that causes them to bond with their partner.

Most of the research on vasopressin comes from the study of prairie voles. Like many humans, prairie voles form monogamous commitments and pair-bond for life. Prairie vole couples mate exclusively with each other, share nests, and even raise their offspring together. The males are especially protective of their mates and nest. Only 3 percent of all mammals exhibit these behaviors, so prairie voles are valuable models for understanding the neurobiology of pair bonding during We Time.

High levels of vasopressin are stimulated, in both men and women, when there is a crisis or emergency and we are urgently needed. On the other hand, high levels of oxytocin are stimulated, in both men and women, when there is a crisis or emergency and we depend on someone else to help or protect us. The pair bonding in We Time stimulates vasopressin in men and oxytocin in women, as long as she needs and appreciates his support and he is providing the support she needs most. This increases his attraction to her as well as her sexual and romantic responsiveness to him.

If, in an emergency, she provides the support he needs, her vasopressin increases and his oxytocin increases. This may feel good to each of them in the moment, but because he has less vasopressin, his attraction to her will decrease, and because she has more vasopressin and less oxytocin, her interest in sex and responding to his romantic efforts will decrease. Rather than staying in love with him, eventually she will feel like his mother rather than his romantic partner.

The pair bonding in We Time
stimulates vasopressin in men
and oxytocin in women.

Unlike oxytocin, which is produced when we get or anticipate getting what we need, vasopressin is produced when we are
needed or anticipate successfully fulfilling someone else's needs.
The more we are needed, the more vasopressin is increased.
Likewise, the more we feel we need someone and can get the
support we need, the more oxytocin is increased.

Challenging or novel situations in which we are neverthe-
less confident of success can particularly stimulate vasopressin,
because these situations also boost dopamine levels. Vasopressin
is most triggered when dopamine levels are high and testosterone levels are not depleted. This is why a man needs enough
time in his cave to rebuild his testosterone—he needs it to be
motivated for We Time.

In psychological terms, men come out of their caves when
they feel needed by their children or partner as long as they
anticipate being successful in fulfilling their family's needs.

One of the obstacles keeping men from leaving their caves
is that they don't understand how much they are needed to
provide the new emotional support women require in a Soul
Mate relationship. Lauren Gray's new insights, which show how
important it is for women to take more Me Time as well as You
Time and We Time, also clarify a man's new role in providing
the help a woman needs to find her happiness and lower her
stress levels.

Although a woman is more independent today than in years
past, she still needs her partner, just in a new way. Being aware
of this is particularly important in a world where women no longer need men as much for their security and survival. If a woman

is unaware of her new emotional needs to return to her female side and so questions why she needs her partner, his vasopressin drops in her presence and he is less motivated to come out of his cave. If he is single, he is less motivated to make a commitment or even get married.

A woman's new awareness of the emotional support she needs to lower her stress increases her ability to appreciate the support her partner can provide, which in turn increases his motivation to come out of his cave. The more he feels he can succeed in fulfilling her needs, the more vasopressin he will make, and the more attracted to her he will feel.

The more a man feels he can succeed in fulfilling his partner's needs, the more attracted to her he will feel.

Without understanding a man's need for cave time, women often take it personally and feel rejected. When he pulls away to take care of his own needs to rebuild his testosterone, she feels neglected. But with this new understanding of her own needs for Me Time, she can more fully embrace his need for cave time and give herself permission to take her own Me Time.

So often women feel that they give more and get less because they are expecting him to provide the support she needs for We Time, instead of recognizing that for the eighteen days of her third phase, she actually needs less We Time and more Me Time.

As women learn to get the We Time they need during the five days of her second phase, they can more effectively enjoy their Me Time during their third phase. With a greater appreciation of her Me Time, instead of sitting around waiting for her partner to come out of his cave, she can use that time to get more Me Time for herself.

Instead of feeling neglected when he goes out to play basketball with his friends, she can take that time for self-nurturing
activities or social bonding. When he is glued to the television
watching football or *Game of Thrones*, if she is not interested in
watching, too, she is free to take her Me Time. This new insight
creates a win-win situation in relationships.

How to Support a Woman's Me Time

The support a woman needs during her third phase will generally be some way that her partner can help her in taking Me
Time. It can be as simple as not complaining when she is talking
on the phone to a friend for a long time or encouraging her to
take a gardening class. But even more powerful are the things a
man does without complaint that free up her time to do more for
herself: handling the emergencies that come up.

Although my wife has a job outside the home, she still doesn't
expect me to do an equal amount of the routine nurturing activities around the house, like shopping, cooking, cleaning, and
caring for the children. She is happy about that because in return
I don't expect her to do an equal amount of the non-routine
activities that most men are generally happy to do—as long as
they get their cave time as well as the appreciation they need.

Below is a list of testosterone-stimulating activities that,
whenever practical, a woman should not be expected to do unless
she wants to. When a man takes on these testosterone-producing
actions, it can help his partner create more Me Time in the third
phase of her cycle. In her second phase, these same activities will
provide the pair bonding she needs to feel fulfilled, particularly
when he does them with a positive attitude without complaint.

When a man eagerly takes on work challenges that most
women don't want to do, it stimulates a lot of oxytocin in women

and vasopressin in men. The more his actions are noticed and acknowledged with appreciation, the more vasopressin, along with testosterone, gets produced.

Most of the examples on this list are drawn from my life in just the last few months. While taking the time to write out this list, I also began to appreciate more what I do.

These examples of the many ways a man supports his wife and family at home are in addition to what he does to earn money at work. This list can be helpful for her to read because if a husband lists all the ways he helps her, it can sound a bit like complaining and this is a big turnoff. Although he is giving his all, he will often say things like, "Oh, it's no big deal," or "It's my pleasure."

The Many Ways a Man Supports His Wife and Family at Home

1. He drives the car when they go on trips.
2. He runs errands and drives the kids to school and to practices.
3. He coaches the children's teams.
4. He helps the kids with homework.
5. He does the sandbagging when storms come.
6. He puts the chains on the tires in the winter.
7. He goes down to light the water heater when it goes off.
8. He fixes the computer, printer, and telephone when they go down.
9. He fixes the fence when it is broken.
10. He picks out the right refrigerator when it breaks.
11. He plans the summer vacation and makes reservations.
12. He studies the map to navigate.

13. He makes reservations when they go out to dinner.
14. He picks up dinner if she is tired.
15. He washes dishes if she asks for his help and at least brings back his plate and washes his own dishes.
16. He goes out in the cold to take out the trash and recycling.
17. He goes out in the dark to check out an unusual sound.
18. He carries the heavy bags and groceries.
19. He packs the trunk when going on a trip.
20. He changes a flat tire, or oversees someone else doing it.
21. He picks her up at the airport.
22. He fixes leaky pipes or talks with a plumber if he can't.
23. He talks to the kids when she is too upset to do so.
24. He talks with neighbors when there is a complaint.
25. He shops around for the best deal on a loan.
26. He shops for the best price for plane reservations.
27. He breaks down the boxes that come from shopping online.
28. He mows the lawn or rakes up the autumn leaves, trims the hedges, and carries heavy loads of weeds and fertilizer bags, or hires someone to do it.
29. He talks with the cable company (for hours) when it stops working.
30. He buys, hooks up, troubleshoots, and supervises the repair of the stereo, TV, cameras, video recorders, and players.
31. He researches, purchases, assembles, fixes, or supervises the repair of whatever breaks down, including bikes, tires, swing sets, toasters, phones, door locks, gate locks, basketball nets, lawn mowers, sliding doors, broken windows, blown fuses, and house alarm systems.
32. He puts down the toilet seat rather than her having to put it up for him.

33. He finds and supervises the contractor when remodeling and oversees the work. He is responsible for making changes, complaining, or asking for more.

34. He takes time to read the financial pages in the news to follow trends and make sure they are making the best financial decisions.

35. He cleans up the brush and pan when painting the house or apartment.

36. He sets up rattraps and buries dead animals.

37. He is responsible for purchasing and understanding insurance plans. When claims are made, he oversees the process to make sure they are paid correctly.

38. He searches the attic for holiday supplies.

39. He hangs heavy pictures, wall hangings, clocks, and phones.

40. He oversees any gun or weapons purchase, cleaning, and usage for either hunting or protecting the family.

41. He takes charge of vacation details such as local attractions, dining reservations, and accommodations.

42. He climbs ladders to change lightbulbs and test for mold in the house.

43. He resets the clocks during time changes or power outages.

44. He sets up umbrellas by the pool on sunny days.

45. He stays updated on the latest smartphones and how to operate them. He goes and gets their phones updated and gets the best carrier for the best deal.

46. He does all of this and more without complaining or feeling resentful that he is giving so much as long as he can see that it is helping her to find her happiness.

All of the *non-routine* activities listed above, which are commonly performed by men, provide an excellent pair-bonding burst of oxytocin that supports her in shifting gears from You

Time to taking Me Time. A man is happy to take on these stressful challenges as long as he sees that it is giving his partner the support she needs to find her happiness. His doing *routine* activities like cooking and cleaning can also create a burst of oxytocin for her if he is doing something she clearly doesn't want to do or doesn't like doing.

A man is happy to take on these stressful challenges as long as he sees that it is giving his partner the support she needs to find her happiness.

The idea of men and women equally sharing routine cooking, cleaning, and nurturing responsibilities works in theory but rarely in practice, and it certainly doesn't support the hormones of passion and attraction.

If a woman doesn't want to equally share in the testosterone-stimulating responsibilities—and most women do not—it is unrealistic to expect a man to still share equally in all the different estrogen-stimulating nurturing activates. Certainly our roles can overlap, but we need to remember that too many non-routine testosterone-stimulating activities increase a woman's stress and too many estrogen-stimulating activities increase a man's stress.

When a man is not too stressed from work or when he feels appreciated at home, many of the activities in the list above can actually be cave time activities. Likewise, if a woman is not too stressed from work or when she is getting plenty of emotional support from her partner, many of the routine nurturing activities of homemaking can be great Me Time and We Time for her.

Popular articles talking about how romantic it is for a man to do housework can be misleading. In Norway, two separate studies of nearly 10,000 couples reported that in marriages where men did as much of the housework as women, couples were more likely to get a divorce. Certainly in the beginning, the novelty of a man vacuuming produces more dopamine in a woman's brain, which can be exciting, but when the novelty wears off, so does the dopamine. What is more supportive over the long run is a man who will do many of the testosterone-producing tasks along with providing the new emotional support most women need to return to their female side.

This doesn't mean men shouldn't vacuum, cook, wash dishes, or the like. Every couple works out their own division of routine jobs according to their preferences, energy levels, and work schedule. It just means that, for most men, at home his primary focus should not be on the routine nurturing jobs but instead on taking cave time as well as non-routine testosterone-stimulating jobs. His cave time gives him the extra time and energy he needs when those emergencies arise.

Another Reason Women Become Overwhelmed

One major issue that can arise when a man is a particularly good provider or works really hard to make her happy is that a woman feels that she has to take on more things to do in order to balance all that he does for her. This is why it is so important for her to know that her taking time to relax and enjoy her Me Time is the greatest gift she can give him.

Taking time to relax and enjoy her Me Time is the greatest gift she can give him.

To review: Women experience the pair bonding of We Time by giving to their partners and then receiving caring, understanding, and respect in return. Men experience the pair bonding of We Time by giving to their partners and then receiving their trust, acceptance, and appreciation. When he does things for her, he doesn't need her to do more for him in response. Instead, he needs her love.

So many great husbands have wives who are overwhelmed because they take on more to do in order to feel worthy of their husbands' support. They take on more things that stress them out because they don't know how happy it makes their husbands to see their wives benefiting from their efforts and hard work!

On the other hand, many husbands who do a lot for their wives and families will think taking responsibility for all the non-routine activities should be enough and then unknowingly sabotage their efforts to please their wives by not providing the extra emotional support, like affection, compliments, conversation, attention, and romance, that they need!

Men mistakenly give less affection and attention because they think working hard for the family is plenty of support.

It is this new insight, that women need a man's pair-bonding support, either for fulfillment during the second phase or to transition to Me Time in the third, that can inspire and motivate men to give more in their relationships. With a greater awareness of how a man can succeed in helping his partner to feel happier, he will need to spend less time in his cave, and when he comes out he will have more to give.

In my marriage, Bonnie appreciates my taking cave time, because she knows it means that, when I come out, I will create quality We Time with her as well as support her in taking her Me Time. In the past, when she didn't recognize or feel the value of her Me Time, my eager willingness to encourage and support her Me Time was not recognized as support and thus resulted in less pair bonding. The more a woman can appreciate her own Me Time, the more she can appreciate her partner's willingness to help her get more Me Time.

The more a woman can appreciate her own Me Time, the more she can appreciate her partner's willingness to help her get more Me Time.

Without this insight, his support for her Me Time may make her feel like he doesn't want to be around her. This confusion can go the other way as well. Some women don't take Me Time because they are afraid their partner will resent their having a good time without them.

One woman said to me, "Oh, I can't take Me Time. If I were to have fun when I wasn't with my partner or tell him I wanted to take time away from him, he might think I didn't love him." This kind of attitude can suffocate a man and prevent him from feeling motivated to come out of his cave and spend more time with his partner.

Having said all this, there are some men who at first will feel left out when a woman is enjoying her Me Time, but this will quickly change when he sees that he gets credit for her happiness. These needy men are just too far on their female side and, very quickly, as they experience their partner in a happier state and appreciate them more, these men will return to their male side and feel more secure.

Emergency Man

Within every man is an emergency worker. His testosterone levels rise when he is needed. When a man understands that women today need his help more than ever, not just for We Time but for Me Time as well, and that he can provide what his partner needs to be happy and fulfilled, he automatically experiences a new sense of motivation.

When a man understands that women today need his help more than ever, he automatically experiences a new sense of motivation.

In traditional Role Mate relationships, a man spent most of his life in You Time at work and then in Me Time in his personal life. To various degrees he would experience the fulfillment of We Time by taking credit for his wife's happiness if she enjoyed and appreciated the support he provided for her.

To various degrees, a man in a Role Mate relationship felt the benefits of We Time by taking credit for his wife's happiness.

In a Soul Mate relationship, a man continues to experience the joys of We Time by taking credit for his contributions to her happiness. But with new relationship skills and by recognizing the new needs of his partner to find balance, he is naturally more motivated to come out of his cave and fulfill her more personal needs for love, romance, and affection.

Men have always been motivated to make women happy. Today, they just don't yet understand how they can help. There is so much misguided but well-intentioned pressure on men to think, react, and respond like women. This imbalance not only increases a man's stress, but a woman's as well.

Men do not need to become more feminine. When he is stressed, to balance his male and female sides, he needs to take cave time to return to his male side instead of spending more time expressing his female side. A greater understanding of how he can be more successful in respecting and caring for a woman's new needs increases his ability to rebuild his testosterone during cave time so that he will have more to give when he comes out.

With a new understanding of the challenges women face in balancing their You Time with We Time and Me Time, and of a man's capacity to solve this new problem, he is automatically more motivated to help. He has a bigger reason to come out of his cave. By giving her what she needs, he fulfills to a greater extent his need for We Time as well.

Balancing Her Different Needs

Even with a supportive partner, a woman can face many other, more internal, obstacles to balancing her different needs for pair bonding, social bonding, self-nurturing, and selfless service in You Time, We Time, and Me Time. Here are three examples:

1. **Parental Issues:** Unresolved issues from a woman's past, such as from an unavailable father or an unhappy, over-dependent mother, can prevent a woman from depending on a partner and creating the pair bonding necessary for the We Time she needs. The thought of needing

someone feels like weakness rather than just accessing a part of her female side.

To avoid intimacy she will become addicted either to overworking in You Time or to the social bonding or private time of Me Time. In both cases, by avoiding pair bonding, she will have greater stress.

2. **Sibling or Friendship Issues:** Unresolved issues with siblings or friends in childhood may prevent a woman from social bonding. She may then be drawn only to the self-nurturing aspect of Me Time. This does help to lower her stress by making progesterone, but she will miss out on the joys and pleasure of social bonding.

We have already discussed the need for self-nurturing and social bonding during Me Time. Time spent self-nurturing gives her more progesterone to restore her testosterone and support her male side, and the time spent in social bonding gives her more progesterone to freely express her female side. But by using only self-nurturing to lower her stress and avoiding social bonding, over time her female side can become suppressed and her male side can become overexpressed.

3. **Lack of Positive Role Models:** When a woman has no role models of strong or successful women who are also happy and fulfilled, it may prevent her from seeking the benefits of You Time. Without the confidence to express her independent male side, her female qualities of interdependence and vulnerability can make her too needy for We Time.

Instead of taking time for self-nurturing during Me Time, she will be drawn to overexpress her female side through social bonding. The overexpression of her female desire to nurture others and experience interdependence in her relationships suppresses her male side. As a result, she tries too hard to please everyone and loses her sense of self. What others think of her overshadows her own inner confidence to express her independence in balance with interdependence.

Equally, when women do not have positive role models of how they can successfully express their male side while enjoying a loving, stress-free, and happy family life, they can suppress their female side in their quest to be financially independent and successful. As a result, she resists the idea of needing a partner in life. Unable to feel the more vulnerable qualities of her female side, she is unable to fall in love or feel attached to a partner.

In all three of these examples, without the support in her past to express both her male and female sides, it is more challenging for her to find happiness and hormonal balance, but it is possible. With an increasing awareness of her different hormonal needs at different times of the month, by practicing these new skills she can overcome her past and create a lifetime of love.

While this book can make a big difference, as with any new skill some coaching can make it easier. Lauren Gray's online blogs at MarsVenus.com provide additional helpful support for women to balance their You Time, We Time, and Me Time.

The Golden Rule for Soul Mates

The Golden Rule of a Soul Mate relationship is when a man or woman feels they are not getting enough attention, love, and support, they should shift their attention to taking more cave time or Me Time. Couples today get too enmeshed with each other and then they lose their passion. Even in phase two, during her five-day love window, if she is not getting the pair bonding she needs, there are many ways to get it other than from her partner. The dance of intimacy requires independence as well as interdependence.

The dance of intimacy requires independence as well as interdependence.

Happiness in relationships is always about balancing You Time, We Time, and Me Time. The poet Kahlil Gibran beautifully expresses this concept of balancing We Time with Me Time in his enduring book of poetic essays, *The Prophet*. He said,

> *Let there be spaces in your togetherness: And let the winds of the heavens dance between you . . . stand together, yet not too near together: For the pillars of the temple stand apart, and the oak tree and the cypress grow not in each other's shadow.*

In the last four chapters we will explore in great detail the particular support women need from men to create quality We Time, as well as the new emotional support men need to be fulfilled. I have saved the best for the last four chapters. With this new insight, men and woman can give and receive the loving support they need most and deserve.

10

SHE NEEDS TO BE HEARD
AND HE NEEDS TO BE
APPRECIATED

M en's and women's main complaints about each other come down to women not feeling heard and men not feeling appreciated. Men often talk too much and don't listen enough, while women take on so much to do that it is difficult for them to fully appreciate the support a man can provide.

In reading about the Venus Talk I describe in chapter six, a man who is more on his female side will often ask, "But what about me? I have feelings to talk about!" The Venus Talk is a powerful process for a woman to return to her female side and for him to return to his male side. It does not mean he does not have feelings or should never share them.

Talking about feelings is a good way for a man to connect with his partner, but it is not a good way to lower his stress. There is a time for him to talk and a time for him to listen. If he feels stressed, angry, or defensive in response to something his partner has said or done, and he thinks he needs to share those feelings to feel better, doing so at that moment will only make matters worse for himself and his partner.

If he is upset over something that happened during his workday and feels an urgent need to complain about it, he should first make sure that he has connected with his male side to lower his stress before sharing with his partner. Talking about his feelings to his wife at times of stress will increase his estrogen and actually increase his stress.

When a man shares defensive feelings with his partner, it only makes matters worse!

After he has taken cave time to rebuild his testosterone and rebalance his hormones, it is a much better time to share his thoughts, feelings, and experiences with his partner. However, she will connect more with him when he shares more positive feelings and fewer negative emotions. For example, when I do share something upsetting to me with Bonnie, I will always include something good I am learning from it so that I don't give the impression that I am a powerless victim seeking her sympathy (though if a problem or conflict is really big, then occasionally it is fine to look for and accept a little sympathy).

Women depend on their partner to stay grounded in his confidence and competence. A woman will often say she wants to know what he is feeling, but most of the time, she just wants reassurance that he still loves her or that everything is okay. When a man is quiet, if a woman feels insecure in some way, she will feel an urge to find out what his feelings are in order to feel connected. At these times, it is better for her to connect with her partner by taking time for him to hear her feelings. She will then both feel connected and be able to return to her female side to find balance.

Women often say they want to know what a man is feeling, but most of the time, they just want reassurance that he is not upset with them.

Quite often when a woman is talking, a man will detach and think about what she is saying. Woman often misread his "thinking" facial expression as angry.

During a seminar, in an experiential exercise, women were asked to observe their husbands' facial expressions when they were relaxed, thinking, happy, and angry. Most women were shocked to see that there was little difference between their partners' expressions when they were angry and when they were relaxed or just thinking.

For example, Melanie had been married to Tom for twelve years. She was shocked when she and Tom did this exercise because, for their whole marriage, at times when Tom was relaxed or just thinking, she had thought he was angry. While some men are more expressive, many men actually look the same when they are thinking intently or just relaxing as they do when they are stressed or angry.

Melanie said, "This completely changed my marriage. So many times I thought he was angry with me and he wasn't. I would always want to know what he was feeling or I would just back off, having no idea of why he was upset with me. Now, I feel so much more relaxed and safe around him. I don't feel like I have to walk on eggshells or avoid upsetting him more by asking for his help."

Talking About Feelings

For both men and women, talking about our negative emotions and feeling heard increases estrogen and reduces testosterone.

If a woman is stressed, she needs to share her feelings to come back to her female side. Even if a man doesn't fully relate to her experience, it can still help her lower her stress. In addition, the more she is able to share her emotions, the more he will be able to understand and connect with her, regardless of whether he is able to relate directly.

But when a man is stressed, the last thing he should do is share his negative feelings with his wife, even if he is not complaining about her. If he needs a sounding board, he should first do some cave time activity to increase his testosterone and calm down. He could talk to another man, a coach, or a therapist; pray or mediate; or do some social exercise like hiking, golf, or going for a walk with his male friends. Then afterwards, if he is still upset, he could once again revisit his feelings by writing them out in a journal.

If a man is upset and he needs a sounding board, he should first calm down and then talk about his feelings to another man, not his partner.

The reason a man's stress can go down when he talks to another man about his feelings is that when men share experiences, it tends to reinforce and validate their male sides and increase testosterone. So if a man talks with another man, it increases his testosterone along with his estrogen.

In the case of sharing his thoughts and feelings with a therapist, coach, or friend, this person does not have to be another man. It certainly can also be a woman, just as long as she is not dependent on or intimately connected to him. This distance means he doesn't have to be concerned with what she thinks of him or with editing himself.

When a man is not a whiner or complainer, it helps his female partner to feel safe and supported in his presence. This is often what it means when, in the military, a man learns to "suck it up." While modern psychology teaches that men should share their feelings, it actually weakens a man's access to his male side if they do it in the heat of the moment. Sure, it can feel really good at the time, but it pushes a man too far to his female side and lengthens the time it will take to return to his male side.

Research with traumatic stress in the U.S. Army has demonstrated that getting men to talk about their feelings while in the combat zone is nonproductive and results in more PTSD. What has proven to work better is talking about their feelings later, when they are out of combat. Waiting until they are relaxed and safe is the most effective way to heal a deep emotional wound.

Getting men to talk about their feelings while in the combat zone is nonproductive and creates more PTSD.

This is a very controversial point. So let me say again: *This doesn't mean a man should ignore or suppress his negative emotions.* He should just not express them to his romantic partner to find relief. Instead he should first do something to increase his testosterone levels to come back to his male side. This will dramatically lower his stress.

Doing so is not suppressing his feelings but simply taking some time to cool off. Directly talking to the person he is upset with will only make him more upset and shut that person down. Even when his partner is not the person he is upset with, before he can come back to his male side, he needs to first express his male quality of detachment and independence, not vulnerability and interdependence. As long as he has a negative emotional "charge," he should not share his feelings with his romantic partner.

Not only does this work better for him, but it is better for her as well. Whenever a woman listens to a man share his feelings, when he needs her support to feel better, it will bring her more to her male side. If she is already too far on her male side, this will not only increase her stress but also can kill the romance.

Sharing Feelings Can Create More Stress

Some women are successful in getting their husbands to "care and share" like a girlfriend and then wonder why the passion is gone. A woman may feel confused or guilty because all his sharing and caring becomes a turnoff. Unable to make sense of this situation, she may conclude he is just the wrong guy, instead of realizing that any man will become the wrong guy if she gets him to share with her the way she does with her female friends.

He, too, becomes frustrated because he is just trying to make her happy and do what she has asked of him, and he can become bitter and resentful because he feels rejected or unappreciated. Consider this example:

June and Alex had been married two years. After begging her husband to open up and share what he was feeling, rather than process his feelings alone, he started to open up and talk more about his feelings with her.

A few sessions later, June said to me in private, "I still love him, but I don't want to stay married. Now that he tells me all his problems and feelings, I am turned off to him. I feel bad about that but I can't help it. I don't know how to tell him I don't want to hear his feelings. When we got married, I didn't realize he had so many problems. Now I feel more responsible to help him. I don't want to feel like his mother. I want a grown-up man."

In this example, June's desire to hear his feelings was an example of expecting a man to fulfill her need for a girlfriend, someone who shared the same feelings about life as her. But when he did share his feelings, even though she could relate to some of them, it didn't make her feel better.

In retrospect, June saw that her desire to hear his feelings was strongest when he was most distant. When she thought she wanted him to share all his feelings, she was really looking to fulfill her own feminine need to be assured that everything was all right and he still loved her.

When a man is distant or quiet, women want to know what a man is feeling primarily to get the reassurance that he still loves her.

Without this insight, many women, like June, push their partners to share what they are feeling when they become quiet or distant. Then when a man does share, she becomes confused because listening to what he feels and shares doesn't feel that good. What she doesn't know is that the best way to get the support she needs is by doing the opposite: sharing her own feelings. Instead of listening to his female side share feelings, which pushes her to her male side, sharing her own feelings will bring her back to her female side.

June eventually learned that it was more effective for both of them if her partner processed his feelings silently. Then, once his stress went down, that was the time to hear his more positive feelings and get the personal love she was looking for.

In listening to Alex's problems, June actually began to worry more about him. Rather than feel like she could depend on his support, she felt like she had another job to do. She needed his personal love to help her connect with her female side and stimulate her anti-stress feminine hormones, but as he expressed his feminine side, she would move to her masculine side. Instead of lowering her stress, his sharing was increasing her stress and pushing her away.

**Listening to a man's vulnerable feminine side
when a woman needs to find her own feminine side
can trigger her masculine side
and increase her stress.**

Listening to Alex's feelings has a different effect on June than if her girlfriend Liz shared the same feelings of insecurity. When June listens to Liz's feelings, June becomes more feminine, but when she listens to her husband's feelings, she becomes more masculine.

This distinction is true for two very big reasons.

Reason One: Dependence

June depends on her husband Alex to share their financial and domestic responsibilities. June doesn't depend on her girlfriend Liz for that same support.

If Liz is insecure and afraid of losing her job or is overwhelmed with too much to do, it doesn't directly impact June. By listening to her friend, June's stress levels do not increase because she is not depending on Liz.

But if June's husband is afraid of losing his job, that certainly impacts her well-being and raises her stress levels. If her husband is overwhelmed, that means he is less available to her if she needs extra support or help. Particularly at a time when she is stressed and needs help to return to her female side, the last thing she needs is to feel more stressed.

It is challenging for a woman to listen and remain detached when his insecurities threaten her well-being.

When Alex shares his insecurities, instead of feeling reassured by Alex's love and support and being able to return to her female side, June's masculine side responds to give Alex the reassurance and support his female side needs. Instead of returning to balance, June goes further out of balance.

When June is already stressed, it is best for Alex to take on the male role by listening while June gets to benefit from coming back to her female side. As mentioned, silent listening expresses our male side, while sharing feelings expresses our female side.

Silent listening expresses our male side, while sharing feelings expresses our female side.

Without this insight, June would continue to pull away from Alex, feeling guilty for not being a more empathetic listener. Her inner pressure to be a good listener would eventually disconnect her from her female side. At a time when June needs to come back to her female side to find balance, Alex's sharing his feelings can make her feel worse instead of better.

Reason Two: Empathy

Because they are both female, when Liz shares her feelings, emotions, and experiences with June, her feelings tend to be more aligned with the kind of feelings that June feels. By listening to Liz and fully relating to being in her situation, June's own feelings are validated, which stimulates her female anti-stress hormones. When she listens to Alex's feelings, because they are different, she doesn't get the same validation.

On the other hand, if Alex has more feminine characteristics, even though Liz might have similar feelings, sharing his insecurities or feelings of being overwhelmed lessens Liz's ability to feel that she can depend on Alex for support or help. It is already very challenging for women to ask for help; hearing his need for help makes it even more difficult for her to consider asking him for more.

Because she loves him, she will instinctively want to either comfort him with reassuring motherly love or try to help him solve his problems. In both cases, as a result, she will feel that she cannot depend on him to be there for her.

Because a woman's survival depends to some degree on her partner, when he talks openly about his mistakes she will automatically become hypervigilant about reminding him what he can do to avoid making the same mistakes in the future. Not only does this constantly remind him of his mistakes, but it also serves to make him feel overly dependent on her.

One time, I left my passport at home. Everything worked out fine with a little last-minute excitement of my having to get special permission to enter Sweden without a passport. But for years after that, Bonnie would consistently remind me to take my passport, until finally, as I was packing for a trip one day, I playfully showed her my passport and said, "I will always remember my Sweden adventure so now you don't ever have to remind me again," and she stopped. While this kind of unsolicited advice is well meaning, it can wear down a man's testosterone.

The solution to this new challenge of when and how to share feelings is often timing. There are times when he can share, but *not* when she needs to come back to her female side or when he is trying to come back to his male side. And, importantly, it is never the right time to share your feelings if it is going to sound like a complaint to your partner.

It is never the right time to share your feelings if it will sound like a complaint to your partner.

Complaining Versus Requesting

Relationships are great in the beginning because we accept our partners just the way they are. The newness and challenge at the beginning stimulates high levels of dopamine in the brain, which temporarily increases our ability to overlook our partner's shortcomings. Then, eventually, as routine, comfort, and familiarity set in, we take on the role of trying to improve them, fix them, correct them, or change them in some way. This is a slow poison that kills passion and love. Wanting to improve someone feels like love but it is not. Changing ourselves to do what works instead of trying to change our partner, letting go of judgment, and finding forgiveness are the true expressions of love.

When we complain in a relationship, it's because we don't like something and we want our partner to change in some way so that we can get what we want. It's fine, even good, to want more support, but complaining is not the way to get it. Every complaint has within it a request. But when we complain, our requests sound more like demands.

The more we push our partners to change, the more resistance they have to hearing us and responding productively. By rephrasing our complaints as requests and not demands, we can convey the same message in a more positive way. To make a request even more effective and positive, keep it brief. The more words you use, the more resistance you will create in your partner.

Here are a few examples of how to rephrase your complaints into short requests using as few words as possible to provide reasons or justifications for your requests.

Complaint	Request
You keep forgetting to take out the trash.	Would you remember tomorrow to take out the trash? It starts to smell bad when it sits in the garage for an extra week.
You left your trash all over the kitchen counter again.	Would you clean up the trash you left on the kitchen counter?
You didn't answer your phone again. I can never reach you.	When you leave today, would you remember to leave your phone on so that I can reach you? I really like being able to stay in touch.
You keep leaving your clothes on the floor in the bedroom.	Would you remember to pick up your clothes in the bedroom?
You were correcting me again in public and I don't like it.	Would you not correct me in public conversations? Unless it is really important, it would feel much better to me.

When you are stressed, by holding in your complaint and doing something to first lower your stress, you can take extra time to reflect on what the request hidden within your complaint is. Then, when stress levels are low and you are feeling both connected and loving, that is the time to make your request.

Another way to get more support and sound even less demanding is to merely let your partner know what you like. Instead of making a request, which requires an immediate yes or no answer, make a statement. Let this statement be an "FYI," or "For Your Information Only," with no demand or requirement for an immediate response.

Sometimes, you will get more support from an "FYI" with no demand or requirement for an immediate response.

Here are a few examples of FYI statements:

Request	FYI Statement
Would you remember to take out the trash?	Tomorrow is trash day. I love it when you take the trash out in the afternoon.
Would you clean up the trash you left on the kitchen counter?	After you make your morning smoothie, I love it when you remember to clean the kitchen counter.
Would you remember to leave your phone on so that I can reach you?	I am not going to see you today. I love it when you keep your phone on so that I can reach you if you are late.

Would you remember to pick up your clothes in the bedroom?	I love it when you pick up your clothes. The bedroom looks so nice.
Would you not correct me in public conversations?	I had so much fun last time we went to Dave's house. I love it when you laugh at my jokes, but not so much when you correct me in front of others. I would prefer you do that in private.
Would you turn out the lights when you leave a room?	I noticed you turned off the lights in the living room. I love it when you turn out lights when you leave a room.

Agree with your partner that when one of you makes a request or FYI statement, no response is required other than, "I hear you." This gives your partner time to consider your request before making a commitment to change their behavior or fulfill your request.

Particularly with men, the less pressure they feel to immediately respond, the more willing they will be to lovingly consider a woman's request and do their best to adjust their actions. By not pushing him for an immediate response, it supports him in making up his own mind. This increased independence supports his male side so he will have more to give.

In a relationship, the best time to make requests is when you and your partner are not feeling any stress. You can soften a request so it doesn't sound like a demand by saying something like, "When you get a chance, I would really appreciate it if you would clean up the garage," or "There is no urgency about this, but I would really love it if you would clean up the garage."

I know this sounds laborious, and it can be at first, but it prevents a lot of tension and actually takes much less time in the end. Take a moment to consider the benefits. Imagine:

- How good it feels to know your partner is not making any demands on you to change.
- What a loving gift you are giving them by not making any demands on them to change.
- How good it feels to trust that because you are not throwing a tantrum or making a demand, they will consider your request to the best of their ability.
- How good it feels not to depend on your partner changing or being perfect to make you happy. What a freedom you give yourself and your partner! This is a glimpse of the higher love that it is possible to achieve.

To ensure clarity and brevity while you are still learning how to do this, I recommend first writing out your request and then reading it to yourself for practice. It can then be delivered on paper, read out loud, or spoken without the script when you are both in a good mood.

Sharing Your Preferences

Some couples I've worked with simply have one envelope labeled "Preferences": when they have requests, they write them out and put them inside. First, they point out in the least number of words what they would like changed. Then they phrase their request as a nondemanding preference expressed in a friendly and loving way. Sharing requests in this way ensures that one is not expected to give an immediate response. For some it also feels much less demanding or controlling. This works best when each person only shares one preference a week and that preference is sandwiched between loving comments.

Here are a few examples of a preference note:

- "The other day you forgot to bring out the trash. I really appreciate when I don't have to do it and I know you don't always forget. I really love it when you remember to take out the trash. Thank you. I love you."
- "The other day the counter was really sticky after you made your smoothie. I really love it when you remember to clean the counter. I know it doesn't happen all the time. Thank you. I love you."
- "The other day you were thirty minutes late to dinner. I didn't see you all day and didn't know where you were. I really love it when you keep your phone on so that I can reach you when you are late. I know you are not late all the time and that you often have your phone left on. When I can't reach you, I worry. Thank you. I love you."
- "The other day I picked up three days' worth of your clothes. The bedroom looks so nice when you pick up your clothes. I know you don't always leave your clothes on the floor and you do so much for me in other ways. I would love it if you would remember to pick up your clothes. Thank you. I love you."
- "The other night at Dave's party I was having such a fun time. I felt embarrassed when you started correcting me in front of others. I appreciate your love and I would also appreciate not being corrected. I know you mean well and it certainly doesn't happen all the time. Thank you. I love you."
- "This week, on several occasions, the light was left on in the living room. I know that you turn the light out on many occasions but not always. I love it on the days when I can move through the house and not have to turn the lights out. I am trying to not waste energy because

our electric bill is getting higher each year. Thank you. I love you."

Agreeing to write each other preference notes means you can feel safe the rest of the time that you will not be confronted by complaints. Another benefit of writing your preferences down in note form is that your partner can respond with a brief note in return, thanking you and if needed also letting you know a better way to express your preferences.

They might say something like: "Thank you for your note. I will work on it. I love you."

Or they might say something like: "Thank you for your note. I will work on it. In the meantime, this is how I would love to hear this request. Instead of saying that I never put the toilet seat down, I would love to hear in your words that you know many times I do put the toilet seat down and that you appreciate that. Then in your note let me know that you would love for me to put the seat down *all* the time. Thanks for listening. I love you, too."

Letting your partner know your needs is important, but it's even more important to appreciate what they do right. Women feel most appreciated when they are heard and respected, but men feel most appreciated when they receive a positive reaction to their words and actions and, whenever possible, a neutral reaction to their mistakes. When a woman overlooks or minimizes a man's mistakes, he feels even more appreciated. And when your partner is already getting many messages of appreciation, it is always easier for them to hear and respond to your requests.

Appreciating Your Partner

The most powerful way to support a man's testosterone levels and bring out the best in him is appreciation. Many women share what they don't like, but do not express out loud as often what they do appreciate.

When women feel supported, they have a much greater capacity than men to feel and express appreciation. One of the main reasons men love to be with women is that women can feel so much appreciation for what men do for them. However, most women don't fully utilize this superpower to bring out the best in men. Just as a man on his female side will often complain about having to listen rather than share his feelings when he is stressed or defensive, women on their male side often resist the idea that men have a greater need to be appreciated.

Here are three easy messages to help increase a man's testosterone levels:

- Whenever possible, when a man speaks, if he makes sense, then say to him, "That makes sense."
- Whenever possible, when a man speaks, if he has a good idea, then say to him, "What a good idea."
- Whenever possible, when a man speaks, if he is right, then say to him, "You are right!"

Women often have these positive feelings inside but don't realize how important it is to say them out loud or how good it feels to him when she does. After using any of the three phrases listed above, watch how his posture and face change. He will pause and stand up a little straighter. With increased blood flow to his brain from the surge of testosterone he feels, his face will brighten. He will be proudly thinking, "What did I just say?" This support is easy to provide, increases his testosterone, and brings out the best in a man.

Just as men love to be appreciated, women love to be heard. When a woman is talking, he can give her the best support by showing more interest. Here are three easy messages to help increase a woman's estrogen levels:

- Whenever possible, when a woman speaks, look at her and say, "Tell me more about that."
- Whenever possible, when a woman speaks, look at her and say, "What else?"
- Whenever possible, when a woman speaks, look at her and say, "Help me understand that better."

The more a man shows interest in what a woman is saying, feeling, liking, wanting, or needing, the more supported she will feel. It is often surprising to men how much more women have to say when they feel it is safe to share and their partner is interested. When a man shows interest in what a woman is saying, she feels he is interested in her, and that is a big oxytocin and estrogen producer. By showing interest she will also feel that he appreciates her more.

Many times, a man is not that interested in what she is saying, but because he is always interested in making her happy, when he realizes that she will feel personally supported if he listens, then he becomes more interested in what she has to say.

Why Women Don't Feel Appreciated

In the book *Work with Me*, which I wrote with Barbara Annis, another expert in gender intelligence, we explored a variety of common misunderstandings or blind spots between the sexes at work. We surveyed over 100,000 men and women in the workplace and this study revealed a large gap in men's and women's understanding of each other. With many of the questions we asked, we got completely different answers from members of the other sex.

One huge difference was in the area of appreciation. Our study showed that while men believe they are appreciating women in the workplace, they are failing to show this appreciation in a way that was meaningful to their female coworkers. The survey responses made it clear that men and women require different kinds of support to feel appreciated at work, and that a significant misunderstanding is taking place.

Men and women require different kinds of support to feel appreciated at work and at home.

This same misunderstanding also happens in the home. Women often feel that their partners don't appreciate them. This confuses their husbands, who love their wives and feel they do appreciate them. Eventually, after years of hearing that she doesn't feel appreciated despite believing he is showing that appreciation, it becomes too hard for him to continue freely extending his heart.

Understanding our different ways of expressing and receiving appreciation was one of the first important gender insights I had over thirty-five years ago. At that time I had a counseling practice and taught weekend relationship seminars. I didn't yet understand gender differences so my seminars focused on healing the past, building self-esteem, overcoming anxiety, and teaching techniques for increasing intimacy.

Helen had been my executive assistant for several years. She came to me one day and said, "John, I think it's time for me to move on. I want to quit."

I was surprised because I thought we had a great relationship and I had recently given her a big raise. I said, "I'm surprised. Why do you want to quit? Are you not getting paid enough?"

She said, "I appreciate the raise. But I just don't feel appreciated."

That really shocked me because I felt so lucky to have her support. I completely appreciated her. Helen handled my calls, appointments, payments, rescheduling, and bookkeeping; printing flyers, setting up my seminars, marketing the seminars, enrolling participants, paying the bills; and the list went on and on. She did everything I needed and there was no drama. Everything went so smoothly.

I asked, "Helen, help me understand why you don't feel appreciated."

Then she said, as if the answer was obvious (and it was, to her), "You have no idea of everything that I do for you."

She was right; I didn't have any idea. But that's why I appreciated her so much. She got things done and I didn't have to get involved. I could just do my job.

What I didn't understand is that just paying her a really good salary and giving her complete freedom to do things her way did not communicate to her that I appreciated her the way that those actions would have to me. I thought she would know that she was appreciated because I never complained or criticized her work. I often told her she did a great job and said "thank you" frequently. She was so good at her job that I rarely had to ask her to do anything. That's because I did appreciate her so much.

From her point of view, however, all that didn't add up to make her feel valued and appreciated.

I then asked, "Would you wait a couple of weeks before you make a final decision and let me try to change things?"

She said, "Okay, but I don't think it will do much good."

Over the next couple of weeks, I made one change that made the difference: I simply asked more questions about what she was doing, and then gave her the space to share her feelings as well. By taking an extra five minutes a day to find out her challenges, frustrations, successes, and failures, I helped her feel seen, heard, and more appreciated.

**By taking an extra five minutes a day
to hear a woman's frustrations,
she will feel seen, heard, and more appreciated.**

Although I appreciated her before, as I began to understand in greater detail all that she did for me, my clients, and my seminars, she then felt seen and confident that I understood all the effort and work she gave to her job. She then began to feel my appreciation. And after the couple of weeks were up, she decided to stay, and continued working for me many more years. By understanding her emotional needs, which were different from mine, I was able to give her the extra support she needed to feel appreciated.

Our Different Needs

Most men have no idea how universal this need to be seen and heard is in women. On Venus, she wants a man to understand the process: her feelings, her challenges, her ups and downs, her setbacks, her victories, and her struggles. This is what makes her feel appreciated. On Mars, he, too, wants to be seen, but less for how he feels than for what he can do. He wants to be appreciated primarily for the results he can produce or the outcomes he has created.

**A woman can feel a man's appreciation
when he clearly understands all that she does.**

Just as she needs to feel appreciated, so does he. But when she does not feel appreciated by her partner, he also ends up feeling unappreciated. When she says that he does not appreciate her, it is impossible for him to feel like she appreciates him. A different approach might be for the woman, rather than communicating that a man doesn't appreciate her, to be more specific instead by saying, "I would like you to know more about what I do. That will make me feel even more appreciated."

So many times in our relationships we think we are giving the love our partner needs, but we are unable to successfully communicate our love and support because we don't understand how we are different. To bridge this gender gap, at work and at home, we need a true revolution that allows men and women to come together with greater freedom to express their authentic selves in a context that understands, appreciates, and supports our differences.

By letting go of old stereotypes, each person is free to access and develop all male and female characteristics that are unique to them. But at the same time, if you are a man, on a biological level you will have certain hormonal requirements that are different than those of a woman.

Likewise, if you are a woman, you have hormonal needs that are dramatically different from a man's. Based on these hormonal differences, men and women experience stress, love, and success in different ways, as if through different filters.

Here are two patterns I see very frequently:

1. A man under stress who expresses his more vulnerable and nurturing female side during the day continues to express his female side at home by talking more to his partner, attempting to feel better through connecting. He thinks this is helping, but as he talks more his female hormones increase and his masculine anti-stress hormones decrease. As a result, his stress levels increase. Over time, he will tend to become more needy, dissatisfied, or demanding.

   Without insight into how his hormones are affecting him, he will not conclude that his inner dissatisfaction comes from being too far on his female side. Instead, he will have a long list of justifiable reasons why his partner is unsupportive of him.

   He will be absolutely certain that he is the more loving partner of the two of them even as he lists all her shortcomings. He thinks he is more loving because he gives more, and wants more in the relationship, but he doesn't see that, by judging her so harshly, he is not being a loving or supportive partner.

2. A woman under stress who expresses her more independent male side during the day continues to express her male side at home by talking less, attempting to feel better through withdrawing. As her testosterone levels increase, she will become overwhelmed with the urge to do more and more, taking on a long list of responsibilities that continue to extend her to-do list rather than taking some time to relax. She becomes absolutely certain that she has to take on more responsibilities and that she doesn't have any time for herself.

   Without insight into how her hormones are affecting her, she will not realize that the major source of her stress is that she is too far on her "Mr. Fix-it" problem-solving male side and has disconnected from her female side that needs to feel heard and nurtured.

   She will think she is being loving by taking on these extra responsibilities, but she is not being loving to herself at all. When we don't love ourselves, others cannot feel loved in our presence. If we are dissatisfied with our own imperfections, then our partners lose trust that they will be loved if they are not perfect.

In both of these patterns, the problem is a failure to recognize the need to return to balance. Here's how understanding their gender-specific needs would have helped the people in these examples return to balance:

1. A woman under stress expresses to her partner her more vulnerable and nurturing female side by talking about her feelings connected to problems at work. She is free to complain about her work but holds back from complaining or

correcting him. He is not required to agree with her nor make any suggestions but just listen and try to understand. If she is heard, her anti-stress hormones are produced and her stress is decreased.

As her stress goes down, her heart opens; she appreciates her partner's support and any feelings of neediness decrease. Her need to complain to him *about* him disappears because her need to complain has been fulfilled by sharing problems that have nothing directly to do with him.

2. A man under stress expresses his independent male side by going to his cave, not talking about his problems but rather putting them aside for the moment. This rebuilds his anti-stress hormone and decreases his stress.

By restoring his depleted testosterone, he gains biological support for increased energy and is then better able to focus and express his interest in his partner. He appreciates her for the space she grants him and becomes interested in spending more time with her. Because she gave him his space without demanding more, he is eager to support her more and responds in a positive way to her requests.

Each of these examples reinforces what is basic common sense: if we have different hormones for lowering stress, then when we are stressed, what is good for one sex is not always good for the other—something we'll look at in more detail in the coming chapters.

11

HIS LOVE NEEDS,
HER LOVE NEEDS

The Beatles ushered in the new age of Soul Mates in the sixties with their big hit "All You Need Is Love." But this universal awakening to the possibilities of love and peace was immediately followed by a reality check. Creating love and peace takes much more than just the intention. Love alone, without insight and new skills, is not enough.

The Rolling Stones ushered in the seventies with their song "You Can't Always Get What You Want." This was then followed by Barbra Streisand and Neil Diamond's big hit going into the eighties, "You Don't Bring Me Flowers," and U2's "I Still Haven't Found What I'm Looking For" as the nineties approached. "Since U Been Gone," the Kelly Clarkson hit, represents relationships in the new millennium.

All of these songs reflect our authentic longing and search for a higher love; they also reveal greater disappointment, pain, and emptiness. With higher expectations we have greater disappointments.

With higher expectations
we have greater disappointments.

Today we are experiencing a spiritual crisis of increasing anxiety, depression, violence, and sickness because we have moved away from being Role Mates without the insights for becoming Soul Mates. With a greater freedom to choose our destiny we are also faced with increased pain. Both men and women have glimpsed a higher love but are unable to sustain this love and find lasting fulfillment. To solve this problem we need to learn a new way to express the love in our hearts and fulfill our new needs.

As I mentioned in the Introduction, women today have a greater need to feel loved and supported on a personal level, and men have a greater need to feel successful. And as we have already seen, with the increased opportunities for women to express their more independent male side, they require a new kind of personal support to return to their female side to find hormonal balance and lower their stress levels.

In other words, although women today no longer need men as much for financial support, they have a greater need for personal support. Through providing this new personal support, a man can experience a new kind of personal success that comes from his ability to apply new relationship skills. In this chapter we will explore in greater depth her new love needs for personal love from her partner and his new love needs to achieve personal success in his relationship.

Women need more personal love;
men need to feel successful in a more personal way.

Through first understanding our new needs for love, and then learning how to fulfill these needs within a Soul Mate relationship, we can begin to access our inner potential to dramatically reduce our inner stress and reclaim the love and happiness in our hearts.

As discussed, this change in our needs is not just psychological; it is reflected on a biological, hormonal level. By using our relationships to balance our male and female sides, we trigger anti-stress hormones. But this works differently for women and men. Let's look first at how it works for women.

Personal Love Lowers a Woman's Stress

Acknowledging that a woman has a male side is different from saying she is a man. Every woman has a male and female side and her own unique balance of male and female qualities, just as every man has a male and female side and his own unique balance of male and female qualities.

Although a woman has both feminine and masculine qualities, she may have to suppress her female qualities to succeed in the working world. This suppression increases her stress. By coming back to her female side and stimulating the production of her female hormones through nurturing personal activities like sharing her feelings or going on a romantic date, she will reduce her stress level.

Yet to do this effectively, a working woman needs a new kind of love when she returns home: personal love. A man's instinctive and automatic expression of his love—being a good provider—is no longer enough. Now she needs small expressions of his personal love similar to the kind of love and support a man automatically gave when he was dating her. This kind of attention, interest, and romantic love helps her return to her female side.

When women didn't work full time outside the home as often, their many responsibilities during the day of being a homemaker, mother, and nurturer supported the expression of their female side. In a traditional Role Mate relationship, a man's efforts to provide financial support and handle any emergencies that came up were enough for her to feel the kinds of love she most needs: his caring, understanding, and respect.

In a traditional Role Mate relationship, a man's efforts to provide financial support and handle any emergencies was enough.

But today a woman requires a different kind of support to feel these aspects of love. He may provide financially, but she, too, has a job. The more financially independent she is, the less his financial support creates the pair bonding she needs to produce estrogen and oxytocin.

In addition, women today do not have the extra time—or, often, the freedom—to support the expression of the many qualities of their female side. In a Soul Mate relationship, a man's deliberate attempts to express more personal love can help her shift from expressing her male side to fully feeling and expressing the different qualities of her female side.

A man's deliberate attempts to express more personal love can help a woman shift to her female side.

This return to her female side makes her feel more feminine and also stimulates her anti-stress hormones. It may take some effort at first if she has conditioned resistance to expressing her female qualities because she considers it a weakness, but eventually it will feel really good.

Women sometimes confuse
their feminine side with weakness.

All of this also applies to stay-at-home mothers. Because the world today is so fast paced and parenting has become so much more challenging, even a woman financially dependent on a man will still require more personal love to lower her stress.

The chart on the following page clarifies the distinction between the traditional material love provided in Role Mate relationships and the more direct personal love that creates a Soul Mate relationship.

- At the top of each section, I've listed the three kinds of love a woman most needs to feel loved and fulfilled: caring, understanding, and respect. These are the same kinds of love she has always needed; this much has not changed.
- The first column lists how a man's love was demonstrated in a traditional Role Mate relationship.
- The second column lists how his love can be demonstrated in a more personal and direct manner to create a Soul Mate relationship.
- The third column lists the many ways his love, both direct and material, supports her in expressing her unique blend of masculine and feminine qualities.

Certainly other kinds of loving support also feel good to a woman, but these three, expressed in a deeply personal manner, have the most power to stimulate her female anti-stress hormones.

For the following chart:

- *Women:* Take a few minutes to underline and reflect on which needs are most important to you. It's okay if they are all important.
- *Men:* Take a few minutes to underline and reflect on what qualities of your partner's female side, in response to your loving support, make you feel most successful in making her happier.

Different Kinds of Love a Woman Needs

His Traditional Material Love	His Direct Personal Love	Her Response to His Love
1. She needs to feel he *cares*.		
He supports her financially.	He provides reassurance.	She feels more trusting and receptive.
He provides physical protection.	He gives romantic attention.	She feels self-assured and relaxed.
He solves problems for her.	He shows interest in her feelings and experiences.	She feels safer being vulnerable, and feels gratitude and appreciation.

He handles emergencies.	He provides affection and hugs.	She feels more warmth, acceptance, and softness.
He is willing to endure hardship to fulfill her needs.	He anticipates her needs and offers to help.	She is more comfortable asking for support and appreciates his efforts.
2. She needs to feel he *understands her*.		
He fulfills his traditional role as provider.	He listens more and does not interrupt with solutions.	She feels safe to express herself.
He makes sacrifices without complaining.	He shows empathy.	She feels supported and is willing to show vulnerability.
He is quick to correct his mistakes.	He apologizes.	She shows forgiveness.
He doesn't ask for help (is self-reliant).	He acknowledges how much she gives.	She admires his abilities.
He holds back his anger.	He compliments her beauty and attractiveness.	She is encouraging and optimistic.

3. She needs to feel his *respect.*		
He commits to staying married.	He considers her needs equal to his own.	She demonstrates her appreciation.
He works hard at his job to make money.	He validates her feelings and contributions.	She shows her approval.
He stays sexually monogamous.	He provides foreplay and plans dates.	She feels sexually responsive.
He wants the best for his wife and family.	He gives her the space to be and express her authentic self.	She feels genuinely happy.
He provides strong leadership.	He compromises.	She feels cooperative and is willing to compromise.

When a modern woman feels her man's personal love, along with his traditional love, she can be much more loving in return. If she is naturally more masculine, she may need or appreciate his traditional material love less, but his more direct personal love can greatly assist her in coming back into balance when she is stressed. For the woman who is naturally more feminine, she will greatly appreciate both his material and direct personal love.

Regardless of whether a woman is more masculine or feminine, when she can feel love, trust, and appreciation in response to a man's personal love, her stress melts away and her heart opens with gratitude and kindness.

Personal Success Lowers a Man's Stress

Just as women have new personal love needs, a modern man has new love needs as well. Traditionally, a man's success at work earned his partner's love. Fulfilling a woman's need for financial support gave his life and hard work meaning—a sense of mission and a higher purpose. When a woman no longer needs or depends on a man's money or success, his life suddenly has less meaning—unless he learns to create a Soul Mate relationship.

In a Soul Mate relationship, a man can fulfill his need for a sense of mission and purpose by providing the personal love that a woman needs in order to cope with stress. Certainly women have a need for a sense of mission and purpose as well, but in a man, it is the fulfillment of this need that produces his anti-stress hormones; the testosterone produced by success helps to lower a man's internal stress but does not help lower a woman's stress.

When a man feels successful, it increases his testosterone, his anti-stress hormone.

The more independent a woman is, the more she needs to receive a man's personal love when she is stressed. Her loving response to his more direct personal love assists her in coming back to her female side. At the same time, it generates a feeling of personal success for him. This new sense of personal success can fulfill a big part of his sense of mission and purpose in life—as long as he understands that he really is making a big difference.

This insight helps to motivate women to make sure he gets this message of appreciation each time he takes a step in giving more personal love. Certainly women also can relate to the need to feel appreciated for what they offer. But a man's need for appreciation to raise his testosterone and lower his stress is greater. When a woman learns to give her partner the appreciation he needs, she will get so much more in return.

A woman's happiness gives a man a greater sense of meaning in his life.

A man's greater need for appreciation to lower his stress can at first seem counterintuitive because women so often feel that their partners don't appreciate them. Almost every woman who is unhappy in her relationship will emphasize this feeling. In most cases it is true that he doesn't appreciate her as much as she would like, but what she actually needs to lower her stress and feel happier in the relationship is more of his respect. She can more easily get the appreciation she needs from her friends or her work. What she needs most from the man in her life is his respect. When he gives her the respect she needs, her female anti-stress hormones (oxytocin, estrogen, and progesterone) are produced.

A man needs appreciation to lower his stress levels.

On the other hand, when a man is disconnected from his heart and becomes angry or mean, he almost always demands more respect, but what he really needs for feeling happier in the relationship is more appreciation for his actions, ideas, sacrifices, and efforts. It is the communication of appreciation that produces the male anti-stress hormone testosterone that can lower his stress.

**When a man demands respect,
what he really needs
is to be appreciated more.**

It's true that everyone needs and loves both appreciation and respect, but what women need most to cope with stress is more respect, and what men need most to cope with stress is more appreciation. In the last three chapters we focused on a woman's hormonal needs because as men learn to respect her needs then in response women can give men the appreciation they need.

When a woman is doing more for a man, she is respecting his needs but not necessarily appreciating him. Quite often a woman will give more but simultaneously resent that she is getting less, in which case she is clearly not appreciating what he does for her. Rather than resent him, he would prefer that she do less and appreciate him more.

When women complain they don't feel appreciated, they are looking for love and support in the wrong direction. When a woman learns to do less for a man but appreciates more what he does for her, not only does he become more caring and supportive, but he can actually appreciate her much more.

**When women complain
that they don't feel appreciated,
they are looking for love in the wrong direction.**

Her heartfelt, loving appreciation is best communicated through messages that she *trusts* he is doing his best, that she *accepts* he is not perfect but is perfect for her, and that she recognizes his successes and *appreciates* his efforts even when he does not always fulfill her highest expectations. This is the particular love that men need most to feel personally successful in their relationship.

Certainly a woman also needs a man's heartfelt trust, acceptance, and appreciation. But a man's appreciation for a woman is like the dessert after the nutritious meal of his caring, understanding, and respect. Eating dessert feels good but it will not nourish the body. On the other hand, her heartfelt and expressed trust, acceptance, and appreciation is, for him, the main meal. Her appreciation makes him feel successful, which is the most important thing a man needs to lower his stress. By contrast, her respect, understanding, and caring is his dessert.

Love Gives New Meaning to a Man's Life

Through experiencing a woman's personal love in response to his personal love, a man can gradually stop comparing his success with that of other men and discover a new sense of satisfaction with himself—a sense of personal success. While he will also want to express more of his potential to make a difference in the world, with his partner's generous love he can be fulfilled in the moment. His personal success in his intimate relationship makes him feel both that he is enough and that he can be better.

A woman's love helps a man to feel fulfilled in the moment even as he also wants to make a bigger difference in the world.

When he experiences the power of his personal success by making such a difference in the life of the person he loves most, he then experiences a greater freedom in other areas of his life apart from any attachment to the results of his actions. He wants to please and serve others in his work, but if they don't appreciate his efforts, it doesn't bother him as much. He feels confident that he is doing his best and that is all he can do. He is not attached to having everything turn out the way he expected. He does his best to fulfill his mission in the world and that is always good enough for him.

In modern relationships, the opportunity to climb higher is greater but the fall is much greater, too. When a man doesn't have concrete proof that he has earned a woman's love by providing some kind of meaningful support in her life, his life has less meaning.

It would be like baking bread every day that nobody eats. Even if you were paid to keep baking bread, if no one eats it, your life loses its meaning. A man's sense of meaning and purpose—his personal success—is fulfilled when he earns the love and appreciation of his partner.

With this new insight a woman can focus her energy and attention more on learning to receive and respond with love to his efforts to support her different needs than on demonstrating how much she *cares* for him, *understands* his feelings, or *respects* his different wishes and wants.

The chart that begins on the following page clarifies the distinction between the indirect love provided by women for men in a traditional Role Mate relationship and the more direct personal love women can express to create a Soul Mate relationship.

- At the top of each section, I've listed the three kinds of love a man needs and has always needed to feel loved and fulfilled: trust, acceptance, and appreciation.
- The first column lists how a woman's love was demonstrated in a traditional Role Mate relationship.
- The second column lists how her love can be demonstrated in a more personal and direct manner to create a Soul Mate relationship.

- The third column lists the many ways her love, both direct and indirect, supports him in expressing his unique blend of masculine and feminine qualities and lowering his stress while leading to the fulfillment of her new needs for personal love.

This new understanding of a man's emotional needs gives a woman greater power to bring out the best in her man and to get more of the support she deserves. Certainly other kinds of loving support also feel good to a man, but these three, expressed in response to his efforts to fulfill her needs, have the most power to lower his stress and increase his energy and motivation to give more.

For the following chart:

- *Men:* Take a few minutes to underline and reflect on which needs are most important to you. It's okay if they are all important.
- *Women:* Take a few minutes to underline and reflect on what qualities of his male side, in response to your loving support, make you feel most loved and supported.

Different Kinds of Love a Man Needs

Her Traditional Love	Her Direct Personal Love	His Response to Her Love
1. A man needs to feel *trusted* that he is doing his best.		
She depends on his financial support and doesn't ask for more.	She depends on his emotional support to lower her stress.	He becomes more caring and reassuring in his support.

She depends on him for protection and is glad to see him return safely from work.	She lets him know what things she would like to do for a romantic date in the future and asks him to decide and provide.	He feels more confident about planning dates because he knows what she wants. He feels more successful because, by picking what they do, he gets to take credit. He plans more dates than he otherwise would.
She looks to him to solve many of her problems.	She shares her feelings of her day to feel more intimate, not for him to solve her problems.	He feels more connected to her and more motivated to make her happy.
She greatly appreciates that he handles emergencies at home.	She warmly receives his hugs and affection as a way of reducing her stress.	He feels greater warmth in his heart and a greater desire to connect.
She is careful to appreciate what he has the energy to do and does not ask for more.	She asks for his help and lets him know what works and does not work for her without complaining.	He feels a greater ease in giving his support, knowing that little things make a big difference.

2. A man needs to feel *accepted* the way he is.		
She does not complain about his limitations.	She makes requests rather than complaining and asks for more in small increments.	He is more willing to provide support by listening and trying to understand her feelings.
She does not express disapproval of his mistakes.	She expresses her feelings but never to shame or punish.	He feels like he is good enough for her and then wants to be better.
She does not correct his behavior.	She forgives his mistakes and doesn't demand apologies.	He wants to make her happy and feels regret for his mistakes.
She does not make demands for more time and attention.	She appreciates his efforts to give her what she asks for.	He can access a deeper love and attachment for her. He is motivated to give more.
She does not burden him with her problems.	She asks for his help and appreciates what he is able to contribute.	He is more flexible about helping her.

3. A man needs to feel *appreciation* for the difference he makes.		
She is not bothered by his small mistakes or lack of manners.	She is happy, delighted, and fulfilled in their relationship.	He has greater respect for her wishes and is more open to make changes for her.
She works hard to make a beautiful home and happy family.	She works hard to communicate her needs in a way that supports him as well.	He is able to validate her feelings and needs and wants to support her.
She never says no to his sexual advances.	She says yes to sex because she enjoys it as well.	He feels like Superman and loves himself and her more.
She tries to be a good and loving wife for her husband and a good mother for her children.	She is grateful for his support as she discovers and expresses her authentic self.	His life has more meaning and purpose, which makes him happy.
She follows her husband's lead and appreciates his guidance.	She shares with her husband in cocreating their relationship.	He is more cooperative and flexible when making decisions together.

When a man feels a woman's direct personal love, along with her traditional love, in response to his actions, he becomes even more loving. If she is more financially independent or naturally more masculine, her direct personal love becomes even more important, because she has less of an opportunity to express traditional love. If she is more dependent on him financially or has more female qualities, he will greatly appreciate both her traditional and direct personal love.

Regardless of whether a man has more male or female qualities, when he becomes more caring, understanding, and respectful in response to her appreciation, acceptance, and trust, his stress melts away and he feels a surge of energy, confidence, and motivation to be the best he can be.

The Purpose of Life on Mars and Venus

The purpose of life on Mars is to make a difference and the purpose of life on Venus is to be happy.

A man is always happiest when his partner is happy. Her happiness is the symbol that he has made a difference in her life—that he is needed by her and that he is successful in caring for and respecting her needs, desires, and wishes. Certainly he is happy with his own success, but that success is only meaningful if it is in service of others that he deeply loves.

There is an old story that illustrates this idea beautifully:

A long time ago, a man was making bricks from mud. He looked rather bored, lifeless, and tired. He was asked, "What are you doing?"

He said, "I am making bricks from mud."

Another man was doing the same thing but he looked much more energetic. He was asked, "What are you doing?"

He said, "I am making the best bricks from mud."

Another man was doing the same thing but he looked even more energetic and was excited. He was asked, "What are you doing?"

He said, "I am making the best bricks from mud to earn more money to get married one day."

Another man was doing the same thing but he looked even more energetic and excited, with a smile that radiated happiness and fulfillment. He was asked, "What are you doing?"

He said, "I am supporting the happiness of my wife and family by earning more money by making the best bricks from mud."

This story illustrates how the context in which we do things makes all the difference in how we feel. The context gives our actions meaning. A man's greatest happiness and fulfillment comes when his life has great meaning.

In a similar way, a woman's greatest happiness comes when she is freely giving love and support from a place of gratitude and appreciation for all the support she has in her life. A life of meaning and purpose is dessert for women but the main meal for men. A life of love and happiness is dessert for men but the main meal for women.

As a man learns to successfully respect a woman's new, more personal needs, as listed in the chart on page 274, then he will be happier, because his partner will be happier. And as a woman learns to appreciate her partner more, she will also be happier.

When a woman is giving her support from a place of appreciation, she is fully on her female side, generating stress-reducing oxytocin and estrogen. Once she is stress-free, she can then freely give of herself without feeling resentful.

A life of meaning and purpose is the dessert for women but the main meal for men.

A woman is happiest when she can give her love freely without feeling like she is giving more and getting less. If she is getting less, then she needs to give a little less to her partner and give more to herself through increasing her Me Time. By respecting her own needs through taking more time for social bonding and self-nurturing, she will begin to appreciate her partner more.

A woman is happiest when she can give her love freely without feeling like she is giving more and getting less.

Most couples today get stuck in a chicken-and-egg scenario. She gives more and he gives less. She resents him and he gives even less. In this example, does his lack of support cause her resentment, or does her resentment cause him to give less? Both are true.

To break free from this self-defeating cycle, if a woman wants to be happy and get more from her partner, then when she begins to feel resentful, rather than continuing to feel stressed and unloving, she can apply the new Soul Mate hormonal insights.

Rather than justifying her resentment and her inability to appreciate her partner by focusing on what she is not getting, she should focus on doing things to come back to her female side. She can do this by creating pair bonding in a way that is not dependent on her partner, and then take more Me Time to increase her progesterone.

**Rather than justifying not appreciating her partner
by focusing on what she is not getting,
a woman should come back to her female side.**

She doesn't need him to create the progesterone she needs to lower her stress if she is in the third phase of her cycle, which is two-thirds of her month. And if she is in the second phase of her cycle, even if she can't get the oxytocin and estrogen she needs from pair bonding with her partner, she can get it elsewhere. As we discussed in chapter nine, there are many ways she can pair-bond with others without always depending on her partner. If she is in the first phase of her cycle, then she can get the support she needs from her work.

By taking time for pair bonding to create oxytocin and estrogen, or through taking Me Time to create progesterone without waiting for her partner to give more, her stress will go down. By returning to her female side, she is able to let go of her resentment, open her heart, and freely give her love and appreciation—the fuel her partner needs to be more attentive, supportive, and appreciative of her.

Respect Versus Appreciation

Men strengthen their male side by caring for and respecting the needs of others. The feedback of appreciation he receives from making a difference increases his testosterone. As discussed, when men take action to make a difference, it increases their testosterone but also uses it up. When he gets feedback that his job is done and he has succeeded, then when he goes to his cave to relax, he can more efficiently rebuild his testosterone. But if he doesn't feel successful, just taking time to relax won't fully rebuild his testosterone. When men don't feel appreciated, their testosterone levels begin to drop.

When men don't feel appreciated, their testosterone levels begin to drop.

The most important lesson men in boot camp are taught to help them find their masculine strength, courage, and power is to respect others. They may hate their drill sergeant, but they learn to respect his orders. They salute the rank, not the man. In many cases, as part of this lesson, a man will have to stand at attention, be criticized by his leader, and respond without any attitude of complaint, just saying, "Yes, sir."

It is not necessary to go to such extremes to learn respect, however. Just apply the new ideas in this book.

In a Soul Mate relationship, when a man's partner needs to talk, he can strengthen his muscle of respect by being fully present and listening without any attitude of complaint. When he feels the urge to interrupt, he doesn't. Instead he says, "Tell me more," "What else?" and/or "Help me understand that better."

Respecting others increases a man's inner power. A woman's appreciation of a man allows him to respect her more.

Respecting others increases a man's inner power.

For a woman to awaken a man's heart so that he can respect her more, she needs to focus on her ability to receive his love by letting go of resentment. Once women are caught in the trap of resentment, it is hard to get out, unless she recognizes that she is giving too much and expecting too much in return. Instead of expecting more from him, she needs to give less and expect more from herself in terms of Me Time.

**Feeling resentment is
a signal to take more Me Time.**

When you appreciate someone, you are acknowledging their success in fulfilling your needs or the needs of someone you care about. When both men and women are successful at doing something, it increases testosterone. But when women are too far on their male side, the last thing they need is more testosterone. This doesn't mean she doesn't need to feel appreciated: we all do. But appreciation is not the loving message that will help her find hormonal balance.

**When you appreciate someone,
you are acknowledging their success
in fulfilling your needs.**

All of the different kinds of love and attention listed in the chart on page 274 are the most potent for helping a woman return to her female side. Instead of needing a man to appreciate what she has done for him, what a woman needs much more from a man are specific actions, reactions, and verbal expressions that communicate his caring, understanding, and respect.

It should be crystal clear that if a man wants a woman to be happier, just sitting back and thanking her for all that she does for him is not going to work. Instead, she needs him to respect and honor her needs by providing her with the different kinds of personal support that increase her estrogen and oxytocin.

With this new insight into our hormonal differences, it is clear that for women to lower a man's stress and open his heart, he needs her patient and loving acceptance to validate his efforts. In the same way, to lower her stress and open her heart, a woman needs a man's patient and loving understanding to validate her feelings. With her acceptance, he gets to feel he is good enough for her, and with his understanding, she gets to feel worthy of his love.

Giving and Receiving Love

When we give the love our partner really needs, we will get the love we really need in return. A woman has the power to increase her partner's ability to care about her, understand her feelings, and respect her needs by giving him the kind of love he needs most.

Appreciation, along with loving acceptance and trust, are the biggest testosterone producers in men. When a woman responds to her partner's actions with more trust, acceptance, and appreciation, she will receive more caring, understanding, and respect.

Loving acceptance means greater acceptance of his imperfections. When a woman is complaining, rejecting, nagging, criticizing, or disapproving, it is much harder for a man to feel her acceptance of him.

Trust does not mean believing that he is perfect or that he is always right, but rather it is about trusting that he has positive intentions. He needs to get the message from her, again and again, that when he shows up, his best is good enough for her.

When women feel they are giving more, often what they are giving is the kind of nurturing support a *woman* wants and needs—caring, understanding, and respect—and not the aspects of love just described that can increase a man's energy and motivation to give more personal love. When she is busy demonstrating her caring, understanding, and respect, she just increases his estrogen and oxytocin, and not his testosterone.

**If you want your man to give you more,
then give him more
trust, acceptance, and appreciation.**

In doing so, she shows *respect* by doing more things for him but does not *appreciate* what he does for her; she *cares* more about him but does not *trust* that he is doing his best or that he loves her; and she makes excuses for him by *understanding* his limitations, but she still corrects him or gives advice rather than *accepting* him just the way he is.

Certainly she also wants to be accepted just the way she is, but to support a man, he needs her loving acceptance even more. While she needs more understanding, he needs to feel her acceptance. When she focuses primarily on *understanding* her partner, she stimulates oxytocin and estrogen in him, but when she focuses on *accepting* him, it increases his testosterone.

Men particularly need more acceptance when they are stressed because acceptance stimulates more testosterone in him and lowers his stress. Likewise, women need more understanding when they are stressed because understanding stimulates more oxytocin and estrogen in her and lowers her stress.

Acceptance means not correcting or trying to improve someone. It is not trying to change your partner. Acceptance to a man may sound like this: "It is no big deal; next time, would you give me a call when you are late?"

**Acceptance may sound sometimes like this:
"It is no big deal; next time,
would you give me a call when you are late?"**

Nonacceptance but understanding may sound like this: "I know you tend to forget the time, *but* it is very upsetting to me when you don't call." The clear message in this case is that, though his forgetfulness is understood, he is being rejected for it.

A rhetorical question that communicates nonacceptance while implying that she is trying to understand is even worse. That would sound like this: "I can't believe you did that. Why can't you remember?" From his perspective he has just been punched in the stomach; the implied message is that he is not good enough.

Acceptance doesn't mean that a woman can't ask for more support or that she should be a doormat. Certainly she can ask for what she wants. But her requests work best when they are not backed by complaints or a list of unhappy feelings. (We will learn more about how to create a complaint-free marriage in chapter thirteen.)

Her caring, understanding, and respect may feel good to him, particularly if he has a stronger female side, but it actually lowers his testosterone. Lower testosterone can make him sleepy or passive.

A woman often demonstrates her caring in two different ways that dramatically lower a man's testosterone. The first way is by giving unsolicited advice. If he is not asking for advice then her attempts to give advice imply his way is not good enough.

The second way is by worrying so much about him that she becomes stressed. This will not only lower his testosterone but also increase his estrogen, leading him to become stressed, defensive, or angry.

Both unsolicited advice and excessive worry imply that she doesn't trust him, and because trust is his primary need, her "caring" makes his testosterone levels drop further.

**Her caring, understanding, and respect
increases his oxytocin and estrogen
and not his testosterone.**

Without this new information, trying to connect with the opposite sex can feel like an impossible task. But by remembering that men are still from Mars and women are still from Venus because our hormonal needs are very different, men can develop the ability to support a woman's new and different personal love needs and women can learn to support a man's new and different love needs for personal success. With this new information for creating a Soul Mate relationship, men and women, although very different, can fit together perfectly.

12

MARS AND VENUS COME TOGETHER

W ithout a positive way to understand our differences, when men and women try to connect we can collide instead of coming together in harmony. To avoid this common outcome we must be vigilant in remembering men and women are not the same and that this is a good thing. Respecting and appreciating our differences can actually bring us closer together.

With greater acceptance of our differences, men and women can come together in harmony.

Couples often collide rather than come together because what is good for men is not always good for women and vice versa. For instance, if a man has had a hard day but his wife happens to be very happy from her day, her happiness can easily cheer him up and make him happier. Whenever she is happy, he feels appreciated because he tends to automatically take credit for her happiness. On the other hand, if a woman has had a really hard day but her husband comes home talking about how happy he is, his exuberance can make her feel worse.

In this example, what is good for him—her happiness and appreciation—is not necessarily as supportive to her. To make this distinction even clearer, imagine the following scenario, which is a composite of several couples that I have counseled. It makes this point very clearly:

> *Bill works sixty hours a week while his wife stays home to care for their two children. When Bill comes home one day after a particularly stressful week at work, his wife June says, "After taking the kids to school today I went out to lunch with my friend Susan. We had all organic food and talked for hours. I am so lucky to be married to you. I have such a flexible schedule and can afford good food and time to spend with friends. I then went shopping and got two pairs of shoes and two new dresses. I didn't have time to make dinner, so would you take us out to dinner tonight?"*

She says all of this with a tone of voice that says, *I know how hard you work so that I can live the sort of life I've always hoped for. I am so happy. Thank you.* When expressing appreciation to a man, a woman's tone of voice is 90 percent of the message! Tone of voice reveals one's real feelings. She can say all the right words, but if she secretly feels resentful, that resentment will come through, and he will not feel appreciated.

When expressing appreciation to a man, a woman's tone of voice is 90% of the message!

In this situation, because she really does appreciate Bill, it will satisfy one of his requirements for feeling loved: appreciation. Her happiness gives meaning to his hard work and helps melt away his stress. The qualities of his male side like independence, toughness, detachment, competence, sacrifice, delayed gratification, and power are being acknowledged and appreciated; as a result, he feels successful and his testosterone levels will rise. He is needed and he has fulfilled his mission and purpose. Now let's turn this situation around and imagine an opposite scenario:

> *June works sixty hours a week while her husband stays home to care for their two children. One day when June comes home, Bill says, "After taking the kids to school today I went with Jim and played eighteen holes of golf. I beat him for the third time. I have such a great life. Today I bought the new Warcraft video game. Can't wait to play it tomorrow after I play tennis with Tom. I am so lucky to be married to you. I didn't have time to make dinner, so would you take us out to dinner tonight? I know how hard you work. Your support makes me so happy. Thank you."*

Most of the time, a woman in this situation, particularly if she had a challenging and stressful day, will not feel any better just because he is appreciating her hard work. Her stress does not melt away due to his happiness. In many cases, the opposite will occur. Rather than be happy that she is providing him with the opportunity to be so happy, she will resent that she is stressed at work while he is home playing golf, tennis, or video games.

If you are a woman putting yourself in June's position, your blood is probably already boiling. This scenario is a great example of how appreciation alone is not what a woman needs. Certainly she needs and enjoys his appreciation, but it does not stimulate her female hormones to lower her stress.

As mentioned in the previous chapter, in relationships we often give what we would want most from our partners, which is not always what our partners want or need most, and vice versa, particularly in male and female intimate relationships. Without clear insight into our different primary emotional needs, we miss opportunities to be more loving and supportive of each other.

But when we do understand our different primary emotional needs, we can focus our support in ways that have the most positive impact on our partners. Although the support men most need from women includes appreciation, acceptance, and trust, they are not the biggest love priorities for women.

How to Validate a Woman's Feelings and Appreciate a Man

Appreciating someone helps them to feel successful; this supports the hormones of their male side. The major source of stress for a woman today is that she is too far on her male "doing" side and she needs to come back to her female "feeling" side. Certainly a man's appreciation for what she does will feel good, but it doesn't lower her stress, and if she has already had a very challenging day it may make it worse.

At work, when June is on her male side, she does need more appreciation, but at home she needs more support for her female side. As long as she focuses on longing for his appreciation, she is missing the opportunity to get the caring, understanding, and respect she needs to come back to her female side.

In the scenario above, if feeling appreciation for June's hard work is not the answer, what is? What can Bill say to support his wife and stimulate the estrogen and oxytocin that will help her to cope with stress when she gets home?

Instead of saying some magic words of appreciation, he can make the biggest difference by hearing her, validating her stressful feelings, giving her a hug, or doing something to help her.

**A man can make the biggest difference
in a woman's stress
by hearing her and validating her stressful feelings.**

When a man provides the support listed in the chart of women's primary needs in the last chapter, he will help her lower her stress and simultaneously fulfill her most important needs. It is a win-win situation: she feels his respect, caring, and understanding, and in return he gets to feel successful at providing the support she needs most.

**When a woman is happy and fulfilled,
a man takes it personally and feels appreciated.**

When a woman is stressed, one of the first things she will feel is unappreciated. Because she is out of balance, she is looking in the wrong direction for support. When she thinks she needs more of his appreciation, what she really needs is more of his caring, understanding, and respect.

This is why when a woman is stressed and asks a man to appreciate her, it will have little impact. In her mind, although she has asked for his appreciation, she will then feel words are cheap. What she wants is action.

**When a woman is stressed,
one of the first things she will feel
is unappreciated.**

She may not recognize it but on a biological level to lower her stress levels she needs more estrogen and not testosterone. To balance her hormones, she needs to talk about her day and feel his empathy. She needs to ask for his help so that she has less to do. And most important, she needs to discuss specific romantic date activities she would like him to provide for her. When she feels he is attending to her emotional needs, then she will feel the caring, understanding, and respect she requires, and also begin to feel greater appreciation for him.

The Power of Validation

When a woman feels stressed, although she may ask for a man's appreciation, the last thing she really needs is him expressing profuse verbal appreciation. Thanking her for her hard work is not what she needs to hear. Telling her how great his life is because of her and how happy he is may actually make her feel worse. She also doesn't need his advice on how she could look at the situation in a different way. No advice is needed; instead, she needs him to listen more and then validate her feelings.

Instead, few words are needed to validate her feelings. What she needs is body language that says he is interested and that he cares. After patiently listening to her complain about the stresses of her day (but not about him), instead of giving advice or sharing the stresses of his own day, he can respond with a brief validating phrase and then give her a hug.

Few words are needed to validate her feelings.

Below are some validating comments for men to offer women. They are short and simple; they validate her stress as well as demonstrate his caring empathy. Validating her feelings is the opposite of trying to cheer her up or explain why she should see the silver lining when she has problems or challenges. These statements acknowledge her male side by mentioning what she does for others or the sacrifices she makes while also supporting her female side by expressing caring. They acknowledge that he has heard her without judgment and with empathy.

After each statement, I have included the phrase, "Let me give you a hug." It may sound repetitive or artificial when listed out in this fashion, but offering the hug is important. After listening for a few minutes, the surge of oxytocin from a hug helps her and him to feel complete. It is like the period at the end of the sentence.

At times of stress, a woman does not get tired of hugs or a man offering to give her a hug, just as a man never tires of hearing validating comments like, "Good idea," "That makes sense," or "You are right!"

Occasionally, while giving the hug, he can also whisper in her ear, "I love you so much."

- "You do so much for so many people . . . Let me give you a hug."
- "There is always so much to do . . . Let me give you a hug."
- "No good deed goes unpunished . . . Let me give you a hug."
- "With all that you do for them, they are not giving you the support you deserve . . . Let me give you a hug."

- "You give so much and they don't acknowledge all that you do . . . Let me give you a hug."
- "You shouldn't have to do it all, you give so much . . . Let me give you a hug."
- "You are so responsible. They are lucky to have your support . . . Let me give you a hug."
- "You are so good at what you do . . . Let me give you a hug."
- "You are so patient with them . . . Let me give you a hug."

By not giving suggestions or solutions but a hug instead, he is supporting her female side. As a result of successfully supporting her female side, his testosterone goes up because feeling successful in supporting her also gives him the support he needs.

When she is stressed, the last thing he should do is talk about how happy he is or try to talk her into feeling happy. A man's happiness makes a woman happy only if she already feels happy. If a woman is stressed, she doesn't want or need to hear about how wonderful a man's life is. When a woman is unhappy, for a man to talk about how happy he is, it is like rubbing salt into a wound.

**When a woman is unhappy,
for a man to talk about how happy he is,
it is like rubbing salt into a wound.**

The opposite is true for a man. If a man is stressed and his wife is happy and fulfilled, if she takes the time to express how wonderful her life is, it will make him feel appreciated and actually lower his stress. A woman's happiness makes a man happy. Without this insight, some women hold back from either taking time to enjoy their life or expressing their happiness and joy so that they don't make him feel worse. She does not know that her joy and happiness will always make him feel better. Whenever she is able to authentically express her happiness, her female hormones increase and her stress levels go down.

The Power of Appreciation

When I return home from work trips, my wife greets me with a smile and a hug. She will first ask me how my trip was. After a few brief minutes, she will then, also briefly, tell me various good things that happened in her life while I was gone. She feels free to express her positive feelings because she knows that it will make me feel better and not worse.

She also knows that a little later it is fine for her to talk about her stress in a Venus Talk as well, but only after she's made it clear to me through her tone of voice when I first arrive home that she is a happy woman. Her happiness dramatically lowers my stress and makes coming home a joy for me.

A woman's happiness dramatically lowers a man's stress and makes coming home a joy.

Knowing that she is giving me the support I need, and that in exchange she will eventually get more support from me, is the perfect pair-bonding experience to stimulate Bonnie's oxytocin and lower her stress—as long as she feels confident that she will get that extra attention from me at a later time.

Bonnie knows that when I feel appreciated, it supports me in being more attentive and interested in her, and that if she needs to talk about problems at a later time, I will be able to hear her negative feelings and challenges fully and with more empathy and caring.

Just the act of choosing the best time to express her positive feelings, or when to share her negative feelings to ensure she will be fully heard, dramatically increases her oxytocin and estrogen. Her anticipating that she will be heard after I have taken some cave time stimulates her anti-stress hormones.

**Just choosing the best time
to express her positive or negative feelings
increases a woman's oxytocin and lowers her stress.**

A woman choosing when and how to share her authentic positive or negative feelings is very different from her suppressing her feelings, positive or negative, because her partner is not interested in what she has to say.

In this example, my wife is choosing the right time to share her feelings so that she can support me while also receiving the attention, interest, and support she needs in return. By sharing her positive feelings she is able to freely express her loving, vulnerable, and receptive female side; later, when I am out of my cave, she can share her other feelings of frustration, disappointment, and concern in a Venus Talk if she feels the need. Or she may ask for my support in some other way so that she can take her Me Time.

Women often assume that "sharing her vulnerability" means only sharing her feelings of hurt, unhappiness, or fear. But negative emotions are only one expression of vulnerability. When a woman shares her happy, excited, and appreciative feelings, she is also expressing her vulnerability, and men love it.

Vulnerability means that she is sharing the part of her that can be affected by others because she needs their support. When she gets what she needs, she is happy, and when she doesn't get what she needs, she is not.

**By sharing her positive feelings,
a woman is able to freely express
her loving, vulnerable, and receptive female side,
and men love it.**

In the most basic terms, by expressing her appreciation she gets to feel my immediate caring, understanding, and respect. Then, when I am more relaxed, she can share about the stresses in her life. As she appreciates my listening, I am able to respect her need to share her feelings even more.

Without an understanding of how men are different, women do not access the full female power of their appreciation to pull forth the best from their partner.

**Without an understanding of how men are different,
women do not access their full female power
to pull forth the best from their partner.**

Women often share their complaints or the details of things that are going wrong in their lives with each other as a way of connecting and feeling good. Sharing complaints so that they can connect allows them both to express their nurturing female sides.

For example, Carol shares how busy and overwhelmed she is and Jane eagerly says, "I know; me, too!" Jane then has the opportunity to talk about her life as well, which stimulates more feel-good hormones.

If a woman shares her positive feelings of happiness and appreciation and her female friend is not in such a positive place, then it can make her friend feel worse. But when she shares her positive feelings of happiness and delight with a man, it actually increases his interest in her. This greater interest she receives increases her female hormones just as sharing her negative feelings with a woman does.

A man is most attracted to a woman who is happy, but to fully activate his automatic desire and motivation to please her, he also needs to feel she needs his help. He can only earn her appreciation and be her hero if she needs him. A man is most motivated to support or please a woman when he feels not only appreciated but also needed.

**For a man to be motivated,
he needs to feel appreciated but also needed.**

Her happiness increases his testosterone so that when she needs his help or support, he has the added motivation and energy to do more for her. This increase in testosterone activates his romantic feelings, as well.

The power of appreciation can be confusing because appreciating a man on its own doesn't motivate him to do more for a woman. Instead, it creates the conditions in him so that, when she needs him, he is automatically and hormonally more energized to fulfill her needs and requests.

Think of her appreciation for him as putting money in his bank account. The money sitting in the account does nothing for her directly, but when she has a need and he has plenty of money in his account, then he is able to spend his money for her benefit. If he has no money in his account, then even if he wants to help her, he has little to give.

When a woman greets a man with a happy smile at the end of his day, if his testosterone is low it can free him to feel his need to relax and take cave time, rather than feeling pressured to help her despite really needing cave time. Because he feels her appreciation, he is able to more efficiently rebuild his testosterone. Then, when he feels needed by her in some way, he will have the energy and motivation he needs to be her hero, whether she needs more We Time or support to take more Me Time.

Any time a woman has something positive to share, she should know that, by doing so, she is giving her partner a gift so that he will have more to give her when she needs his support.

Awakening the Alpha Male

The primitive part of our brains is actually the same as a monkey's. Researchers often call the limbic system of the brain the "monkey brain." Of course humans are very different from monkeys, but certain instincts are similar.

In a monkey tribe, the strongest male and leader of the tribe is the Alpha male. The female members are most attracted to him and mate primarily with him. Hormone tests reveal he has twice as much testosterone as the other male monkeys. He is the Alpha and the rest of the males are Beta. When the Alpha monkey dies and he is replaced by one of the Beta monkeys, that Beta monkey's testosterone levels double in one day.

This phenomenon reveals how a man's position or status affects his hormone levels. If he becomes the CEO or president of his company or a successful entrepreneur who answers primarily to himself, this role automatically increases his testosterone levels. If he answers to others or is dependent on the approval of others, his estrogen is higher and his testosterone is lower. A man's independence and success in the workplace dramatically increases his testosterone; likewise, his failures lower his testosterone.

Deep inside the brain, a man's instinct is to be the Alpha male of his tribe, if he can. With higher testosterone, he will not only attract more women, but also be healthier and live longer. (This is often why young men want to become rich rock stars or super famous in sports or the movies. They want the money but also the attention of girls.)

But because we are no longer living in small tribes, there will always be someone in the world who is bigger, richer, younger, more competent, or more successful. Even if a man is the leader of his company or earns a million dollars a year, the growing number of global billionaires will dwarf his success. Every list of *Forbes*'s most successful or richest people in the world is a blow to his efforts to be the Alpha male and can keep his testosterone down.

In the modern world of men, there will always be someone who is bigger, richer, younger, more competent, or more successful.

The good news is that men are not monkeys. A man's status is not limited to his dominance over other males. Instead, he has Alpha male status whenever he comes home to a woman who loves and appreciates him. A woman's love, in the form of her trust, acceptance, and appreciation, powerfully boosts a man's testosterone levels by awakening the Alpha male in him.

When a man feels a woman's love and admiration, it awakens the Alpha male in him.

Though this support is most powerful when it comes from his partner, it can come from his work as well. I was on a long flight to Japan to teach a seminar while I was working on this book. The whole flight, including runway delays, was fourteen hours straight. While I was busy writing, others were sleeping. After about twelve hours, a flight attendant—a woman—stood by me and said with a tone of amazement and appreciation for my dedication as a writer, "You have been working this whole flight without stopping . . . wonderful!"

It made my day! Her acknowledgment of my endurance felt so good, I had to keep writing for the last two hours.

Any time a woman appreciates a man's efforts of hard work, he will feel good because it produces a surge of testosterone in him. This is true even if she is not his partner (although his partner's appreciation is more effective). When his partner truly appreciates and delights in a man's competence, strength, or endurance, it makes a much bigger difference because she also knows and accepts all his failures and mistakes. Her appreciation in that moment erases the shortcomings in his past, and then they can both be in the moment, loving and appreciating each other.

Any time a woman appreciates a man's hard work, it will feel good and lower his stress because it produces a surge of testosterone in him.

As I've mentioned, when a woman appreciates a man—because that is what he needs most from her—he can fully appreciate her in return. Doing more for a man is not what he appreciates the most; it is her appreciation of him that he can appreciate the most.

On that flight to Japan, if I had been a woman, the best thing the flight attendant could have said would be something like, "You have been working the whole flight; you must be so tired. Can I bring you something? A glass of water, a snack, or a pillow to rest?"

But I am not a woman, so if she had said that to me I would have felt a little annoyed, though appreciative of her offering, and then felt like going to sleep. Instead I got to feel like Superman, the Alpha male, a hero!

If a woman reading this feels more like I did and wants to be acknowledged for being the Alpha woman, but would be annoyed if the flight attendant had also offered a little empathy and support, then it is a sign that she needs to work a little harder to find and support her female side, particularly if she is stressed in her life or not getting what she needs to be happy with a man.

If a woman wants to be acknowledged for being the Alpha woman, it may be a sign she needs to find and support her female side.

Love Languages on Mars and Venus

In the example at the beginning of this chapter, when June doesn't feel appreciated, Bill needs to translate "I don't feel appreciated" into Martian language. Although it sounds to him like she needs him to say, "Thank you for all that you do," it really means "I need you to do more for me. I need your caring, empathy, understanding, and an offering of help, and then I will be able to feel your love and appreciation."

In this case, the most powerful way for Bill to lower June's stress is not by merely expressing his appreciation for her but by doing things for her that support her need to feel seen, heard, cared for, and touched.

In practical terms, Bill would do this by listening more to June's feelings about her day, doing things that make her feel that he is contributing to her happiness, and giving her his attention and interest rather than just enjoying and appreciating her nurturing support. When she feels stressed and unappreciated, what she really needs is to experience that her partner respects and honors her needs—that she is a priority and that he cares about her.

In the chart of women's primary needs in the last chapter, we saw that it is mainly expressions of respect, caring, and understanding that stimulate a woman's anti-stress hormones, not merely expressions of appreciation. Her male side needs the appreciation, but when she is stressed, her greatest need is to come back to her female side.

When a man is stressed, his greatest needs, as shown in the second chart in chapter eleven, are to feel trusted that he is doing his best, accepted just the way he is, and appreciated for his efforts to fulfill her personal and material needs. When she responds with appreciation for his efforts, acceptance of his mistakes, and trust that he is doing his best, this personal, loving response is, to men, like gold.

**When a woman responds with appreciation
for his efforts, acceptance of his mistakes,
and trust that he is doing his best,
this loving response is, to men, like gold.**

While a woman needs a man's caring, understanding, and respect to lower her stress, in response a man needs her trust, acceptance, and appreciation to lower his stress. These are the different love languages of men and women.

Focusing on his successes and not his failures is much easier for a woman once she realizes that it is not automatic for a man to provide the personal love that supports a woman's new emotional needs. For centuries men have shown their love by providing financial support. Now, suddenly, that is not needed as much. Just because he loves her, it doesn't mean he knows how to express that love in a language that makes her feel cared for, understood, and respected.

To her that shift may seem obvious because she can feel her new needs, but to him it is all new and different. A man's new challenge in marriage is that, in addition to providing traditional support from having a job to make money, he also needs to provide a new kind of emotional support.

This more personal expression of love is still very new to him. He is learning a whole new language. In some ways, it goes against everything he has learned about being a man. When a woman understands that this is not so easy for him, but that he is still willing to try, it can increase her appreciation of his efforts.

Focusing on his successes and not his failures is much easier when women understand giving personal love is a whole new role for men.

Why Couples Break Up

Without these new insights that reveal our different emotional needs, it is inevitable that the passion in a relationship will dissipate.

So many people, when asked if they are happy in their relationship, will say they are, because they are giving the kind of support that they need while assuming that one day, they will get the same support back. But when men and women keep giving what they need and not what their partners need the most, then eventually, instead of coming together, they collide.

In some cases, it happens abruptly, as if without any warning: that happy couple you know suddenly announces they are getting a divorce. They go from madly loving each other to hating each other. Or they are happy with each other but still decide to get a divorce while remaining friends. In both cases, the reason they previously believed they were happy in their marriage was that they were ignoring their different primary needs. At a certain point, those needs could no longer be ignored.

Certainly, ending a relationship as friends is a good thing. But when this happens, they should not pretend that they were *really* happy together. This kind of denial sets the groundwork for them to fail in their next relationships.

If men and women are to be happy together, they must clearly take responsibility to first be happy on their own. Then they must apply the new insights in this book for giving their partner the love they need. Without these new insights, both men and women will continue to give the sort of love they themselves need rather than focus their efforts on giving the love their partner needs most, and this misunderstanding can eventually end their relationship.

In the next chapter, we will put together all the new insights in *Beyond Mars and Venus* to give you the practical skills you need to create a lifetime of love.

13

THE COMPLAINT-FREE RELATIONSHIP

All the new insights into our new needs have been leading up to one thing: how to have a complaint-free relationship. For many men and women, the thought of never having to hear another complaint sounds like heaven. In a complaint-free relationship, love is sure to grow. But complaints are a part of life; life is not perfect, and quite often it is really hard. To not complain is to hide a part of our authentic self.

Sharing complaints is actually not the real problem; it is sharing your complaints about your partner with your partner! A complaint-free relationship does not mean you can never complain; it means you don't complain about your partner to your partner. You can still complain about other things.

**The problem with complaining
is sharing your complaints about your partner
with your partner!**

Men and women are sensitive to complaints in different ways. When a man complains to a woman, it often makes the woman more overwhelmed. She will tend to give more in answer to his complaints, but will feel overwhelmed and resentful as a result. When a woman complains to a man, it makes the man feel controlled. In response, he will eventually stop caring about making her happy and give less.

Complaints are a necessary part of life, but we need to upgrade our skills in communicating them so that our partners can hear us in a way that makes them feel supported rather than unappreciated, rejected, criticized, or controlled. Learning to talk so that our partners can hear us is the most important skill in a relationship.

Why Complaining Doesn't Work

What men and women think they are saying when they complain is often not what their partner hears. For example, when a man complains to his partner, "You are not home enough," what a woman hears is that she is not being a "nurturing," "cooperative," or "loving" partner. Her reaction is to feel that he doesn't understand all that she tries to do. What she hears is she has to do more to make him happy.

She is also turned off because she feels he is being needy, and to be nurturing, cooperative, and loving she has to give more. In most cases she feels that she is already giving as much as she can, so to give more makes her feel overwhelmed.

My wife Bonnie, like most women in these high-stress times, has a tendency to feel overwhelmed. To support her, I have basically given up verbalizing any complaints or blame. If I don't like something, I wait until I am not feeling annoyed or upset and briefly make a request letting her know what I would like from her in the fewest number of words I can.

**A woman is turned off by a man when he complains,
because she feels he is being needy
and she then feels pressured to give more.**

If my complaint is, "You are too busy, you don't spend enough time at home," I convert it to a request and instead say, "Let's plan to spend more time together. Let me know when you can go over our calendars."

If I sense that she may become defensive in response to my request, I soften it with an FYI: a "For Your Information Only" statement, as I described in chapter ten. Sharing an FYI means I am just informing her of my preferences and do not require an immediate response or action.

I could say, "We have been so busy lately. Sometime soon, I'd like to schedule something fun we can do together."

Or I may ask that she just consider a request. I could say, "Would you think about ways we can spend more time together? I had so much fun when we went for lunch at D'Angelo's."

As we discussed in chapter three, "nurturing," "cooperative," and "loving" are three primary female qualities. The seemingly harmless statement that she is not home enough can feel more critical to her than a man intends because it focuses on her female side, where she is most vulnerable. Being nurturing, cooperative, and loving are qualities that stimulate her estrogen, so they are more important for her well-being.

If a woman says to a man, "You are not home enough," it affects him differently than when a woman hears it from a man. It gives the message that he is not giving enough and therefore he is not succeeding in making her happy. She doesn't realize that, instead of hearing that she loves him and really appreciates being with him, he hears that he is not good enough, that once again he has failed to make her happy.

**A seemingly harmless statement
feels more critical to a woman when it focuses on
her female side, where she is most vulnerable.**

If she wants him to spend more time at home, then her communication would work much better if she simply said, "Let's plan to spend more time together. I love being with you. Let me know when you have time to go over our calendars."

Hearing that she loves being with him raises his testosterone and makes him much more willing to sit down and plan some special time together. A nondemanding request motivates a man best because it gives him the information he needs to give more in a relationship without saying that he has failed her in any way.

**A request gives a man the information he needs
to give more in a relationship
rather than the message that he is not good enough.**

A Man's Greatest Vulnerability

Criticism affects men and women differently, depending on where we are most vulnerable. A man's greatest vulnerability has to do with feeling controlled. Even a small complaint or criticism expressed in an emotional tone of unhappiness is kryptonite to a man.

Here is a list of complaints, big and small, that will affect a man:

"You are always working."

"You didn't do what I asked."

"You didn't call me to let me know you were late."

"You only think about yourself."

"You are not listening to me."

"You never plan any dates."

"You are no longer affectionate."

"I don't feel like you love me anymore."

"You left the lights on in the bathroom."

"Why can't you pick up after yourself?"

"You ate all the cherries in the refrigerator."

Each of these complaints is about his competence, a quality of his male side, so they strike him where he is more vulnerable. Feeling attacked, he will become defensive and to various degrees minimize her message, discount it, complain back, or simply push her away and stop caring about anything she says.

It is often surprising to women which of these are the most offensive. If she links her complaint to emotional unhappiness, then, ironically, the smaller it is, the more annoying it is to a man. If I am two hours late for dinner and I didn't call, then I can easily understand why she is upset or unhappy with me, but if I left the light on in the bathroom or I ate all the cherries in the refrigerator, then her complaint is much more annoying.

If a woman links a complaint to emotional unhappiness, then ironically, the smaller it is, the more annoying it is to a man.

If a woman simply comments, without any emotional charge, "You are not around these days; I miss you," or "Hey, you ate all the cherries; next time save some for me," then it doesn't upset him and he is better able to validate and remember her needs or request next time. However, when her complaint is backed with feelings of unhappiness, it affects him negatively.

A man's male side primarily identifies with feeling successful. As long as he wants to succeed in making her happy, any complaint that is backed up with the emotional charge of her unhappiness pushes his most sensitive buttons. The right or wrong wording has some importance but the message communicated by the tone of her voice and her facial expression have a much greater effect.

When a complaint is expressed in a tone of voice that reveals her unhappiness with him, he will feel controlled. The message he hears is that to make her happy, he "must" spend more time at home or "should" never eat all the cherries. From his point of view, it can sound like a mother scolding a child. Her complaint sounds like a demand that he has to do what she says if he is to make her happy.

When a woman complains in a tone of voice that reveals her unhappiness, a man will feel controlled.

On the other hand, a nondemanding request frees him to decide on his own to adjust his actions. This supports his independent, assertive, and problem-solving masculine side. Even if he does not fulfill that particular request, he will feel more inclined to support her in other ways.

His natural resistance to doing everything she wants is not a rejection of her, but a way to ensure he has the energy and time to do what he needs to do as well. In a complaint-free relationship, his gradual behavioral adjustments in response to her requests are his gifts of love, rather than obligations. A man will always give more when the message he gets from his partner is that he is already a good and loving partner and that she needs his help.

The message that he is good enough keeps his testosterone up, and her request for help creates a pair-bonding experience that stimulates the production of vasopressin in him, which not only increases his motivation to give more but also increases his attraction and desire to bond with her.

If a man immediately yields to a woman's every complaint, either to keep peace or to please her, he gradually begins to lose his sense of confidence and competence when in her presence. He no longer feels like he is making his own decisions but instead becomes overly dependent on her direction or approval.

When a man finds himself saying "I'm so sorry" all the time, it increases his oxytocin and estrogen, which are associated with his female qualities of interdependence, emotion, nurturing, and cooperation. These are positive qualities, but when they are triggered too much in her presence it will lessen his male hormones, which depend on him feeling more independent, analytical, decisive, confident, and competent.

To repeatedly hear and yield to her complaints affirms within him that he is incompetent or not good enough. If he feels that she sees him as incompetent, then he is certainly not getting the trust, acceptance, and appreciation he needs to keep his heart open.

In short, repeated complaints, combined with the emotional message that he has failed to make her happy, become to a man's mind a controlling message, which either shuts him down or suppresses his male side. And as we've seen, when a man suppresses his male side, to please his partner or for any other reason, it automatically pushes him toward his female side. Moving too far on his female side lowers his testosterone and increases his estrogen, and over time he becomes excessively needy and dependent on her approval, or overly emotional, passive, or moody.

Women tend to be completely unaware that their complaints sound controlling to a man. In my three-day Soul Mate seminars for singles and couples, we explore in great detail all of the most common general complaints men and woman have about each other. We go into separate rooms where men and women list their complaints, and then we bring out the lists to explore them together. Because the complaints are anonymous, no one takes them personally or gets defensive.

Women often complain that they give more than they get, and men will complain that there is no point in giving more because nothing they do is enough to make their partners happy. But while women are not surprised to hear that a man's biggest complaints have to do with her complaining and nagging, they are completely surprised and baffled to hear that men also feel controlled.

Without understanding the differences between men and women, women often think that by complaining, they will get men to do more because, as I explained, when a man complains, a woman feels pressured to do more. But to a man it has the opposite effect: when a woman complains, he eventually *loses* his motivation to give more.

Complaining makes men do less, not more.

Most of the time, a woman's intent in complaining is not to control. However, to be happy, she does want his support. When she recognizes that complaining really doesn't work, she can then be more motivated to stop complaining and instead wait until she is feeling happy and appreciative of his support. Then, and only then, she can make specific requests for a little more. As I mentioned in the Introduction, making requests in small increments and then giving big rewards is the secret of getting more in a relationship.

Preventing Defensiveness

When Bonnie does complain to me about me (which is not that often), to prevent my own defensive reactions I will listen up to the point where I start to get a little defensive and then simply say, "I hear you."

That ends the conversation and completes the communication. It lets her know that I have been taking in what she has said and will certainly consider it.

It is such a relief for both of us to have this simple tool. My job is to not let her push me further in my defensiveness, while her job is then to trust that I have heard her and will do my best with the information I received. If I need more information, I will ask. But I am very unlikely to do that when I am already feeling defensive.

After making a complaint, many women will wait for some kind of warm, friendly response like, "Oh, I am so sorry, I will try better in the future," to complete the communication. This is the response she expects because it is the kind of response she would give to signal that she heard the person, particularly if she had disappointed them.

**A woman mistakenly expects a man
to respond to her complaint by saying,
"Oh, I am so sorry, I will try better in the future,"
because that is what she would say.**

But for a man, particularly if his partner's complaint is backed with feelings of unhappiness, it activates the fight-or-flight center in his brain, which I described in chapter five. It is a mini-emergency; his testosterone automatically rises to solve the problem, and his estrogen (temporarily) goes down.

Due to this hormonal reaction, he will automatically disconnect from his emotions to silently analyze her complaint and consider how to solve this problem. This is called "mulling it over."

In that moment, he is quietly reflecting on what she has said; any further conversation will usually interfere with this process. Her unfulfilled expectation of a more female, empathetic response from him just increases his resistance to changing his behaviors in response to her needs.

When hearing a woman's complaint, a man automatically withdraws from his emotions to mull over the challenge or problem.

When he detaches from his feelings, she will feel this disconnection immediately; she then feels a need for some reassurance that he is not mad at her, that he has "heard her," or that he will consider the unmet need that she is complaining about.

But for him to say more than "I hear you" at this point requires him to talk about his feelings and reactions to her complaint; this will only interfere with his ability to mull over what she has said. It will increase his stress and prevent him from feeling her need.

In my marriage, when I simply say, "I hear you," that lets Bonnie know two important things:

1. I am sincerely considering her request, and if I need more information I will ask for it.

2. If she continues talking about her complaint or asking more questions, my automatic defensive reactions will prevent me from easily considering her request and adjusting my behavior as I see fit.

"I hear you" gives a woman the message she needs that her partner has heard her and is considering what she has said without negatively affecting a man's ability to process her request. It signals that they are equals—he is not her servant, who changes with her every complaint—and gives him the space to consider her complaint or request without being "expected" to do something. The more space he is given for his reaction, the more he is able to feel his respect for her and his desire to support her.

When he says "I hear you," it doesn't mean for sure that he will correct whatever she is complaining about, but it does mean that he will consider it more than he would if she continued to complain about it. It means that, based on his priorities and needs, he will also consider her priorities and needs. And the more successful he feels in the relationship overall, the more he is likely to be willing to give more.

When a man is starting to get defensive, blood flows to the fight-or-flight center in the back of his brain and it becomes more difficult for him to hear another point of view. The last thing he is able to do when he is defensive is feel empathy or compassion for her needs.

**When a man is defensive,
the last thing he is able to do
is feel empathy or compassion for her needs.**

My daughter Lauren teaches women this technique: when a man doesn't know to say "I hear you" or doesn't say "I am so sorry," but is just silent, instead of intently looking at him and waiting for some caring or compassionate response, a woman should say, "You are thinking about this, right?"

This makes it easy for him to say "Yes," and gives her the reassurance she needs that her message has been received as much as is possible at that time.

Expecting a heartfelt feeling of regret to immediately come out of his mouth at a time when he is feeling defensive is unrealistic and unproductive. For him to consider what she is saying without a defensive reaction, he has to temporarily pull away from his emotions. If she is upset with him, each additional word she speaks increases the amount of time it will take for him to return to his compassionate side.

By not pushing him further to his defensiveness, she makes it easier for him to receive her message. In addition, by converting her complaints into requests, she supports him in making his own decisions on how to help her. If he is getting defensive, then the more she pushes, the more he will resist what she has to say.

In my marriage, when my wife does complain about something and I start to defend myself, she will often just walk away, or if we are on the phone, she will just hang up. While this may sound cold, I appreciate it. We both understand the importance of preventing emotional and hurtful arguments.

Keep in mind, it is rare for her to do this, but when she does, because we have prevented an escalating argument, she is able to let go of her upset more quickly. When we connect again, she does expect and appreciate an apology from me if my mistake or defensiveness was hurtful or upset her.

Saying "I hear you" doesn't mean I never say "I'm sorry." It just means I say it a lot less. It also means that, at times when I hear a complaint and get defensive, I have a way to give her the message that I am considering her request. Usually if I do something that disappoints or upsets her a lot, and I am not feeling defensive, then of course I will feel a wave of empathy, caring, and compassion, and say, "I am so sorry. I didn't mean to upset you. My mistake."

The Value of Complaining

While complaining about your partner to your partner does not work, there is another case, as we've previously discussed, where complaining is a valuable tool: when a woman talks about and shares her feelings (just not about her partner) upon returning home from work. If she does not, she is missing an opportunity to come back to her female side to balance her hormones.

When women do not talk about their feelings, they miss the opportunity to relax.

One of the reasons women don't talk about their day is that men often don't listen. If a man is more on his male side he will quickly become distracted or disinterested, or interrupt with solutions. However, if he is more on his female side, he will want to talk more than her, and if she has complaints about her day, he will respond with more complaints about his day. While this seems reasonable to him, it provides her with social bonding, not the pair bonding she needs to come back to her female side.

Whether a woman is more masculine or feminine, learning to share feelings in a way any man can hear will help her to feel better and relax. On the other hand, men who talk more than their wives miss out on a unique pathway to lowering their stress levels by coming back to their male side: listening. Listening is often considered to be a more feminine action, but it actually strengthens a man's masculine side.

Listening is often considered more feminine, but it actually strengthens a man's masculine side.

After spending all day on her male side, it is a big challenge for a woman to come back to her female side. And when a woman feels stuck on her male side, it affects her partner as well, because a man will tend to move more to his female side in an effort to connect with her. As he moves to his female side, it can then push her further into her male side. As a result, instead of lowering their stress, both end up increasing it.

In light of my example with June and Alex in chapter ten, consider Jackie, who manages a real estate firm and over fifty employees. During the day she is on her male side. She is constantly putting out fires, making decisions, and solving problems. But when she returns home, her workday is not over. She just feels overwhelmed, with more to do. In a practical sense she is stuck in her male side with more problems to solve.

Jackie said, "My husband Jonathon tells me I should just chill out. But there are things that I have to do. There is just not enough time to get it all done. Then he wants to talk about his day. I try to listen but I really don't want to. I don't know why but it turns me off. I feel embarrassed that I am so judgmental, but it is how I feel. I don't know how to tell him to stop talking without being rude or hurting his feelings. Listening to him has become another thing I have to do!"

Jackie needs to come back to her female side, but she doesn't know it. She is stuck on her male side, believing that she will feel better if she gets everything on her list done. But as long as she is suppressing her female side, her to-do list will never end, and the activities that could nurture her female side will always be at the bottom, if they make the list at all.

When a woman is suppressing her female side, her to-do list will be never-ending!

An insight from my seminar changed her life. There, Jackie learned that the major cause of her stress was not her never-ending to-do list but the stress she was feeling due to hormonal imbalance. It was not the pressure to do more that was causing her stress; rather, it was her hormonal imbalance that was increasing the pressure she felt to do more. Women feel this increased pressure when they are too far on their male side; without the support of their female hormones, what they can do will never feel good enough.

**The pressure to do more
is not the cause of a woman's stress
but rather the symptom of hormonal imbalance.**

In a follow-up session after the seminar, Jackie said, "Now we are talking more and I am more relaxed. The difference is I talk and Jonathon basically listens. I don't have to listen to his complaints about his job, nor pretend to be interested in him and ask a lot of questions. Instead he just asks me questions and listens. I feel heard and he feels appreciated. Afterwards I go in for a hug and it feels really good. I can feel my whole being softening."

Without an understanding of our different hormonal needs to cope with stress, Jackie would have felt it was rude to have a one-way conversation. After all, when friends talk, it is never one way. Both people talk and both listen. And of course Jackie and Jonathon continued to have back-and-forth conversations when they were not stressed. But Jackie learned the power of sharing her feelings and complaints for a limited amount of time as a powerful tool to come back to her female side, and Jonathon learned the power of listening without giving any suggestions as a powerful tool to come back to his male side.

Like Jonathon and Jackie, you, too, can learn to use your relationships to find hormonal balance to support the full expression of your unique self. Through giving the support your partner needs most and getting the support you need most, you can create a lifetime of love. Providing the safety for you and your partner to grow in love through creating a complaint-free relationship as described in this chapter is a choice you can make today.

Four Stages of Relationships

Unsolicited advice or suggestions, criticism, complaints, and judgments are simply not loving behaviors and always make things worse. Even if you are only "trying to help," if your suggestions are not requested, they are unproductive. Yet we find it difficult to stop criticizing and complaining because, when we are stressed and don't know what to do to find balance, we tend to react automatically, often in ways that simply don't work.

When we are stressed, blood flow to the prefrontal cortex of the brain, where we can choose our responses based on what works, stops. But by learning to manage stress effectively by balancing our hormones, and with a clear commitment and intention to be loving and supportive of our partner and ourselves, we can move through the following four stages of a relationship. This journey not only creates a lifetime of love but also helps us to develop individually our full potential for happiness and success:

Stage One: In this stage, communication with our partner is primarily based on what we believe is right or wrong and not what is loving and kind. It is based on what we believe is good or bad according to our social conditioning or our own expectations and standards of behaving. This leads to attempts to manipulate our partner into making the changes that we demand through punishing and shaming.

Punishing and shaming come from a primitive part of the brain. When we are stressed, blood flow to our reasonable and loving part of the brain is redirected to more primeval parts of the brain, and our automatic reaction is to attempt to control our partner.

Stage Two: Here we recognize that the things we did in stage one don't really work. Now, when we are stressed, rather than continuing to make the same mistakes or repeat unproductive behaviors, we take action to lower our stress by balancing our hormones. Then we analyze what works and what doesn't work, and then do what reasonably can work.

No one is perfect, so we can't stay in stage two all the time. But at least when we do make mistakes, we can then take some time to recognize how we contributed to any dispute, problem, escalation of tension, or mistake.

When there is drama, fighting, cold wars, or theatrics, instead of dropping back to stage one, we recognize we are stressed and do something that is not dependent on changing anything about our partner to feel better. Then, when we feel better, without requiring our partner to change for our happiness, we can then consider how to interact in a way that works better for our partner and for ourselves.

In stage two, we practice holding back reactions that simply don't work and instead respond with intention in ways that make sense and do work. Whenever there is a problem, we first take time to lower our stress, then reflect on what we did that didn't work and what we can do that will work better.

Stage Three: In this stage, through practicing what works and what doesn't, we begin to discover our inner compassion and wisdom as well as other aspects of higher love. This higher love is what allows us to express our full potential in life. It is what gives us patience, confidence, acceptance, and lasting love.

There are still challenges in stage three, but there is little drama; the passion and love is stronger and deeper and our commitment to love is much greater. We recognize that all challenges in a relationship are opportunities to become a more loving person. By overcoming our inner resistance to finding and expressing love during times when it is difficult to do so, all aspects of our lives become easier and more fulfilling.

In the first stage, we easily get upset, complain, yell, withhold our love, punish, shame, or criticize just to communicate the simple message, "This doesn't work for me. I would prefer you do something else."

In the second stage, we realize that we can set boundaries and disagree without drama or demands. We can be flexible and patient.

Now, in the third stage, our demand for perfection is replaced by a liberating acceptance of what cannot change, an appreciation for what can change, and the wisdom to know the difference.

Stage Four: In this stage we fully accept that relationships and life will always present new challenges to our ability to find a greater love within ourselves. It is a radical acceptance that life is not perfect, our partner is not perfect, and problems and challenges will never go away, but all of that is okay.

In this stage we feel much less resistance toward life's inevitable challenges, less attachment to getting everything we want when we want it, and less avoidance of the things we want to do or be. In stage one, these obstacles are like big speed bumps that slow us down. Now they are simply unexpected turns in the road of your life, which bring opportunities for gaining new insights and greater inner strength, wisdom, and love.

Getting to this stage in our relationship gives us the freedom to be all that we can be, and to do what we are here in this world to do. It is in this stage, after growing in compassion and wisdom and other aspects of higher love, that we experience the freedom of unconditional love.

This unconditional love, particularly for and from our intimate partner, provides us with great comfort, always reminding us that while life is not perfect, we are here to make it better—for our partner, our family, and the world. No one can do it all, but we can each do our part; that is all we can do, and that is beyond good enough.

A New Chapter in Your Life

I hope that the journey of moving from Role Mates to Soul Mates has been as fulfilling for you to read about as it has been for me to write about. It is the result of forty years of teaching these important insights to create more love in the world.

Each month I travel and teach my relationship seminar to thousands of people around the world. But it is not enough. Millions and millions of people long to experience a higher love, but without understanding our new needs for love they continue to be disappointed. Even one insight toward understanding our differences may save a relationship or help someone find love. I know this book can help. I hope that you feel this way as well and will share this book with your family and friends.

The new insights in this book are easy to understand but hard to put into practice. We have a lifetime of past training and conditioning that can sabotage our success. We must be vigilant in order to be accountable for our mistakes as well as to forgive others.

These new insights are easy to understand but hard to put into practice.

It is unrealistic to expect that you or your partner can immediately or completely let go of past habits for relating to each other. We need to be kind to our partners and ourselves by recognizing this is not easy. Even the most brilliant and successful people in the world fail in their relationships. With this in mind, we can then fully appreciate and celebrate our gradual progress as well as forgive our setbacks.

At times when it seems your relationship is not giving you the love you want and need, at least now you will know why it isn't working. By letting go of blame you can shift gears to lower your stress and open your heart again and again.

Rather than assume you and your partner (or future partner) will put these new insights into practice perfectly, expect that you will move forward two steps and then one step back. That has been the case in my life and for most of my thousands of clients and seminar participants.

After years of practice being a Soul Mate, it will certainly become much easier and most of the time totally effortless. Inevitably, however, you will be tested again and again to rise to a higher level of love, wisdom, and compassion. It is only by being challenged that we can take our next step to develop and express more of our inner authentic and unique potential.

I hope you don't expect perfection of yourself in applying these many new insights, or demand it of your partner. When your relationships are not working, remember that this takes a lot of practice to master.

**In every relationship at different times,
you will be tested to rise
to a higher level of love, wisdom, and compassion.**

If this book has inspired you, I encourage you to come back to it again and again. Just open up to any page and it will help you. Most of the time, when we are having relationship challenges, it is because we have unrealistic expectations of our partner or ourselves. Coming back to love will help you remember how we are different and can inspire you once again to open your heart and love yourself and your partner more. If you have been moved to apply these new insights, let this moment be the beginning of a new chapter in your life.

As you make the changes to open your heart and keep it open, you make it easier for others to do the same. In my own marriage, I know that whenever I come back to love, it makes it a little easier for others in my life to come back to love, too. It is a gift not only to myself and my wife, but to my children and grandchildren as well. It is this insight that motivates me to be a better person through letting go of resentments and transforming anger into passing annoyance. If I can't find forgiveness, how can I expect it of anyone else? If you and I can't do it, where is the hope for our world and our future?

By putting the many new insights of *Beyond Mars and Venus* into practice, you will experience a lifetime of love and access your inner potential to experience a higher love. With that love as your foundation, you can develop and express your full creative potential in service to the world.

Always remember you are needed in this world and that your commitment, character, and higher love make all the difference.

EPILOGUE

GROWING TOGETHER IN LOVE

When a man or woman is able to simultaneously blend their masculine and feminine sides in full authentic expression of their unique self, they are then able to feel and express a higher love. With repeated glimpses of this higher love we are able to grow together in love and passion for a lifetime. With the development of this higher love through our intimate relationships, all aspects of our lives are enriched.

Here is a list of the different expressions of our higher-love potential:

1. **Equal Interdependence:** Through blending our *independent* masculine side with our *interdependent* feminine side, we can create relationships that are equally interdependent. With equal interdependence no one is a victim. With equal interdependence we can recognize how we and not just our partners contribute to our problems. We are free to let go of automatic defensive reactions like blame, punishment, resentment, and judgments.

2. **Deeper Compassion:** Through blending our *detached* masculine side with our *emotional* feminine side, we can listen with empathy and then experience a deeper compassion, which motivates us to be of service. With this blending we can convert our own sadness and grief into greater compassion for others, but only if we are able to heal our own emotional wounds. Through knowing our own inner pain, and with the detached clarity that can change how we feel, we can then relate to and feel compassion for the pain of others beyond sympathy or mere empathy.

3. **Inner Wisdom:** Through blending our *problem-solving* masculine side with our *nurturing* feminine side, we can access an inner wisdom that helps us discern what works and what does not work in life and relationships. This inner wisdom acknowledges our limitations and the limitations of others. With this blending we can convert our own mistakes and regrets into greater wisdom.

4. **Daring Courage:** Through blending our *tough* masculine side with our *vulnerable* feminine side, we can access the daring courage to set boundaries so that we are not taken for granted or taken advantage of. In doing so we can convert our own hurts into the courage to reopen our hearts and give more love. We are free to admit our mistakes, forgive our partners, and find new ways to express more of what we have to offer the world.

5. **Win–Win Compromises:** Through blending our *competitive* masculine side of wanting to win with our *cooperative* feminine side of wanting our loved ones to win, together we can learn to make compromises where both partners win. With this blending of competition and cooperation, we can convert our feelings of anger, betrayal, and jealousy into shared success. Without giving up our needs, we can find ways to support our partner's needs.

6. **Brilliant Creativity:** Through blending our *analytical* masculine side with our *intuitive* feminine side, we can be more creative in finding solutions to life's challenges and adapting to stressful circumstances. We can find creative ways to support our partners and others without having to sacrifice our integrity. Through accessing our creative potential, challenges roll like water off our backs. With this blending of analysis and intuition we can convert our worries into brilliant creativity. Every mistake becomes a lesson that was necessary for taking one step closer to your goals. Rather than feel stuck, we can go with the flow and face our challenges with grace.

7. **Effortless Patience:** Through blending the *inner power* of our masculine side with the *loving nature* of our feminine side, we can convert our frustrations into opportunities to develop and express effortless patience. "Silence is golden and patience is a virtue," the old saying goes. Our increasing patience gives us the ability to stay silent at those times when our automatic defensive reactions are to say or do something to blame, correct, criticize, intimidate, shame, or punish our partners.

8. **Unattached Persistence:** Through blending our masculine *assertiveness* with the *receptiveness* of our feminine side, we can let go of feeling helpless and powerless in our relationships and more effectively ask for what we want and need by communicating it as a preference and not a demand. We can convert our disappointments into unattached persistence to get what we need and to achieve our goals.

9. **Authentic Humility:** Through blending our masculine *competence* with the *virtuous nature* of our feminine side, we can freely express ourselves while trusting that doing our best is good enough. We can relax from overachieving or from feeling the pressure to be perfect. We are free to be

transparent, acknowledging our strengths along with our limitations and failures. We are freed from perfectionism and can rejoice in the success of others as if it were our own. With belief in our own competence paired with a sincere desire to express our virtue, we can convert our embarrassment when we make mistakes into authentic humility.

10. **Inspired Curiosity:** Through blending our masculine *confidence* with the *trusting nature* of our feminine side, we can awaken the higher love of inspired curiosity. When listening to our partners, rather than reacting to protect ourselves or in a way designed to get what we want, we can be curious about their thoughts and feelings and recognize their positive motivations to love or be loved. We are eager to see the good in situations and wonder how we might be able to help.

11. **Heartfelt Gratitude:** Through blending our masculine *accountability* with the *responsive nature* of our feminine side, we can awaken heartfelt gratitude for the opportunity to be alive and of service. We are automatically motivated to correct our mistakes, keep our word, and sustain a willful intention to serve the well-being of our partner. With this blending of accountability and responsiveness we can convert our fears into heartfelt gratitude for all that we can have and can give.

12. **Grounded Innocence:** Through blending our masculine *goal-oriented* nature with the *process-oriented* nature of our feminine side, we can develop a grounded innocence that permeates our wants, wishes, and needs. We are consciously aware of a primary and consistent motivation to do only good and be true to ourselves as well as to others. We can forgive our mistakes and imperfections and feel with

certainty our worthiness to be loved. This frees us to see the good in others as well as forgive them for their mistakes.

The Pot of Gold at the End of the Rainbow

All of these expressions of higher love are the pot of gold at the end of the rainbow. When we learn to give and receive love through blending our male and female sides, our highest potential for love, happiness, and success can emerge.

Even in nature, it is the blending of sunshine and rain that gives rise to a beautiful rainbow, which reveals all of the colors of visible light. In a similar way, we, too, can gradually develop and express all of the different talents and gifts that remain dormant within us as we grow together in love.

The pot of gold will always be a little beyond our reach, but bathed in the different colors of the rainbow, we will continue to enjoy the moment even as we eagerly want more and more.

As we learn to love ourselves and become Soul Mates, we make it safe for others to open their minds and hearts to a greater love as well. This is the ultimate freedom, and it is one we can all experience by making a commitment to love and continuing to do our best to do so.

Growing together in love does not require perfection. If we were already perfect, there would be no growth. Learning to experience unconditional love is only achieved by facing our own imperfections and making changes in ourselves.

Growing together in love is our hero's journey to discover and express our highest potential through compassion, wisdom, and equal partnership: equal partnership with our partner, and equal partnership with our own male and female sides.

For bonus information, and to download a free copy of the e-book *How to Get Everything You Want in Your Relationships*, please stay in touch with me and my daughter Lauren Gray at MarsVenus.com.

ACKNOWLEDGMENTS

I want to thank my wife, Bonnie Gray, for her continued love and support in our personal relationship as well as in the office. I could not have written this book without her support, her wisdom, and her insight.

Having family support is everything to an author writing about relationships. For this, I thank our three daughters and their partners, Shannon and Jon, Juliet and Dan, and Lauren and Glade, and our adorable grandchildren, Sophia, Bo, Brady, and Makena.

So many thanks go to my team that makes this work happen. Hallina Popko, my executive assistant; Jon Myers, my marketing director of MarsVenus.com; Marcy Wynne, director of customer service; Glade Truitt, web designer and director of video production for my daily online blog; Rich Bernstein, president of Mars Venus Coaching; and all of the Mars Venus Life Coaches around the world. Special thanks to my daughter Lauren Gray for her popular video blogs at MarsVenus.com and for developing online relationship training for women only.

Extra thanks goes to Warren Farrell, who is a close friend and brilliant authority for understanding how men and women can understand and communicate with each other to create lasting love. Many of his ideas from our weekly walks are sprinkled throughout this book.

I want to thank my agent, Frank Weimann, and my other friends who held the vision that this book is truly needed at this time.

I want thank Glenn Yeffeth, CEO and Publisher at BenBella Books; Alicia Kania, Senior Publishing Associate; and Jessika Rieck, Senior Production Editor, for their continued support in publishing this book, along with my editors, Leah Wilson and James Fraleigh, who helped keep these many new ideas clear and concise.

ABOUT THE AUTHOR

John Gray is the #1 relationship expert in the world. He's the author of the groundbreaking book *Men Are from Mars, Women Are from Venus*, the best-selling relationship book of all time. His numerous relationship and health books have sold over 50 million copies in 45 different languages in 150 different countries. For the last forty years, John Gray has helped millions of people improve their relationships, communication, and health. He follows his own advice and has been happily married for over thirty-one years.

John regularly gives workshops and talks around the world helping men and women better understand and respect their differences in both personal and professional relationships. His approach combines specific communication techniques with healthy nutritional choices that create the brain and body chemistry for lasting health, happiness, and romance. His many books, blogs, and free online seminars at MarsVenus.com provide practical insights to improve relationships at all stages of life and love. An advocate of health and optimal brain function, he also provides natural solutions for overcoming depression, anxiety, and stress to support increased energy, libido, hormonal balance, and better sleep.

He has appeared on *The Oprah Winfrey Show* many times as well as *The Dr. Oz Show*, the *Today Show*, *CBS This Morning*, *Good Morning America*, *The Early Show*, *The View*, and many others. He has been profiled in *Time*, *Forbes*, *USA Today*, and *People*.

John Gray lives in Northern California with his wife, Bonnie. They have three grown daughters and four grandchildren. He is an avid follower of his own health and relationship advice.